Nicholas Perrin is Franklin S. Dyrness Associate Professor of New Testament at Wheaton College Graduate School, Illinois. He was formerly research assistant to Tom Wright, the internationally renowned New Testament scholar. Nick has taught at Biblical Seminary (Hatfield, Pa.), co-founded Covenant Classical School (Naperville, Ill.) and served as senior pastor at the International Presbyterian Church, London. He completed his Ph.D. at Marquette University in 2001. In addition to writing numerous articles, Nick is the author of *Lost in Transmission: What We Can Know about the Words of Jesus* (Thomas Nelson, 2007), *Thomas, the Other Gospel* (SPCK, 2007), *Thomas and Tatian: The Relationship Between the* Diatessaron *and the* Gospel of Thomas (SBL, 2002), and is the joint editor, with Mark Goodacre, of *Questioning Q* (SPCK and IVP, 2004). Nick lives in Wheaton with his wife, Camie, and their two sons, Nathaniel and Luke.

JESUS THE TEMPLE

NICHOLAS PERRIN

Baker Academic

a division of Baker Publishing Group
Grand Rapids, Michigan

First published in Great Britain in 2010

Society for Promoting Christian Knowledge
36 Causton Street
London SW1P 4ST
www.spckpublishing.co.uk

Published in the United States by Baker Academic
a division of Baker Publishing Group
P.O. Box 6287, Grand Rapids, MI 49516-6287
www.bakeracademic.com

British Library Cataloguing-in-Publication Data
A catalogue record for this book is available from the British Library

Library of Congress Cataloging-in-Publication Data is on file
at the Library of Congress, Washington, D.C.

SPCK ISBN 978–0–281–05872–3

Baker Academic ISBN 978–0–8010–4538–7

1 3 5 7 9 10 8 6 4 2

Typeset by Graphicraft Ltd, Hong Kong
Printed in Great Britain by Ashford Colour Press

Produced on paper from sustainable forests

For N.T.W. and M.E.A.W.

Contents

Preface

'"Who do people say that I am?"' When Jesus, according to the Gospel of Mark (8.27), first puts this probing question to his disciples, they are able, apparently without too much difficulty, to run down a laundry list of responses: 'Some say John the Baptist. Others say Elijah. Still others say one of the prophets.' One might perhaps think that today, after humanity's having two thousand years to reflect on the matter further, there would be fewer, rather than more, credible options for answering Jesus' question. Unfortunately, this is hardly the case. If Jesus were alive now to pose the same question to the person on the street, or for that matter to pastors in their pulpits or professors behind their podiums, the range of responses would be even more wildly diverse.

In the academic arena, at least in the past several decades, research into the historical Jesus has yielded a stunning variety of accounts. As in the past, such pronouncements will work their way down into the Church, through various media outlets, and then finally onto the streets of everyday life. With their children playing at their knees, the proverbial man and woman on the street will form their own judgments as to who Jesus was. Their children will then eventually grow up, a few to be pastors, a *very* few others to be professional students of the historical Jesus. Their Jesus will be similar in some ways to the Jesus of their parents; in some ways, he will be different. And so it goes on. Despite the abundance of primary and secondary sources, history has yet to hand down a final verdict on Jesus of Nazareth. As a figure of agreed-upon history, he has remained elusive as ever – and for better or worse will likely remain so.

So on being asked, 'Why yet another book on the historical Jesus? Don't we have enough such books already?', I would respond, 'No. We don't, actually.' In the first place, despite the social situatedness of all inquiry, I believe in the progress of history, just as I believe that scholarly conversations, even centuries-long scholarly conversations, are getting us somewhere. In advancing a new way of looking at the historical Jesus, in particular, Jesus as one who saw himself as the human embodiment of the temple, I hope to be doing justice to past conversations and perhaps setting the stage for some new ones. Second, in a day when contemporary reflection on the historical Jesus has struggled mightily with translating the first-century Galilean's ethical teaching into compelling contemporary idiom, a fresh appraisal of Jesus' aims holds out the prospect of fresh translations. By historically locating Jesus within the ebb and flow of Jewish counter-temple movements, I believe it is possible not only to do right by the historical facts, but also to bring the various foci of his life to bear in an integrated way. In my humble estimation, it is not Jesus the magician or Jesus the socio-political revolutionary or Jesus the sage who holds best promise for crossing time and history, it is Jesus the high priest *and* temple. Redemptive history has at one time or another managed without a magician, without a revolutionary, and even without messiah. But from the time of Adam it has never managed without a priest and a temple. If the historical Jesus saw himself as the temple, then Jesus himself embraces all of history because – from the ancient Jewish point of view – the temple embraces all of history. Likewise, as I hope shall become clear in the following pages, Jesus the temple enfolds all of life, simply because the temple embraces all of life. One would think that those who profess to follow Jesus would settle for nothing less than a vision of the same dimensions, one that encompasses within its reach all of history and all of life. If they happen to find such a vision in the historical Jesus, history has worked out well for them.

This book would have been impossible without a number of people. First of all, I am much obliged to Rebecca Mulhearn, Philip Law, and Simon Kingston of SPCK, as well as to Shirley Decker-Lucke of Hendrickson Publishers: such have proved themselves as models of encouragement and patience. On the more formative end of things, I have had countless conversation partners, some of whom I have actually been able to interact with face-to-face. I appreciate Warren Carter and Edmondo Lupieri taking on my 'temple-based' papers at Society of Biblical Literature meetings, as well as my interaction with other scholars in or around the same meeting: Stephen Patterson, Marianne Meye Thompson, Kathryn Smith, Alec Lucas, Scott Hahn, Mike Bird, Joel Willitts, and Brant Pitre. My annual Italian lunches with Scot McKnight have also had their formative contribution. I am also grateful that I have had opportunity to lecture on my ideas in their germination stage (thanks to Don Alden of Athens, Georgia) and engage with colleagues in seminar style (especial thanks to Armin Baum and the faculty of Freie Theologische Hochschule in Giessen). I am also thankful to Tom Hastings and Will Storrar of the Center of Theological Inquiry (Princeton), who graciously allowed me a few weeks to finish up this project before jumping into my next one. Of course, I am also indebted to my students and colleagues at Wheaton who have challenged and sharpened my perspective; in this connection, I need to mention two faculty in particular who share my temple interest: Greg Beale and John Walton.

I've had more than a few research assistants, formal and informal. Matthew Farrelly's extensive work on Isaiah 28 is reflected in Chapters 1 and 2. Lane Severson and Katrina Combs should also be recognized. Most of all, I need to give ample thanks to my research assistants Chris Spano, who chased down countless books and articles, and Nicholas Piotrowski, who did the same *a fortiori*, but also contributed from out of his own dissertation expertise relating to Matthew and exile.

The project would have been insurmountable apart from the support of other friends and family. The rather crucial Chapter 3 would have not have gotten off the ground apart from the writing space in the mountains of North

Carolina – all made possible by Drs Philip and Mary Mehaffey. (It goes without saying that Fred and Steve were added inspiration.) All our friends at Covenant Classical School (Naperville, Illinois) were also a great support and inspiration: the integration of our *imago dei* educational model bears no slight analogy to Jesus' all-encompassing program (as I argue it to be). Ron Kneezl provided very sage and thorough comments on the entire manuscript. David Vinson did the same on numerous drafts. I am quite grateful to David (and by proxy his wife Brigette): for the record, the initial inspiration for this book came out of our evening of chips and salsa in San Antonio. Saving the best for last, I happily affirm that my greatest inspiration has been my family: Camie, Nathaniel, and Luke. May I never take them for granted.

There are two more individuals I need to mention, both of whom had an indirect yet nonetheless important role in the writing of this book: Tom and Maggie Wright. I remember reading *The New Testament and the People of God* (1992) many years ago, at first with skepticism, but then by the end asking myself, 'How could it be otherwise?' (Important works of scholarship are almost always greeted with initial skepticism.) In my judgment, Tom would only come to outdo himself in later writings on the first-century Palestinian context and has done more than anyone I know to lend the historical Jesus discussion a fresh vibrancy. Whether one agrees with Wright's arguments or not, all should agree that he has advanced the discussion considerably. For this Jesus scholarship as a whole ought to be grateful.

I too am grateful for this but also for much more. While there are of course junctures at which I part ways with Tom, just as Tom himself sometimes parted ways with his own mentor, George Caird, I am so very thankful for the many ways in which he has given me, as a scholar, both roots and wings. But there's more to life than scholarship, for knowledge passes away. Above all, I am grateful that Tom and his wife Maggie, who in her own way is present wherever the Bishop of Durham is present, have shared with us the gift of friendship. To both of them I dedicate this volume.

Abbreviations

Abbreviations for the titles of ancient sources other than the Bible follow SBL conventions.

ABRL	Anchor Bible Reference Library
ACCS	Ancient Christian Commentary Series
AGJU	Arbeiten zur Geschichte des antiken Judentums und des Urchristentums
AGRL	Aspects of Greek and Roman Life
ALGHJ	Arbeiten zur Literatur und Geschichte des hellenistischen Judentums
AnBib	Analecta Biblica
ArBib	Aramaic Bible
BBB	Bonner biblische Beiträge
BibS(N)	Biblische Studien (Neukirchen, 1951–)
BJRL	*Bulletin of the John Rylands University Library of Manchester*
BK	Bibel und Kirche
BNTC	Black's New Testament Commentaries
BS	The Biblical Seminar
BZNW	Beihefte zur Zeitschrift für die neutestamentliche Wissenschaft
CalTM	Calwer theologische Monographien
CBQ	*Catholic Biblical Quarterly*
CBR	*Currents in Biblical Research*
CL	Cunningham Lectures
ConBNT	Coniectanea neotestamentica/Coniectanea biblica: New Testament Series
DQ	Documenta Q
EJL	Early Judaism and its Literature
EVIPP	Eric Voegelin Institute Series in Political Philosophy
EvQ	*Evangelical Quarterly*
FB	Forschung zur Bibel
FCCGRW	First-Century Christians in the Graeco-Roman World
FTS	Frankfurter Theologische Studien
GTA	Göttinger theologischer Arbeiten
HSM	Harvard Semitic Monographs
HTKNT	Herders theologischer Kommentar zum Neuen Testament
HTR	*Harvard Theological Review*
HUCA	*Hebrew Union College Annual*
IBC	Interpretation: A Bible Commentary for Teaching and Preaching

ICC	International Critical Commentary
ISFCJ	International Studies in Formative Christianity and Judaism
JAOS	*Journal of the American Oriental Society*
JBL	*Journal of Biblical Literature*
JCP	Jewish and Christian Perspectives Series
JCT	Jewish and Christian Texts in Contexts and Related Studies
JETS	*Journal of the Evangelical Theological Society*
JJS	*Journal of Jewish Studies*
JQR	*Jewish Quarterly Review*
JR	*Journal of Religion*
JSHJ	*Journal for the Study of the Historical Jesus*
JSJ	*Journal for the Study of Judaism in the Persian, Hellenistic, and Roman Periods*
JSJSup	Supplements to the Journal for the Study of Judaism
JSNT	*Journal for the Study of the New Testament*
JSNTSup	Journal for the Study of the New Testament: Supplement Series
JSOTSup	Journal for the Study of the Old Testament: Supplement Series
JSP	*Journal for the Study of the Pseudepigrapha*
JTS	*Journal of Theological Studies*
LNTS	Library of New Testament Studies
LSTS	Library of Second Temple Studies
LtSp	*Letter & Spirit*
MBMC	Matrix: The Bible in Mediterranean Context
NCBC	New Cambridge Bible Commentary
NEchtB	Neue Echter Bibel
NFTL	New Foundations Theological Library
NICNT	New International Commentary on the New Testament
NICOT	New International Commentary on the Old Testament
NIGTC	New International Greek Testament Commentary
NovT	*Novum Testamentum*
NovTSup	Supplements to Novum Testamentum
NSBT	New Studies in Biblical Theology
NTOA	Novum Testamentum et Orbis Antiquus
NTS	*New Testament Studies*
NTTS	New Testament Tools and Studies
NVBS	New Voices in Biblical Studies
OBT	Overtures to Biblical Theology
OTL	Old Testament Library
OTP	*The Old Testament Pseudepigrapha*, ed. J. H. Charlesworth. 2 vols. New York: Doubleday, 1985
OxTM	Oxford Theological Monographs
PFBR	Publications of the Perry Foundation for Biblical Research in the Hebrew University of Jerusalem

PNTC	Pillar New Testament Commentary Series
PRS	Perspectives in Religious Studies
PrTMS	Princeton Theological Monograph Series
RB	*Revue biblique*
RBL	*Review of Biblical Literature*
REJ	Revue des Études Juives
RevQ	*Revue de Qumran*
RSB	*Religious Studies Bulletin*
SANT	Studien zum Alten und Neuen Testaments
SBAB	Stuttgarter biblische Aufsatzbände
SBEC	Studies in the Bible and Early Christianity
SBLDS	Society of Biblical Literature Dissertation Series
SBLEJL	Society of Biblical Literature Early Judaism and its Literature
SBLSP	Society of Biblical Literature Seminar Papers
SBLSymS	Society of Biblical Literature Symposium Series
SBS	Stuttgarter Bibelstudien
SBT	Studies in Biblical Theology
SFSHJ	South Florida Studies in the History of Judaism
SHJ	Studying the Historical Jesus
SJ	Studia Judaica
SJT	*Scottish Journal of Theology*
SNTSMS	Society for New Testament Studies Monograph Series
SP	Sacra pagina
STDJ	Studies on the Texts of the Desert of Judah
Str.–B.	Strack, Hermann L., and Paul Billerbeck, *Kommentar zum Neuen Testament aus Talmud und Midrasch.* 6 vols. Munich: C. H. Beck, 1922–61
StudBL	Studies in Biblical Literature
SUNT	Studien zur Umwelt des Neuen Testaments
SynK	Synagoge und Kirchen
TANZ	Texte und Arbeiten zum neutestamentlichen Zeitalter
TDOT	*Theological Dictionary of the Old Testament*, ed. G. J. Botterweck and H. Ringgren, trans. J. T. Willis, G. W. Bromiley, and D. E. Green. 8 vols. Grand Rapids: Eerdmans, 1974–
Themelios	*Themelios*
TLZ	*Theologische Literaturzeitung*
Transeu	*Transeuphratène*
TTZ	*Trierer theologische Zeitschrift*
TZ	*Theologische Zeitschrift*
UUA	Uppsala Universitetsårskrift
VD	*Verbum domini*
VSA	Verbum salutis annexe
VT	*Vetus Testamentum*
VTSup	Supplements to Vetus Testamentum

WBC	Word Biblical Commentary
WMANT	Wissenschaftliche Monographien zum Alten und Neuen Testament
WUNT	Wissenschaftliche Untersuchungen zum Neuen Testament
ZacSNT	Zacchaeus Studies: New Testament
ZNW	*Zeitschrift für die neutestamentliche Wissenschaft und die Kunde der ältern Kirche*

Introduction

Turning the tables

Old prejudices and paradigms die hard. This is as true in the world of New Testament Theology as it is in any other realm of life. Of course, as long as the 'old ways' make sense, it's best to leave well enough alone. The default mode doesn't normally become the default mode without good reason. On the other hand, it is also sometimes true that paradigms establish themselves more on the basis of passing fashions than on the foundation of reliable facts and sound arguments. Conventions go unchecked simply because life is short, and we generally prefer the sense of progress that comes from building on our given assumptions rather than the upheaval of having our sturdiest tables overturned. When old paradigms die hard despite patent counter-indications, it is worth considering whether those sitting at the tables have a particular vested interest in keeping their benches bolted tightly to the floor. After all, when it comes to cashing out the hard currency of history for the sacred mintage of theology, not all coins are equally valuable: some images of Jesus will yield a much more profitable rate of theological exchange than others. The recurring temptation is to accept only that coinage whose face fetches a high market value, a picture of Jesus our culture can comfortably accept. In the meantime, history continues to pay an exorbitant price – that is, until such paradigms are overturned.

As I begin this book, I wish to register my suspicions regarding one particular old paradigm. In my view, too much twentieth-century and now twenty-first-century scholarship has labored under the assumption that there is an un-crossable chasm between the historical Jesus, on the one side, and Paul and the early Church, on the other. Particularly among mid-twentieth-century German scholars, the divide between Jesus and Paul was sometimes seen as being so gaping that it ruled out *a priori* any substantive comparison between the two great figures or any real historical continuity.[1] Jesus was up to one thing; Paul, for whom the earthly Jesus mattered precious little, was up to something entirely different. For all intents and purposes, they might as well have been ships passing in the night.

This is not to say that New Testament scholarship has unanimously embraced this position, for indeed there have been significant dissenters who have dared to crack their whips in the hallowed courts.[2] The thesis of a 'great divide'

---

[1] See Bultmann 1969 [1933]: 220–46; Schmithals 1962; Bornkamm 1977 [1969].
[2] Among the post-Bultmannians such dissent surfaces in Kümmel (1963–4) and Blank (1968).

between Jesus and Paul has been effectively challenged, and I do not intend to reiterate the details of that challenge here. Suffice it to say that the weight of so much earlier scholarship (which, following Bultmann, wrote off a Jesus–Paul linkage as spurious) has proved unable to preserve the legacy of what now appears to be a rather extreme position, and in my view, New Testament theology is all the better off for its impending demise. The old story which holds Jesus and Paul radically asunder is not finally tenable; it requires us to suspend our disbelief indefinitely in regard to too many other stories.[3]

In considering why this take on Jesus and Paul remained so eminently plausible, as it did for so many years, I believe we come face-to-face with two of the most foundational working assumptions in modern Jesus scholarship. The first surfaces in the tacit and misguided decision to abstract the historical Jesus from his Jewish context. This move is in part explained by the prejudices and philosophical mood of the day, for the anti-Semitic sentiments of the nineteenth and early twentieth centuries could only serve to extend the tradition of reinventing Jesus as one who stood opposed to Judaism and its allegedly legalistic trammels.[4] Once you have a Jesus whose attitude to his native religion ranged from glorious apathy to gut-level antipathy, you inevitably also end up with a Paul who, entangling himself now and again with the law, becomes something of a problematic younger brother. Jesus had had the heroic verve to call Judaism on the carpet for its petty externalism and willing subjection to heteronomy (a law outside oneself, namely, Torah); Paul, despite his best Hellenizing intentions, had not managed to make so clean a break. Given the proclivities of an era which sought a Jesus who would liberate the individual from societal restraints like law/Torah, and given that the West had not yet experienced the shockingly horrific culmination of its anti-Semitic tendencies, a de-Judaized Jesus and a de-Judaized Paul made perfect sense.

If the dissolution of Jesus' and Paul's shared Jewish heritage removed one obvious point of continuity between the two great figures, the divide was only further (if not paradoxically) reinforced by the then-attractive assumption that both were fundamentally oriented to the inner life. This applies especially in the case of Jesus. Long before the likes of Bultmann or Bornkamm came on the scene, in a day when Germany and England were steeping in the juices of their own Romanticism, nineteenth-century scholars and laypersons alike tended to look at Jesus as a kind of religious analogue to the

---

[3] For example, that Paul had a fairly detailed knowledge of Jesus' birth (Gal. 4.4), ethics (Gal. 6.2; 1 Cor. 7.10–11), prayer (Gal. 4.6; Rom. 8.15), passion (1 Cor. 11.23; Gal. 4.6), death and resurrection (Gal. 2.20, 3.1; 1 Cor. 15.1–9) is in my mind unimpeachable; that these traditions failed to shape the apostle's theology is incredible. See Wenham 1995.

[4] This is not to suggest (in an *ad hominem* way) that the notion of a *contra*-Jewish-legalism Jesus is necessarily anti-Semitic.

great poets, a kind of first-century Wordsworth.[5] For this Jesus, as for Wordsworth and the great Romantic tradition, the point of departure was the world of experience and feeling. The things which preoccupied Jesus were matters of the Spirit, insofar as the Spirit could be detected within one's breast. Such a Jesus was far too busy meditating on the lilies of the field and the birds of the air to concern himself with the rough-and-tumble social and political realities of the day.

The problem here at bottom is a historical one. The fact remains that the historical Jesus and the historical Wordsworth (or anyone like him) have almost nothing in common. While Jesus spent his influential years preaching the 'kingdom of God' in a world where kingdom language could only be construed as potentially terroristic speech, Wordsworth was musing on intimations of immortality while sipping tea in his garden in Cumbria. Judging by how the Romans were accustomed to treating aspiring messiah-types, it is clear that anyone in first-century Palestine preaching the kinds of things that Jesus was preaching, and doing the kinds of things that he was doing, was inevitably engaging in a do-or-die political venture. While Wordsworth is known to have his own political opinions which cut across the grain of the establishment, there is no meaningful sense in which the projects of the Galilean carpenter and the English poet can be compared. Despite the inappropriateness of this type of comparison, and Albert Schweitzer's acerbically calling attention to it, the incongruity between the presenting facts and an idealized romantic genius seems to have been all but lost on the nineteenth- and early twentieth-century writers whose desperate lack of historical curiosity could only be outdone by the extravagance of their sentimentality.[6] The haunting footsteps of this same Wordsworth-style Jesus can still be heard in lecture halls, pulpits, and bookstores to this very day.[7]

One of the consequences of this romanticized Jesus is our tendency to think that Jesus looked at life pretty much as any thoroughgoing western individualist would. According to this vision, here was a simple and unassuming Galilean who taught others about the spiritual life and brotherly love, but who showed no interest in applying his ethic beyond the level of the individual. Here was a Jesus who was happy to give his own perspective, but one who did not press his claims too strongly or expect his teachings to be taken as much more than suggestion. Finally, here was a Jesus who certainly had no interest in starting a cause or a movement. After all, poetic geniuses aren't known to start causes. (Even Wordsworth had the good taste to leave

---

[5] This finds excellent treatment in Theissen and Winter 2002 [1997]: 42–76.
[6] See Schweitzer 2001 [1906].
[7] Perhaps the experientially driven Jesus of Marcus Borg falls prey to the same criticism which Schweitzer applies to his predecessors. Borg's *Meeting Jesus Again for the First Time* (1995) is one of the best-selling books on Jesus in print.

it to a later generation of readers to start the Wordsworth Appreciation Society.) Just as the model of 'Jesus as romantic genius' remains attractive, so too does its correlate, 'Jesus the radical individualist'.

A romanticized, privatized Jesus lends further reinforcement to the historical wedge between Jesus and Paul. On consideration, it becomes clear at any rate that the two understandings go hand in hand. If Jesus and Paul were up to two very different things, then this implies that the concerns of both these figures overlapped minimally with the goals of the Jerusalem movement, a movement with which Jesus was closely associated in his day and with which Paul was in alliance in his (Gal. 2.6–10).[8] And if the respective visions of Jesus and Paul can both be so easily separated from the vision of the Jerusalem community, then this can only mean that Jesus and Paul were not so much movement leaders but, more harmlessly, relatively isolated thinkers. Thus the assumption of a disjoined Jesus and Paul almost requires a Wordsworthesque Jesus, and, conversely, a Wordsworthesque Jesus clearly did not get much through to Paul. The sundering of the Palestinian carpenter from the Cilician tentmaker dovetailed well with the way in which the European reading public was predisposed to think about the carpenter in the first place. This does not necessarily make such 'sundering' historically inaccurate, but it does go to show that the common move of pitting Jesus against Paul, not to mention broader Christianity, partly depends on certain prior assumptions regarding Jesus, assumptions which are explicable as the by-product of western ideology.

Whatever other historical weaknesses beset the great divorce between Jesus and Paul, the paradigm strikes me as pre-eminently unpersuasive in that it requires both figures to have been almost entirely aloof from the acquired traditions and expectations of the Jerusalem community. While history is largely in the dark in regard to the social history of the Jesus movement in Jerusalem, as a movement it must have acquired some kind of boundary-markers, defining features, distinctive practices, goals – and many other similar such things that characterize a philosophical or religious sect. In this sense, the movement took on a life of its own, a life that continued even after Jesus' death and had some recognizable shape before Paul came on the scene. While corporations and dictatorial governments may have the ability to reinvent official structures and agreed-upon convictions in a short space of time, religious communities, which are bound together by shared answers to certain basic questions ('What is it that we believe?' and 'What is it that we do?'), generally do not. Traditions of faith and practice may undergo transformation in the light of key events (as occurred after the resurrection); they are not normally the kinds of things which may be altogether gutted overnight. There must have been some cord of continuity between

---

[8] On the underestimated role of Peter as a bridge figure between Jesus and the early Church, see Bockmuehl 2007; also on Paul and Jesus, Bockmuehl 2006: 42–4.

the teachings of Jesus, Christianity as Paul found it in post-Easter Jerusalem, and Christianity as Paul would later preach it in the diaspora.[9]

But what was that cord and what was its nature? There have been more than a few ways to answer the question, not all of which are mutually exclusive. But perhaps more can and should be said about a certain passage in Paul, where amidst the apostle's description of his own role in relation to the Corinthians, we find some interesting architectural imagery:

> For we are God's [fellow workers]; *you are . . . God's building.*
>
> According to the grace of God given to me, like a skilled master builder I laid a foundation, and someone else is building on it. Each builder must choose with care how to build on it. *For no one can lay any foundation other than the one that has been laid; that foundation is Jesus Christ . . . Do you not know that you are God's temple and that God's Spirit dwells in you?* If anyone destroys God's temple, God will destroy that person. For God's temple is holy, *and you are that temple.*[10]

The comparison between the Corinthians and God's temple is no 'one off', for later in the same epistle Paul returns to the idea:

> Or do you not know that your body *is a temple* of the Holy Spirit within you, which you have from God, and that you are not your own? For you were bought with a price; therefore glorify God in your body.[11]

And in another epistle to the same church, he returns again:

> What agreement has the temple of God with idols? For *we are the temple* of the living God; as God said, 'I will live in them and walk among them, and I will be their God, and they shall be my people.'[12]

The apostle's identification of the Corinthian believers with 'God's temple', apparently something of an *idée fixe* for Paul, seems to signify one of two things. On the one hand, it is conceivable that he draws on temple imagery simply because it is rhetorically handy for his purposes. In this case, his choice of metaphor may be regarded as effective perhaps, but nonetheless as somewhat capricious – as if he could have just as well compared the Corinthians to, say, fitted bricks in a Roman aqueduct. On the other hand, if we allow that Paul, writing almost two decades before the fall of the Jerusalem temple in 70 CE, identifies his addressees as the temple in a realistic (as opposed to a purely metaphorical or analogical) sense, the implications are nothing short

---

[9] There were obviously highly significant differences between Jesus and Paul as well. Nevertheless, while Paul certainly would come to have considerable influence on his Christian circles, this should not eclipse the fact that the Christianity Paul inherited was one which must have already taken some stand in terms of agreed-upon beliefs and practices. It was *this* Christianity, presumably shaped in some fashion by Jesus, which Paul had signed on to.
[10] 1 Cor. 3.9b–11, 16–17.
[11] 1 Cor. 6.19–20.
[12] 2 Cor. 6.16.

of stunning. On this reading, he is casting the Corinthians, presumably by virtue of their 'in Christ' status, as a fresh expression of the central institution of Judaism, the living and breathing embodiment of the divine presence – and all that while the famed Jerusalem edifice was still standing shiny and tall, carrying on business as usual! This in turn would also presumably imply, again from the apostle's perspective, that certain functions which had been assigned to Herod's temple and its personnel were now being imparted through Christ to the likes of the Corinthian believers. Finally, that would also mean that the Corinthian believers were not merely *like* the temple of God – in some sense they *were* the new temple. And that temple was also Christ. For various reasons (which I will fill out in Chapter 2), I find the second view, linking the Church with the emergence of the long-awaited eschatological temple, to be more compelling.

In this case, the above passages constitute the earliest written testimony to Jesus Christ and/or his followers being explicitly and clearly linked to the forthcoming temple. The pattern is repeated in later non-Pauline texts, including, as has been pointed out in recent literature, the four canonical Gospels (the major sources for biographical information relating to Jesus). Apparently, it was more than a few who were eager to make a point of presenting Jesus and his community as temple; it is also clear that the theme of Jesus *qua* temple retained considerable staying power, well into the second century and beyond.[13]

All this necessarily raises the historical question as to whether the identification between Jesus and the temple, attested so early in Paul (and so amply in later primitive Christianity), can be credibly rooted in the life of Jesus himself. Even if, as I have insisted, there is no reason to rule out a path from Jesus to Paul *a priori*, this is no argument for attributing Paul's community-as-temple tradition to Jesus. The question must remain open. Was it the early Church which, upon reflecting on the events of Jesus' death and resurrection, first developed such notions? Or, alternatively, was there already a shared understanding among Jesus and his followers that they were taking part in something that could meaningfully be described as a 'temple movement'?

Generally speaking, New Testament scholarship seems to have opted for the former version. Considering the state of play on several research fronts, one discovers that the reasons are not hard to discern. A natural bias towards crediting the early Church rather than Jesus himself with this kind of 'temple talk' follows quickly and easily on the heels of two broadly held assumptions: one relating to the perceived nature and function of the temple in Second-Temple Judaism, the other relating to the problem of eschatology in Jesus' teaching. Again, it seems, we must examine our assumptions.

---

[13] See further discussion below in Chapter 2.

When it comes to how New Testament scholars view the temple, I suggest that there is a widespread tendency to construe the temple, as one might expect, in very western – one might even say Protestant – terms. In other words, there is an instinctive propensity to see the temple's *raison d'être* as having exclusively to do with the religious impulse, in particular, the need to be forgiven. 'What was Israel's temple for? Why, blood sacrifices and being restored into fellowship with God of course – little if nothing more.' This kind of unreflective judgment together with the obvious fact that the early Church did indeed thematize Jesus' death in high-priestly terms has no doubt induced innumerable Gospel scholars to infer that whenever the evangelists portray Jesus in temple terms, it is only a clumsy attempt to smuggle post-Easter atonement theology into the life-story of Jesus.

But such narrow and anachronistically modern views of the temple will no longer suffice. True, the temple was the locus for atonement, but, as has now been sufficiently demonstrated, it was more than that.[14] As the convergence point between heaven and earth, and the visible manifestation of Yahweh's presence among his people, the temple retained a significance which far exceeded that generally granted by us who are accustomed to seeing it simply as a means of propitiation or a strictly 'religious' proposition. Somehow, perhaps out of its fondness for abstract categories, post-Enlightenment thought has tended to compartmentalize the various aspects of public life, separating out the religious from the political, isolating both of these from the social, and again distancing all of these from economic concerns. For the first-century Jew, by contrast, all these realities were wrapped into one. There was no separation of church and state, *pontifex* and *imperator*, divine will and common weal. Religious realities were intrinsically political in nature, as well as social, as well as economic. So while it remains true that the temple was the heart of Jewish worship, it was also the hand of economic aid to the poor, the eye of social recognition, and the mouth of politico-religious confession. The Jewish temple was not just a 'religious center', nor simply the seat of atonement: it was a totalizing institution.

But unlike many modern-day institutions which are made to serve the needs of a given society, the temple at Jerusalem was the one and only created reality which was greater than Israel itself. Since the temple was created for worshipping the Creator God, it did not *ultimately* exist for the sake of the people; rather, the people existed for the sake of Yahweh and Yahweh's temple. This was the theory anyway. But as Israel's long and tempestuous history demonstrated, if God's people were willing to break the covenant, Yahweh would also be willing to evict the tenant nation from his dwelling-place. There was, correspondingly, an abiding sense among the

---

[14] See, e.g., Levenson 1985; Schmidt 2001; Han 2002; Stevens 2006.

anxious pious that the long-term political fortunes of Israel would rise or fall on proper worship being offered through the proper personnel. Apart from this, Israel could no longer truly function as Israel. The temple was the singular point on which Israel fixed its national hopes and from which it derived its national identity. The temple was the balance on which Israel's fortunes hung.

In this case it is not surprising that 'temple news', like today's stockmarket report, was a constant focus of intense speculation and scrutiny. A particularly crucial focal point of the nation's watchful gaze was the high priest himself. If the high priest showed himself to be unholy, this was taken not only as an indictment against the office-holder, it was ultimately a sign of divine displeasure against the people. Such was in fact the widespread impression when, following the upheaval under Antiochus IV, the temple priesthood came to be offered and sold to the highest bidder.[15] By the mid-second century BCE, when Hasmonean rule was still settling in, who ended up running the temple, how they did so, and the quality of their character were all highly pressing matters, amounting to something of a national preoccupation. By the time we come to Jesus' day, some five or six generations later, these issues had only come to loom larger. Given the precariousness of Israel's situation under the Romans, and given, too, the unabated egregiousness of the high priests who had been authorized to represent Israel before God during Roman rule, more and more God-fearing Jews were waiting for the proverbial shoe to drop – right from heaven. Within this mix, talk of a divinely initiated regime-change, that is, God's deposing the current temple structure and replacing it with a new one, would have been hot on the lips of many in Jerusalem and beyond.

It is into this world, when Israel was both vexed by and preoccupied with the state of the temple, that Jesus was born. It was in this world that Jesus carried out his ministry. All this forms an important but often ignored backdrop in understanding the historical Jesus. All this, too, puts into clearer perspective the likelihood that Jesus, a thoroughly Jewish and therefore socio-politically engaged individual, saw himself as Yahweh's answer to a debilitated temple. The suggestion, rarely taken up, seems to present itself naturally even on a superficial consideration of Jesus' actions. We might ask, 'On the face of it, which is more likely – that a first-century Jew, who called twelve men (on obvious analogy to the twelve tribes of Israel) to himself and who came into open conflict with temple authorities, referred to his own movement in temple terms, or that he did not?' It seems to me that the answer to this question is self-evident. Along these lines, I believe that E. P. Sanders could not have been more right when he declared, 'I think that it is almost impossible to make too much of the Temple in first-century Jewish

---

[15] The first such highest bidder was Jason (175–172 BCE), who in short order would in turn be ousted by a higher bidder in Menelaus (2 Macc. 4.7–25).

Palestine.'[16] Conversely, I believe that in presuming that Jesus made very little of the temple one way or another, we are flying in the face of historical evidence, context and common sense.

If the first stumbling-stone impeding scholarship in drawing a 'temple line' from Paul back to Jesus is an anachronistically narrow view of the temple, the second hindrance has to do with eschatology. As Paul ruminated on various matters touching church life, he clearly resorted to an eschatological framework which took its basic starting-point in the resurrection. The resurrection had forced Paul to revise his Christology dramatically (Rom. 1.3); it also provided the basis of future hope and, therewith, ethical perseverance (1 Cor. 15.58). It is between the two resurrections, the past resurrection of the messiah and the future general resurrection to come, that Paul situates the scope of his ethics. If my judgment is correct regarding the eschatological import of the above-discussed 'temple passages' from the Corinthian correspondence, we are induced to see the apostle's reasoning also falling within this eschatological frame. The underlying assumption that the Corinthians' physical bodies constituted the long-awaited eschatological temple, the final and incorruptible dwelling-place which God would establish at the end of the age, would of course have been impossible without the premise of the resurrection (1 Corinthians 15). If so, if Paul does identify believers with the temple on the basis of the resurrection, how does this square with Jesus, who, so much scholarship tells us, knew little if anything of his impending death, even less of his resurrection, and was moreover misled by his mistaken conviction that the world was soon coming to an end? Does not the eschatological embeddedness of Paul's temple sayings, together with the seemingly disparate eschatologies of Paul and Jesus, strongly discourage any attempt to derive the apostle's teaching from the Lord?

This too is a large and important question, which depends on the resolution of a host of issues which cannot be addressed here. However, I will offer one point, namely, that while it is true that the resurrection was foundational for Paul's undertaking of 'temple ethics' in the Corinthian letters, and that this has no immediate analogy in Jesus' teaching, I suggest it is equally true that the meaning of resurrection was itself established on a prior and more fundamental narrative, one with which Jesus and Paul would have been equally familiar and one to which, I believe, both would have given credence.

The story begins in what might be considered the charter documents of Israel, where Yahweh summarizes the goals of the Sinaitic covenant as it was about to be installed:

---

[16] Sanders 1993: 262. Similarly, Herzog (2000: 115): 'the role of the temple is crucial'. Writing well over a dozen years ago, N. T. Wright (1996: 405) opines: 'One of the chief gains of the last twenty years of Jesus-research is that the question of Jesus and the Temple is back where it belongs, at the centre of the agenda.'

Now therefore, if you obey my voice and keep my covenant, you shall be my treasured possession out of all the peoples. Indeed, the whole earth is mine, but you shall be for me a priestly kingdom and a holy nation.[17]

The roles and function ascribed to Israel, as expressed here, are at the heart of Yahweh's covenantal purposes. Israel was called to keep the covenant, and as it did so, it would fulfill its calling to be a 'priestly kingdom', that is, a 'kingdom constituted by priests'.[18] In the same cycle of material, there are hints that the nature of Israel's priestly office was not to remain static; it would evolve even as the mode of Yahweh's presence was expected to evolve. This is already alluded to in the Song of Moses, where the redeemer of Israel looks forward to the special 'place' in which God exercises his dynamic reign:

You brought them in and planted them on the mountain of your own possession, the place, O LORD, that you made your abode, the sanctuary, O LORD, that your hands have established. The LORD will reign forever and ever.[19]

On observing the way in which Exodus and sanctuary are so tightly bound together, it becomes clear that the final goal of Israel's redemption was not merely freedom, but the opportunity to establish a proper temple and with it proper worship. This is borne out by later Judaism, which did not see the force of Exodus 15.17–18 as being exhausted on the establishment of the sanctuary in the land. There was to be another temple to come, a cultus of a different order, one made not by human hands but by divine hands. This was to be equated not with Solomon's Temple, nor even with the Second Temple, stunningly refurbished as it was by Herod. No, if Moses was to be understood aright, it was to be the divinely wrought eschatological temple that would prove to be the terminal goal of the Exodus and thus too, on analogy, the ultimate goal of all Yahweh's redeeming purposes.[20] This scriptural notion would come to have quite a reception. For Palestinian Jews laboring under foreign domination, the near-expectation of the eschatological temple was a defining characteristic of the late Second-Temple period.[21]

---

[17] Exod. 19.5–6.
[18] See insightful discussion in Dumbrell 1984: 84–104.
[19] Exod. 15.17–18.
[20] Dimant (1984: 519) calls Exod. 15.17–18 the '*locus classicus*' for the eschatological temple' in Second-Temple Judaism.
[21] Significant primary texts witnessing the eschatological temple include but are not limited to 1QS 8.5–7, 8–10; 9.6; 4Q171 3.10–11; 4Q174 1.6–7; 4Q400 frag. 1.1–2; 4Q404 frag. 6; 4Q405 frag. 8–9; 11Q19 29; *4 Ezra* 10.19–54; *2 Bar.* 4.1–6; *1 En.* 53.5–7; 71.3–13, 89—90; *T. Benj.* 9.2; *Jub.* 1.17–18; *Sib. Or.* 5.420–33; Tobit 13. For noteworthy discussions in the secondary literature, consult Lohmeyer 1961: 10–23; McKelvey 1969: 25–41; Freedman 1981; Sanders 1985: 77–86; Chance 1988: 5–18; Brooke 1999; Ådna 2000: 35–50; Klawans 2006: 128–44.

This eschatological temple was nothing less than the heavenly temple, the basis for Moses' instructions (Exod. 25.40), come down to earth.[22] Thus while the heavenly beings worshipped Yahweh in the transcendent sanctuary, not made by human hands (Dan. 2.34), Israel saw itself as mirroring this activity through its own temple cultus, very much made by human hands. But this was only to be for a season. The sanctuary instituted under Moses was merely a prelude to a final, much more glorious temple. The defeat of the Gentiles, the arrival of the messiah, the full return from exile, the establishment of everlasting righteousness – as important as these events and conditions were, they were ultimately subsidiary to Israel's overriding and everlasting destiny: to render worship *as* the temple. It was this reality on which both Jesus and Paul had their eyes fixed.

Yet they were not alone. As Israel languished under the hand of the Gentiles, other zealous imaginations became increasingly stoked by visions of the eschatological temple's grandeur and increasingly sensitized to the earthly temple's shortcomings. It was also the fact of Israel's continuing state of exile that forced the conclusion that something was radically amiss in the earthly temple. The only path forward was to work towards conforming the earthly temple to the heavenly one. Once the temple made by human hands came to be coordinated with the temple not made by human hands, once God's will was done on earth as it was in heaven, then and only then the heavenly temple would appear and the final age would be ushered in.

But for apocalyptically minded Jews the path to eschatological deliverance was not without its own trials. As the old traditions would have it, God would act to redeem his people in due time, but this moment of salvation, actualized through the messiah, would come only after mounting resistance from the wicked and then finally a period of intense tribulation.[23] Once the righteous remnant emerged victoriously from this time of testing, then and only then would God finally decree the end of exile and establish the everlasting temple. But if so, then what of the mere brick-and-mortar temple that was standing? What would become of it? As it so happens, the broader

---

[22] Jewish restoration eschatology seemed to envisage not so much a re-established equilibrium between the heavenly and earthly temple, but a collapsing of the two into one reality; contra Bietenhard 1951: 196. On the correlation between the eschatological temple and the heavenly temple, see, *inter alia*, Schwartz 1979; Horbury 1996; Ådna 2000: 90–110. The identification of the eschatological temple with the remnant itself certainly surfaces in late Second-Temple texts like 1QS 8.5; 11.8 and 4Q174 1.6 (see, e.g., Wentling 1989, Maier 2008), but this may already be intimated by the likes of Isaiah's reference – read through the lens of Exod. 15.17–18 – to the remnant as 'the work of my hands' (Isa. 29.23; 45.11; 60.21); see now Vonach 2008.

[23] The notion of messianic woes finds its roots in the Hebrew scriptures (Amos 5.16–20; Isa. 24.7–23; Daniel 8—9, 12; Joel 1.14—2.3) and is sustained in Second-Temple apocalyptic literature (*4 Ezra* 7.37–38; *Jubilees* 23—24; *1 Enoch* 80). For an outstanding study, see Pitre 2005, who stands at the end of a long line of interpreters who see the tribulation as integral to Jesus' purposes: Schweitzer 2001 [1906]: 330–97; Jeremias 1971a; Meyer 2002 [1979]: 204–19; Allison 1985, 1998; Wright 1996: 577–611.

scenario also typically included the belief that the destined tribulations would culminate in the greatest national catastrophe possible: the desecration of the temple.[24] Once so profaned, the standing temple was useless for worship and its destruction was imminent. Conversely, once the faithful Jew observed apostasy within the temple, 'the abomination that causes desolation', necessitating 'the end of sacrifice and offering' (Dan. 9.27; 11.31; 12.11), he or she could only conclude that tribulation was underway and that the end was near.

Paul knew the broad outline of this story full well, as did Jesus before him. This I think is almost impossible to deny. Building on previous scholarship which recognizes (rightly in my judgment) the centrality of exile and tribulation in the first-century apocalyptic matrix, I find it entirely likely that Paul and Jesus shared the same basic eschatological map, even if they would have identified themselves as being on different places on the route.[25] True, the historical Jesus could not have anticipated all the events that Paul took for granted – not at least in all their details. But if Paul recognized Jesus as the foundation to this final temple, it is no stretch to propose that Jesus, assuming for the moment that he somehow sought to redefine Israel around himself, shared the sentiment.

In this book, I wish to argue that Jesus of Nazareth saw himself and his movement as nothing less than the decisive embodiment of Yahweh's eschatological temple. This self-perception had both a negative and a positive aspect. Negatively, Jesus' assuming the role of temple underwrote his prophetic critique of the temple administration under the regnant high priest. Censure was justified, in his mind, not least on the grounds that the temple establishment was steadily profaning its office and the cultus itself. As we shall see, this critique was already something of a tradition within Israel long before Jesus even set foot on temple grounds. But as he saw it, the temple's corruption was not merely a temporary lapse on any one individual's part, nor was it an inexplicable or random downturn in pious Israel's national fortunes. Rather it was a clear sign that the promised tribulation was underway, that judgment was about to be carried out against the standing temple, and, finally, that a new and everlasting temple was poised to be established in the midst of the suffering righteous.

As it turns out, Jesus was also convinced – and herewith the 'positive aspect' – that he and his disciples were those suffering righteous and as such

---

[24] See Daniel 9—12, *1 Enoch* 89—90, *Jubilees* 23, *Psalms of Solomon* 1, 2, 8, 17, 18; *Testament of Moses*.

[25] Here I think above all of the work of N. T. Wright (1992, 1996, 2003). In many respects, this project seeks to extend Wright's fundamental premise that Israel considered exile to be among its most pressing problems. Whether or not exile was *the* problem, and whether or not Israel believed itself to be in exile in an absolute sense (as opposed to being 'in exile' in a relative sense, that is, as not yet realizing the full promise of restoration) need not be stipulated for my purposes.

constituted the foundation of this new temple, one which on some level stood in continuity with Herod's temple order, but also, on another level, anticipated an altogether different cultic order. Because the temple had always been intended to embody justice, just as God was just, Jesus insisted that his own movement live accordingly. Following the witness of the Hebrew scriptures, Jesus never separated the office of the temple personnel from the way in which their proscribed attitudes were worked out in practice. Public acts of righteousness on the part of himself and his followers were indispensable, since they provided the grounds for Jesus' essential claim. And his essential claim, though often veiled for political reasons during his ministry, was a simple one: namely, that he and his community were becoming the true on-going temple of God, even as they were the temple and the spatial destination of the soon-to-descend heavenly temple. By living out the long-awaited righteousness of God, a radicalized righteousness, this new temple would ultimately show itself as the focal point of God's saving activity and the continuing cultic apparatus within redemptive history. In Jewish antiquity that cultic role had socio-economic and political entailments and precisely these lay at the heart of Jesus' most defining day-to-day activities.

Towards demonstrating all this, I wish to lay out my argument according to the following structure. I begin in Chapter 1 by showing that Jesus in his provocative call to be the new temple was not entirely different from a number of his contemporaries, who were equally dissatisfied with business-as-usual in the temple precincts, and in some tragic cases, equally vocal about that dissatisfaction. Here I first pay attention to the sects behind the *Psalms of Solomon* and the Qumran covenanteers, and then, by triangulation, to John the Baptizer's following. I argue that not only is there good precedent for Jesus' counter-temple aspirations, but also that it is even possible to establish a set of shared characteristics among these groups. These characteristics arise not only in response to their perceptions of 'official Judaism', but also in their perception of themselves. My first goal within this chapter then is to sketch a simple profile of counter-temple sects, one which also takes account of their significant differences; my second goal is to locate John the Baptizer within this schema.

In Chapter 2, I fast forward to the writings of the early Church, where I take up the question as to how primitive Christianity situated itself vis-à-vis the temple. This is a complicated and highly controverted question, but one which I think admits at least some satisfying answers. To anticipate my argument, I maintain that early Christianity, like the society of John the Baptizer, was also a counter-temple movement. At the end of this chapter, drawing on my study of the Baptizer (which gave birth to Jesus' movement) and early Christianity (which was birthed through the same movement), I propose tracing a solid line, a counter-temple trajectory, which winds through the life and ministry of Jesus. Jesus' status as a counter-temple movement leader can be reasonably secured only after an analysis of like-minded groups which preceded and followed him.

The proposal builds in Chapter 3 on a focused consideration of Jesus' much-interpreted 'Cleansing of the Temple'. Here I argue that his counter-temple concerns come to clearest public expression, negatively, in his criticizing the temple elite for its offense against the poor and the temple, and, positively, in his announcing the establishment of a new temple and himself as its messianic high priest. It was this direct challenge, this calling the temple authorities' oversight into question on every level, that eventually cost Jesus his life. Concurring with so much recent scholarship, I find that the temple action was no sideshow but the climactic epitome of his career. On establishing the socio-economic and political implications of the temple event, it then becomes possible to make sense of Jesus' other activities undertaken earlier in his career.

This becomes the burden of Chapters 4 and 5. In the former, I argue that the Jesus movement's solidarity with the poor was a function of its larger calling to be the eschatological temple. Here I maintain that Jesus' message and actions together betray his own self-consciousness as the eschatological high priest, who was to implement the final jubilee, a once-for-all, exile-ending release for the poor. As an important prerequisite to proper temple worship, jubilee was central to Jesus' program. This declaration of jubilee not only presaged God's final restoration of Israel in the future, but also in the present intimated a set of socio-economic practices distinctive to the movement. Ultimately, Jesus' concern for the poor was a function of his calling as the priestly founder of the final temple.

In Chapter 5, I explore the nature of the kingdom preached by Jesus as expressed by what may be considered his most distinctive actions. Here I begin with healings and exorcism, and end with meals, with (in the latter section) particular emphasis on the traditions of Jesus' mass meals. Both sets of actions are a powerful form of kingdom preaching; both signal the in-breaking of the eschatological temple. When we rightly understand these speech-acts, so I argue, we see that they are indicative of Jesus' affirmation that he himself and his followers constituted a new locus of divine presence. Precisely as the herald of a new temple order, Jesus reconfigured notions of time, space and even humanity; through his exorcisms and meals he posed no mean political challenge to competing kingdom visions on offer.

The book closes with some consideration of historical and theological implications. Inclusion of the former is a matter of course; inclusion of the latter is hardly out of place. For if Jesus saw the establishment of a new temple community as the goal of his life's work, then the modern-day heirs of the same project may welcome newly cut building-blocks of rumination and hope. One would presume that precisely because the temple in Jerusalem was at once a socio-economic, political and religious institution (with corresponding socio-economic, political and religious functions), Jesus' attempt to cast a definitive vision for a better alternative would entail implications not only for the final eschatological moment, but also for the present as well. By understanding Jesus better as a figure in history, his imitators are poised to do better theology and carry out more integrative practice.

Whether one's interest lies primarily in the face of the historical Jesus or in the theological cash-value such coinage may obtain, a historical exploration of the origins of Jesus' co-identification with the temple is long overdue. Thankfully, the path to the temple is not an entirely untraveled one. A hand-ful of Jesus scholars have already made important inroads into the territory I am contemplating, and they have written convincingly.[26] But to date there has yet to be a book-length attempt either to conceive of the historical Jesus' movement within the mix of counter-temple movements or to argue that the imminence of the eschatological temple provided the basic rationale for his most characteristic actions. If the most promising hypothesis is the one which provides the most compelling and comprehensive account of the data, I would humbly submit that 'Jesus as temple' offers a paradigm that might brook equally convincing ways of looking at the famous Galilean, but is nonetheless unexcelled in its explanatory power. It is not the only way to understand the historical Jesus. It is, however, an approach which we can no longer afford to ignore.

Like any book worth its salt, this one builds on the work of others, as well as on certain assumptions. Most fundamentally, I align myself ahead of time with the impressive swathe of scholarship that sees Jesus as an apocalyptic prophet-teacher.[27] Within this circle of scholars there is another one, only slightly smaller: those who find that the Jewish notion of tribulation was of key importance in Jesus' self-understanding. I also believe that Jesus saw the tribulation as being underway in his own time and inferred as much on the basis of, among other things perhaps, the apostasy of Israel's official leadership; that is, the temple personnel and Herod. While I argue out the second point in these pages, one of my basic assumptions, namely, that perception of apos-tasy induced belief in tribulation, finds its warrant elsewhere.[28]

In order to make the overall argument manageable, I have limited the scope of considered data, as any study of this kind must inevitably do. Because the actions of Jesus (with a minimum of interpretive help from the words of Jesus) are sufficient for my case, I rely on little else. This is not to say that Jesus' teachings, conversations, and parables are not important. Most assuredly, they are. But the authentication of Jesus' words demands a level of

---

[26] Among them are Sanders 1985; Meyer 1992, 2002 [1979]; Chilton 1992, 1996; Wright 1996, 2009; Tan 1997; Fredriksen 1999; Bryan 2002; Han 2002; Klawans 2006; Fletcher-Louis 2006, 2007; and Pitre 2008.

[27] By 'apocalyptic' I mean the complex of eschatological expectations, typically but not universally focusing on a cosmic rupture, the appearance of a messianic figure, the full end of exile, judg-ment, and restoration of true Israel – the end of history (though not necessarily the space-time continuum) as we know it.

[28] See note 18 above.

methodological complexity which, for the present volume, I wish to avoid. It will also not go unnoticed that I say relatively little in regard to Jesus' death and resurrection. This, again, is not because these matters are unimportant, but rather because they are important. Jesus' discourses and his final days are better off being relegated to two later volumes, which will follow and build upon the present work. If Jesus conceived of himself and his mission – even roughly so – in the terms I set out, this will certainly have implications for our understanding of Jesus' teaching and execution. Both of these in turn will also impact our appreciation of Jesus the temple, as evidenced in this volume by his actions.

But I am getting ahead of myself. Whether the one whom Paul came to call 'cornerstone' thought of himself along the same lines remains to be seen. The theological desire to make the earthly Jesus the temple does not make him so, for even theology must ultimately make its appeal to history. So then, to history – the history of Jesus – we shall go. And just as Paul had to make a few stops along the Mediterranean coasts before reaching the lord of the Roman Empire, we too will have to approach the one who would become his risen Lord by a seemingly circuitous route. It is a route which begins by giving us a clear view of a few counter-temple movements before our hero's heyday. By better understanding these analogies, we will eventually be in a much better position to understand just what Jesus and his movement were up to.

1

'Who warned you to flee the coming wrath?'

John the Baptizer and the anatomy of counter-temple movements

Introduction

Protest, by its very nature, comes in all shapes and sizes. Some public shows of resistance are explosive and short-lived; others are more protracted, even institutional. Sometimes opposition to the status quo and its perpetuators can be completely open and vocal; at other times, those wishing to express their discontent must do so in muted, even cryptic, terms. Ordinarily a call for change in practices or policies carries with it an attempt to influence the empowered to implement the necessary reforms. But in certain cases the hoped-for change is of a more radical nature. Sometimes the goal is not so much to work within the system, but to reinvent the system altogether. When the utopian dream of a reinvented society is regarded not merely as an ideal but as a matter of divine fiat, the dream becomes totalizing.

That this was the case for at least a sizeable band of messianism within the spectrum of Second-Temple Jewish eschatology has not always been fully appreciated. Looking back, it appears that a good deal of twentieth-century scholarship failed to acknowledge not only the contingency and variation within Second-Temple messianic expectation, but also, correspondingly, the way in which particular social and political aspirations gave shape to messianic concepts. This is not to say, in the direction of some who seem to be over-reacting to Bultmann's concept of messianism as 'dogma', that there was extremely little which could be said in regard to identifiable 'messianic characteristics' in the first century. Nor is this to say that the conceptualization of a messianic figure should be chalked up to a few self-invested pundits whose appropriation of scriptural language was a historically particular expression of their political utopianism. The concept of the messianic figure(s) was born first and foremost out of studied reflection on scriptural traditions; at the same time, these reflections were never separated from the ebb and flow of contemporary realities. Since unfolding history regularly provided the lenses for scriptural interpretation, we cannot lose sight of the fact that messianic speculation was begotten not in the abstract, but from out of the union of textual musings and shifting political fortunes.[1]

To be sure, Israel's life under the successive iron hands of the Ptolemies, Seleucids, and Romans proved to be highly problematic, both theologically and practically. But even if the 'Gentile problem' was a necessary condition for the rise of messianic speculation, this was not in itself a sufficient condition. The ancient Jewish faith was a *religio*-political reality, and so as important as it was to rid Israel of the Gentiles and thereby free God's people from the throes of exile, an even higher item on the agenda revolved around the much-debated question as to what it meant to be true Israel. After all, Israel saw the Gentile occupation not so much as the core problem but as the presenting symptom of Israel's failure to be Israel in the true and best sense. However diverse the solutions within the first-century Jewish faith to this pressing problem, everyone at least agreed on the basic question: 'What does it mean to be a people faithful to Torah and therefore faithful to Yahweh?'

As I have already pointed out, one of the ways that the Jews of the Hasmonean and Herodian period answered this question, in so many words, was by the way they responded – through either approbation or censure – to the one occupying the chair of the high priest. This followed naturally on the assumption, to which I have already alluded, that the identity of the high priest and the identity of Israel went hand in hand. Although Gentile overrule constituted a problem that only God could finally resolve, the issue as to who represented and defined Israel was one which – at least by the middle of the second century BCE – was perceived as being at least partially in *someone's* control.[2] While the faithful of Israel looked over the turbulent waters of the on-going national tempest and held correspondingly strong opinions as to how best to ride it out, at the eye of the storm sat none other than the high priest himself and his temple administration.

Thus it is no surprise that when we survey the course of late Second-Temple Jewish history, we find that it was not the presence of hostile Gentile powers that brought messianic fervor to pitch levels, but the entrenchment of high-level religious leaders (sometimes with the help of the Gentiles) whose credentials and character were highly dubious. If with many scholars we mark the middle of the second century BCE as the first serious signs of messianic smoke, this cannot be directly attributed to Gentile rule (since Gentiles had already been ruling for quite some time); rather, it was primarily the infiltration of those Jews who might as well have been Gentiles inside

---

[1] Whether or not one agrees with his account of the origins of messianism, Laato (1988, 1997) underscores this admirably.

[2] The break in the Zadokite line of high priests under Antiochus IV (175–164 BCE), as well as the precedent of buying the priesthood from the Seleucid ruler, created some sense of 'open season' for would-be high priests, regardless of their personal qualifications.

the temple 'system' that provoked apocalyptic longings for justice and utopian visions of restoration.[3] To remain under Gentile political control and thus in a state of exile was a national tragedy, but a tragedy which was half-tolerable as long as the temple, the nerve center of Judaism, remained operative. However, once Judaism was made to play tail to the Gentiles' head *and* made aware of treachery within the defining symbol of Judaism, a sense of crisis would be inevitable.

Judging by the evidence, it appears that such a crisis was not completely unanticipated. Second-Temple Judaism had long witnessed to a belief that the remnant of God would undergo a period of great tribulation in the days leading up to God's final, eschatological intervention in history.[4] Among other things, this future tribulation would involve widespread apostasy, defilement of the temple, the emergence of a righteous remnant as a counter to the defiled temple, and, finally, the arrival of an eschatological, messianic figure who would usher in judgment and salvation. And so Israel's story of Yahweh's final and lasting intervention, like any good story, involved a beginning, a middle, and an end. Even though divine intervention and the messianic dawn were expected to burst on the scene in the end, there was also a good deal of darkness to be endured at the beginning and middle. They say that the darkest hour is right before the dawn. Ancient Judaism could not have agreed more, even if some first-century pro-status-quo Jews thought of that darkness as either a distantly past or a distantly future reality.

But as far as at least a few groups were concerned, Israel had indeed already entered the proverbial darkness before the dawn. Theirs was the conviction that the temple had been irretrievably profaned – in a catastrophically ironic twist – by the very ones appointed to ensure its sanctity. In the grim light of the temple's violation, there was nothing else for these scandalized groups to do but to uphold Torah properly, endure the indignities inflicted by the wicked establishment, and await divine intervention. And as they waited, they took it upon themselves to be Israel's true temple, the institutional anticipation of the everlasting temple to be built for the age to come. That meant, in positive terms, that these counter-temple movements saw themselves as the sole remaining sign of God's continued faithfulness to Israel; negatively, they also saw themselves as a living and prophetic protest against the failure of the temple. When the consequences of that protest came back on their own heads, this was only further confirmation

---

[3] See Pomykala 1995: 159–216; Fitzmyer 2007; Beavis 2006. At the same time, the effect of the Maccabean crisis (167–164 BCE) on the rise of messianism can be and has been overstated. True, where there's smoke, there's fire. But usually where there's fire, we are also sometimes better off imagining an extended period of preliminary smoldering rather than sudden spontaneous combustion.

[4] Scholars call this period by such names as 'messianic woes' or 'tribulation' or the 'great affliction' (Schweitzer); I will use such terms interchangeably. At the same time, see the important distinction regarding the climactic tribulation, flagged up by Pitre (2005: 49–93, esp. 50).

of their collective priestly role. For it would be precisely through the chosen remnant's suffering, arising out of their clash with the socio-economically empowered false temple, that they would achieve atonement on Israel's behalf.

The remainder of this chapter will show among other things that such associations indeed existed; this in turn will serve the modest goal of establishing that the world of Jesus was *not* a world in which everyone was saying, 'All is well within Zion'. From the historical evidence, it becomes clear that a tradition of counter-temple protest, involving both the embodiment of righteousness and prophetic criticism of untoward priestly practices, had been well in place long before Jesus' day.[5] If this is true, then in my painting Jesus in the colors of a first-century dissident, I am painting a figure who, when viewed against the landscape of first-century Palestine, is hardly alone.

More centrally, I hope in this chapter to stake a specific claim about John the Baptizer. This will be a building-block which I intend to set alongside a similar claim about the early Church (Chapter 2). To anticipate the logic of the argument, it would be helpful to imagine, by way of analogy, boating on a river and encountering from a distance two short concrete piers jutting out towards each other from opposite banks. If one side of riverbank represents John the Baptizer, who matches the profile of a counter-temple movement, and the other side stands for the early Church, which also seemed to think of itself in temple terms despite the fact that Herod's much-adorned edifice was very much still standing, then the question arises as to whether Jesus, who got his start under John and later provided the impetus for the Church, also considered himself and/or his movement as a temple in some sense. To put it crisply, if both John and the early Church can be accurately described as counter-temple movements, then this goes a long way to showing Jesus as a 'counter-temple bridge', especially if there is indication that he shared some of the defining characteristics of such movements.

Towards discerning these 'defining characteristics', I first consider certain basic similarities between two groups: the community behind the *Psalms of Solomon* and the sect which kept the cache of texts we now call Dead Sea Scrolls (DSS). Both these movements, theologically speaking, appear to be rather distant cousins within the large and diverse family known to us as ancient Judaism – not only in respect to each other but also in respect to John. Thus, there is no *a priori* reason for (reductively) supposing that these similarities are to be accounted for merely by one community's inheriting another's genetic code. In this review, I attempt to explain these

---

[5] Notwithstanding the abundance of attestation to a broad-based opposition to the temple in the Hasmonean and Roman periods, there has been all too little attempt, remarkably, to locate Jesus historically within this sea of discontent. Notable exceptions include Sanders 1985, Evans 1989, Meyer 1992, Wright 1996, McKnight 1999, and Horsley 2003.

commonalities by positing a shared perception of contemporary events interpreted within a broadly common eschatological framework. The way in which these groups assessed the temple and then interpreted their own pivotal role in light of that assessment – these I see as characteristic features of Jewish counter-temple movements. Drawing on this limited sample, I am essentially undertaking a charcoal-pencil sketch of such movements.

The point of this profile is to provide a basis for comparison, determining whether John's community may also be deemed a counter-temple movement. To anticipate my conclusion, I believe that John and his following fit the profile splendidly. This end-result is nothing starkly new; I am only making a case which has already been made in less detail elsewhere: like the writers behind the *Psalms of Solomon* and several Qumran texts, John saw himself as the leader of a new-temple movement.[6]

A brief study of two counter-temple movements

The *Psalms of Solomon* sect

No one knows who wrote the *Psalms of Solomon*; the text is formally anonymous. Moreover, there are no dead-obvious clues as to what sectarian allegiance might lie behind this document. I suspect that the author and his community had Pharisaical leanings.[7] Written in the 60s BCE, the *Psalms* not only give us one of the richest troves of pre-Christian messianism, but also offer a glimpse into a community that was unnerved by the priestly regime in Jerusalem.[8] The text consists of eighteen psalms, which, following a recitation of societal ills and pious affirmations, culminate on a hopeful note, the expectation of divine intervention through the messiah. The messiah's coming is not an end in its own right, but simply attends the restoration of proper temple life.

If our standard critical bearings are accurate, the psalmist begins by looking back to the traumatic events of 63 BCE, when the Roman general Pompey battered his way through the north temple wall, cut down the Sadducean backers of the then-regnant high priest (Aristobulus II), and finally entered – perhaps more out of curiosity than anything else – into the Holy of Holies, which was normally restricted to the high priest.[9] Pompey's flagrant breach of the most sacred space, not to mention his Roman soldiers entering sandal-clad into the inner court (a double violation of holy space), was a disaster

---

[6] See Meyer 1992: 253; Wright 1996: 132, 160–2.
[7] Pharisaic authorship is maintained, e.g. by Schüpphaus 1977: 127–37; de Goeij 1980: 16; see also Winninge (1995: 34) and Wright (2003: 162), who persuasively argue for a Pharisaic doctrine of resurrection in the *Psalms* (3.11–12).
[8] On the dating of the *Psalms*, see, e.g., Büchler 1968; Schüpphaus 1977; Atkinson 1998, 2004.
[9] *Pss. Sol.* 1.1—2.2.

of huge proportions. For the faithful Jew, such a tragedy could hardly go uninterpreted. As the psalmist read the situation, Pompey's incursion was ultimately a result of Jerusalem's covenantal unfaithfulness. This was after all Yahweh's regular response to Israel's disobedience: send in the Gentiles, not for weal, but for woe. And if woe meant anything at all, it meant – especially should God's people continue to disobey – the possibility of even more severe woe, perhaps even the Gentiles' leveling the temple grounds altogether.[10]

But for the author, the Gentiles are only a problem in an indirect way. The much more pressing issue was the disobedience of Israel, especially its leaders. This becomes clear in the very first psalm. Assuming the voice of Jerusalem personified, the psalmist writes:

> I cried out to the Lord when I was severely troubled, to God when sinners set upon (me).
> Suddenly, the clamor of war was heard before me; 'He will hear me, for I am full of righteousness,'
> I considered in my heart that I was full of righteousness for I had prospered and had many children.
> Their wealth was extended to the whole earth, and their glory to the end of the earth.
> They exalted themselves to the stars, they said they would never fall.
> They were arrogant in their possessions, and they did not acknowledge (God).[11]

Jerusalem's children, representing both the populace of the city and the priesthood in particular, had gone astray from the faith of their mother. Having acquired wealth, their prosperity only made them arrogant.[12] Then, borrowing the language of Isaiah, the psalmist says that they 'exalted themselves to the stars,' believing that 'they would never fall'.[13] The invocation of this particular passage in connection with Jerusalem is shocking inasmuch as it implies that that which Isaiah predicated of Babylon, the societal embodiment of all wickedness, could now be said of Jerusalem.

Yet the *coup de grâce* is still to come: 'Their lawless actions surpassed the gentiles before them; they completely profaned the sanctuary of the Lord.'[14] Because those who had been entrusted with the temple had in fact exceeded the Gentiles in their unrighteousness, they had – literally the Greek reads – 'desecrated the holy things of the Lord in desecration'. There is simply no

---

[10] *Pss. Sol.* 7.1–6.

[11] *Pss. Sol.* 1.1–6. Unless otherwise noted, all translations of the *Psalms of Solomon* are from R. B. Wright 1985.

[12] *Pss. Sol.* 1.4, 6.

[13] *Pss. Sol.* 1.5. The allusion is to Isa. 14.13. Interestingly, the Gospels record Jesus' censure of Jerusalem (Mark 13.8, 24 par.; Isa. 13.13, 10) as drawing on the same larger prophecy (Isa. 13.1—14.23), which was originally directed against Babylon.

[14] *Pss. Sol.* 1.8.

way to soften the impact of this language. Assuming that the 'holy things' (*ta hagia*) refer to the temple in its broadest sense, encompassing temple grounds and all that lies on temple property, the charge is comprehensive in scope.[15] For all intents and purposes, the temple has been rendered ineffective through disobedience.

Lest the point was missed in *Psalm* 1, in *Psalm* 2 the marauding attack of the pagan armies is again tied back to the priesthood's disobedience.[16] The ill-fated turn of events came about because 'the sons of Jerusalem [i.e. the priests] defiled the sanctuary of the Lord'.[17] Because of all this, too, the psalmist has the Lord call out in the language of Jeremiah 7, a passage which Jesus is later recorded as quoting in his so-called cleansing of the temple, 'Remove them far from me; they are not sweet-smelling'.[18] Per ancient Jewish understanding, a willfully desecrated temple meant that the divine presence had departed or was about to depart, and that exile was imminent; all this would be evinced retrospectively by the temple's patent military vulnerability.[19] Already from this early point in the text, the indictment against the temple priests could hardly be more damning: as the priests fell morally, so too fell the temple.

But apart from greed and arrogance (as if these were not enough), was there anything else about the priests and their behavior that the psalmist found so objectionable? For this question, we have a trail of clues starting in *Psalm* 2: 'They [the Gentiles] set up the sons of Jerusalem [i.e. the priests] for derision because of her prostitutes. Everyone passing by entered in in broad daylight.'[20] Elsewhere we find reference to shameless leering and 'illicit affairs' (*syntagē kakias*).[21] As far as the psalmist was concerned, the fate which the high priest Aristobulus incurred at the hands of Pompey was no surprise; in fact, when the Roman general returned to Rome with the children of the high priests in order to parade them, it was a moment of sheer poetic justice:

> He led away their sons and daughters, those spawned in desecration.
> They acted according to their uncleanness, just as their ancestors; they defiled Jerusalem and the things that had been consecrated to the name of God.[22]

---

[15] See Atkinson (2004: 74), who cites the study of Dimant (1981).

[16] *Pss. Sol.* 2.1–2.

[17] *Pss. Sol.* 2.3.

[18] *Pss. Sol.* 2.3–4; cf. Jer. 7.15, 29. So marginal notes in *OTP* 2.652; Atkinson 2001: 21, 27. On other possible allusions to Jeremiah 7 in the psalmist's attack on the temple, see Atkinson 2001: 72, 89, 90, 209, 214, 271, 273, 313, 324, and 326.

[19] Such is the force of the chosen verb, 'remove' (*aporiptō*). Cf. *Pss. Sol.* 2.21, 9.1; Jer. 7.15 (2×), 29; 8.14 (2×); Ezek. 16.5; etc.

[20] *Pss. Sol.* 2.11.

[21] *Pss. Sol.* 4.4–5. The suggestion of Aberbach (1951) that the phrase refers to political alliances with Rome poorly fits the context.

[22] *Pss. Sol.* 8.21–22.

On the assumption that Aristobulus' progeny are included among these 'sons and daughters', it is unclear whether his children were indeed the offspring of adulterous sexual union or whether they were living emblems of the high priest's choosing to marry outside of priestly lineage.[23] For our purposes, the question is almost beside the point, for other places in the *Psalms* lodge further charges of adultery and even incest, all said to occur in the underground tunnel system beneath the temple.[24] Flouting the demands of priestly purity, the priestly rulers disqualified themselves not least on account of their sexual sin.

But that is not all. The catalogue of sins continues this time with the focus turning to the highest-ranking judicial body in Judaism, the Sanhedrin, presided over by the high priest himself.[25] While it is possible that this passage concerns just the high priest, I think it is more likely to have in view any given member of the Sanhedrin, who is characteristic of the council as a whole:[26]

> Why are you sitting in the council of the devout, you profaner? And your heart
> is far from the Lord, provoking the God of Israel by law breaking;
>
> Excessive in words, excessive in appearance above everyone, he who is harsh
> in words in condemning sinners at judgment.[27]

This would not be either the first or last time that similar charges of judicial heavy-handedness would be brought against the high priest and his ruling council.[28] Nor should we overlook what may appear to be the relatively minor criticisms of verbosity and ostentatiousness.[29] It may well be that such pious grandstanding was understood to be a prelude to a well-known scam targeting unsuspecting widows who had a few pieces of hard currency in their purses and a soft place in their hearts for the observably religious.[30] This is only a suggestion; we cannot be certain.

A related line of polemic, already anticipated in the accusations of greed in *Psalm* 1, bears on the priests' dishonesty in their business dealings, as

---

[23] See discussion in Atkinson 2004: 68–71.

[24] *Pss. Sol.* 8.9–10; cf. *Tamid* 1.1.

[25] On the Sanhedrin, see Saldarini 1992: 975–80; cf. also 1 Macc. 14.44; Matt. 26.57; Josephus, *Ag. Ap.* 2.24 §194; *Ant.* 20.9.1 §200.

[26] So Schüpphaus 1977: 33–5.

[27] *Pss. Sol.* 4.1–2.

[28] In regard to a priest during the Hasmonean period, see *T. Lev.* 16.2–3; in regard to the reign of Ananus, see Josephus, *Ant.* 20.9.1 §§198–203.

[29] Were it certain that such affectation was historically well-founded and continued down into the first century, this would perhaps provide further background to the words of Jesus, recorded in Matthew (6.5, 7), also expressing displeasure at the public display of religious affectation in his day.

[30] Perhaps the best modern equivalent could be found in an email purporting to have been written by an overtly pious billionaire from Nigeria interested in depositing large sums into your bank account. This would at any rate square with the psalmist's mention of these same characters 'scattering orphans' and 'devastating houses' (*Pss. Sol.* 4.10–11; cf. Mark 12.38–40); see Derrett 1972.

well as in their stewardship of the temple's financial affairs: 'They stole from the sanctuary of God as if there were no redeeming heir.'[31] Charges of the priests' embezzling temple funds are not uncommon in ancient Judaism, and apparently the era of Aristobulus was no exception.[32] Not that the Jewish populace winked at the misappropriation of temple funds: on the contrary, the act was considered a treacherous sacrilege (*ma'al*) and as such was desecrating.

No discussion of the psalmist's disquiet would be complete without some mention of the high priest's alleged violation of purity regulations. In the first place, the priests 'walked on the place of sacrifice of the Lord, coming from all kinds of uncleanness; and (coming) with menstrual blood (on them) . . .'.[33] Like the contemporary Qumran sect, the psalmist faults the priests for officiating while enjoying sexual intercourse with their wives during their menstruation.[34] It is also possible that the above-discussed 'sons and daughters . . . profanely spawned' (*Pss. Sol.* 8.21) include offspring born out of unions involving non-priestly spouses.[35] Thus the community's concern for cultic purity, as construed through the community's own halachic interpretation, must have also factored into its break from the temple.

Having reviewed the biting attacks contained in the *Psalms of Solomon*, it remains to be asked to what extent these accusations have a historical basis. Here, alas, we have no easy answer. Obviously, on one level, the diatribe is stylized. One would almost have to expect in a text such as this some heightening of rhetoric and embellishment of lurid detail. At the same time, it will not do to surmise that all this was spun on the loom of baseless rumors. We have very similar charges elsewhere laid at the feet of the Hasmonean high priesthood, not to mention other priestly administrations.[36] Like the *Psalms*, these various texts also explain in detail how the priesthood had gone far beyond the bounds of acceptable behavior. Even if these witnesses share the same ideological goals as the psalmist, there is no evidence of interdependence or collusion among the various polemicists. Because the charges brought up in the *Psalms* are also registered in various other independent camps *and* agree in detail, they must have at least some substance.

Quite apart from this, it is helpful to keep in mind an even more basic point. On the assumption that the texts contained within the *Psalms of Solomon* were not merely private musings, but rather liturgical works written for a

---

[31] *Pss. Sol.* 4.4; 8.11.
[32] 4Q390 Frag. 2, *Tg. 1 Sam.* 2.17; 29.29; *b. Pesh.* 57a; Rom. 2.21–22. See also Chapter 3 below.
[33] *Pss. Sol.* 8.12.
[34] CD 5.6–7; Lev. 15.19–24.
[35] See Atkinson 2004: 69–73. The same author (2004: 78–80) also suggests that the psalmist also takes up the argument of 4QMMT (4Q394–399) and the Sadducees, namely, that pouring water from a clean vessel onto an unclean object renders the vessel unclean. This is possible, but can be little more than a suggestion.
[36] See Evans 1989, 1992.

community in Jerusalem (as is almost certainly the case), it would make no sense at all for the author to have simply dreamed up these charges. Word on the street traveled fairly well in ancient Jerusalem, and if the scorching blast of the psalmist was nothing but hot air, this too would eventually become apparent to his community. In assessing the historical trustworthiness of the *Psalms* then, the course of wisdom would involve neither taking the text completely at face value, nor reading it as the inane diatribe of a delusional muckraker. It appears that at least some in Jerusalem, who could certainly investigate matters for themselves, were convinced that the temple regime was corrupt beyond repair. The ranking priests in Jerusalem must therefore have given these pious folk at least *some* reason for maintaining that conviction, especially as such a belief, once adopted, would only exact great personal cost.

At the same time, the convictions expressed in the *Psalms* did not seem to have been born strictly out of observation; nor does the psalmist view the priestly malfeasance as occurring within some self-contained plane of reality. The improprieties are described in terms of scripture; this is so, not because 'scripture always says it best', but because scripture had already foretold these events long ago. Along the same lines, the world of the *Psalms of Solomon*, like the world of the biblical text itself, is one in which the divine and human converge without contradiction. So, on one level, the divine response is humanly prompted: it was precisely on account of priestly apostasy that the sanctuary fell to the likes of Pompey.[37] But on another level, the psalmist interprets this same unfortunate turn of events as falling within Yahweh's unfolding purposes. The priesthood's unfaithfulness and Pompey's incursion were neither wholly unanticipated calamities nor merely grim reminders that 'the times they were a–changin''; rather, they were manifestations that the line had been drawn and the curse had been cast, according to a divine plan. Once the temple had been profaned, it became clear that Yahweh was on the move and that the appointed hour was at hand. Dark though the hour was, it was the decreed season of evil which was to precipitate the age of redemption.

The focal figure of this redemption in this text is the person of the messiah. In anticipation of his coming, the psalmist cries out: 'Sound in Zion the signal trumpet of the sanctuary; announce in Jerusalem the voice of one bringing good news.'[38] This point in time is presumably identical with the point at which 'the kingdom of our God is forever over the nations in judgment'.[39] It is also the point at which the 'king . . . the Lord Messiah' shall come. If no 'one among them in Jerusalem acted (with) mercy and truth', this messiah will:

---

[37] *Pss. Sol.* 8.23.
[38] *Pss. Sol.* 11.1.
[39] *Pss. Sol.* 17.3.

destroy the unrighteous rulers, to purge Jerusalem from gentiles who trample her to destruction; in wisdom and in righteousness to drive out the sinners from the inheritance ... And he himself (will be) free from sin, (in order) to rule a great people. He will expose officials and drive out sinners by the strength of his word.[40]

In this context, the 'inheritance' is generally understood as the temple; the 'sinners' which the messiah will clear out are the temple officials. He will do so, not strictly with physical force, but by exposing their misdeeds, by the 'strength of his word'. From that point on, the 'Lord Himself is our king for evermore'.[41] The arrival of the kingdom coincides with the expulsion of the wicked leaders from the temple.

On this logic, interestingly enough, those who count themselves among the 'great people', who call the Lord their king, will not strictly be one and the same as ethnic Israel. This is, again, made obvious on observing that, from the psalmist's point of view, those who oversaw the temple would be decisively and lastingly removed from the holy precincts. Obviously, neither the temple officials' office nor their ethnic status was sufficient to save them from the eschatological wrath expressed through the messiah. While this certainly does not mean that the psalmist anticipated early Christianity in its proactive effort to include Gentiles in the covenant, it does imply a reconfiguration of Israel according to the sect's own code. Likewise, an eschatological vision of a restored and re-purified Israel which excluded the temple elite necessarily would have entailed a vision of purity – and presumably an *Ersatz* priesthood conveying true purity – at odds with that which was being promulgated by the same elite. As the newly defined 'innocent lambs' of God, the remnant consisting of the psalmist and his community in Jerusalem set their hope on the day of redemption and vindication.[42]

As they waited, they also identified themselves with the 'poor' of Yahweh.[43] This identification had both practical and theological significance. From the fifth psalm in particular one gathers that the community members were subject to persecution and, consequently, economic deprivation – yet another scarlet stain on the hands of the high priesthood. At the same time, the psalmist seems to find blessedness in his scarcity: 'Happy is (the person) whom God remembers with moderate sufficiency,' whereas 'if one is excessively rich, he sins'.[44] By 'excessively rich' the psalmist obviously has in mind the priesthood he has just been describing in the previous psalm. This suggests that for the psalmist, at least until the day of redemption when God would settle all accounts (in part by making large transfers from the coffers of the

---

[40] *Pss. Sol.* 17.22–23, 36.
[41] *Pss. Sol.* 17.46.
[42] *Pss. Sol.* 8.23.
[43] *Pss. Sol.* 5.2, 11; 10.6; etc.
[44] *Pss. Sol.* 5.16.

wealthy to the poor), the calling of the remnant entailed a life of moderation if not near poverty. This call to poverty was intended to be a sign and a counterpoint to the outlandish greed of the official priesthood.

Yet there is also some indication that the sect's embracing of poverty was related to its priestly vocation of prayer. In *Psalm* 3, which functions as a call to prayer, the psalmist says that the righteous person 'atones for (sins of) ignorance by fasting and humbling his soul, and the Lord will cleanse every devout person and his house'.[45] Such fasting and humbling of the soul would in fact be enacted through the recitation of half the psalms (1, 2, 3, 5, 8, 12, 13, 15, 16), and so it is likely that the community behind the *Psalms of Solomon* sought to secure atonement through their recitation of their text. This certainly would be in keeping with the way in which penitential psalms were used in Qumran and broader Judaism.[46]

One of the prayers included in this collection is a prayer for the messiah's coming.[47] The present moment, the psalmist gathers, is the time of messianic tribulation which immediately precedes the arrival of the Coming One. Top-down apostasy, suffering among the righteous, drought (*Pss. Sol.* 17.19), pagan uprising against Zion – all these were indicators that the eschatological wheel was about to turn.[48] True, messiah would necessarily come, the psalmist reasons, and that in order to deal with the mess in which Jerusalem found itself. At the same time, the sectarians saw their own prayers as a catalyst for this coming. In this respect, the sectarians' prayer had a deeply eschatological orientation. The great wheel of history was about to turn, but only on the axle of priestly activism.

Yet ironically it was on the backs of the psalmist and his community that the great wheel was due to fall. As members of the community prayed, they prayed in expectation that answers to their prayers would be accompanied by suffering: 'When a person is tried by his mortality, your testing is in his flesh ... If the righteous endures all these things, he will receive mercy...'.[49] Judging by the broader witness of ancient Jewish literature, the 'testing of flesh' had at least several functions. First, persecution would serve as a crucible through which the faithful could prove their faithfulness. By enduring suffering for the sake of Yahweh, believers could gain greater assurance of their eventual vindication. It was only the truly righteous, those who had successfully passed the test of suffering, that could offer confident prayer to Yahweh. Second, persecution of the righteous may have been seen as a

---

[45] *Pss. Sol.* 3.8. The word choice may be derived from the scriptural, atoning figure of the 'Suffering Servant', who is humble (Heb.: *na'aneh*) and makes intercession (Isa. 53.4, 7, 12).

[46] Atkinson 2004: 3; Nitzan 1994: 1–32; Werline 1998: 109–59.

[47] *Pss. Sol.* 17.21–25.

[48] As Pitre (2005: 84) rightly notes: 'the *Psalms of Solomon* provide us with an extremely important and very explicit example of messianic tribulation'.

[49] *Pss. Sol.* 16.14–15.

way of forcing God's hand. If the righteous were wronged by the wicked, Yahweh was bound to intervene. Thus a willingness to suffer in order to actualize redemption was seen as having an atoning force. As the community saw it, the eschatological hour of suffering has come in order that the righteous might prove themselves true and in order that they might make, on the basis of that proof, atonement on behalf of Israel.[50] Through their stipulating the impurity of the current temple cult, establishing a new basis of purity issuing from within their own community, and offering up prayer designed to secure Israel's atonement, the sectarians behind the *Psalms* clearly saw themselves as carrying on at least several significant temple functions.

In summary, the *Psalms of Solomon* is a text that provides insight into how a particular Jerusalem-based sect conceived of itself and its opposition as two opposing forces on the brink of redemptive history. According to the psalmist, the temple leaders had reneged on their high calling; they had done so through their scandalous greed, unbridled arrogance, promiscuous behavior, religious pretentiousness, dishonest dealings, temple pilfering, and relaxation of purity standards. Since the impurity and unrighteousness of the priests rendered the temple null and void, the sect understood the appointed hour of tribulation to be at hand and took it upon itself to serve as a kind of provisional temple until the imminent climax. At that time, the messiah would come and establish the kingdom by driving the wicked out from the temple. Until that moment, however, it was the assigned lot of the newly reconfigured people of God, that is, fellow sectarians who subscribed to the sentiments of the psalmist, to function as substitute temple priests. One of the distinctive marks of this new priesthood – in contradistinction to the regnant priesthood – was in its aversion to unnecessary wealth and a corresponding self-identification with the 'poor'. Precisely as the suffering poor, this temple community would also help usher in the longed-for day of vindication. Such was the perspective of those who read, studied and prayed through the *Psalms of Solomon*.

The Qumran sect

From their discovery in the mid–1940s until the present day, the Dead Sea Scrolls (DSS) have been mired in controversy. If there has been any diversion from the smoldering resentment over the painfully slow rate of the documents' public release, it has been the colorful flares of controversy surrounding their historical origins. Whereas scholarship of an earlier day could rest satisfied at de Vaux's judgment that Khirbet Qumran was the scribal hub of Essene Judaism, such assurances are again beset by fresh doubts. The absence of any archaeological evidence of first-century tent-dwellers around the

---

[50] So Atkinson 1998: 107–12.

settlements, along with paleographical evidence attesting to a huge number of scribal hands (suggesting the community was more of a library than a publishing house), continues to raise questions about not only the identity of the DSS community but also the relationship between this community and its texts. The origins and sectarian character of the Qumran community, its history and hypothetical stages of redaction – all these remain at the center of learned contention.

Rather than enter this fray directly, it will suffice for the purposes of my argument to adhere to the following largely uncontroversial premises. First, I will assume, on the basis of archaeological evidence, that the site enjoyed its heyday between 100 and 50 BCE, and it therefore cannot be taken for granted that the Qumran settlement was founded in direct response to the extended leadership crises of the early Hasmonean era.[51] In any event, the mother lode of Qumran theology seems to have been written some time later by authors roughly contemporaneous with the author of the *Psalms of Solomon*, and thus not *too* far removed from the time of John the Baptizer. Second, I am assuming that the Qumran covenanteers kept what documents they did, because they saw them as congruent with their own beliefs. Most people (with the exception of some book reviewers, many lawyers and a great many biblical scholars) do not spend their time poring over texts without at least passing sympathy for their contents. Certainly, given the time and cost of copying texts in antiquity, it is unlikely that the Qumran community went out of their way to obtain manuscripts and preserve texts which they found objectionable. Third, there are no grounds for assuming that the Qumran community was thoroughly monastic or 'other-worldly' in its outlook. The indications that this was a politically engaged movement, whose members had strong opinions about contemporary political events and personages, should be taken seriously.[52] It simply flies in the face of historiographical common sense to suppose that clear allusions to historical contemporaries are ciphers for other individuals altogether whose identities have since been lost to history.

With this prolegomenon in place, I turn now to places in the DSS literature where rather serious complaints are lodged against the regnant priesthood. Since they are not hard to find, I limit myself to two texts. The first, the *Commentary on Habakkuk* (1QpHab), is a retelling of the scriptural prophecy through the lens of the community's experience. One important player within that experience is the Romans (aka the Kittim); another one is the community's arch-nemesis, whom the pesherist sees as jumping off the pages of Hab. 2.5–6:

---

[51] On the dating of the collection, see Vanderkam and Flint 2002: 20–33.

[52] For example, it is very likely that the people behind the DSS were supportive of Alexander Jannaeus, the Sadducean-supported king who took revenge on 800 Pharisees by crucifying them and slaughtering their families. This is apparent from the text *In Praise of King Jonathan*.

And indeed, riches betray the arrogant man and he will not last; he who has made his throat as wide as Hades, and who like Death, is never satisfied. All the Gentiles will flock to him, and all the peoples will gather to him. Look, all of them take up a taunt against him, and invent sayings about him, saying 'Ho, one who grows large on what is not his, how long will he burden himself down with debts?'

This refers to the Wicked Priest, who had a reputation for reliability at the beginning of his term of service; but when he became ruler over Israel, he became proud and forsook God and betrayed the commandments for the sake of riches. He amassed by force the riches of the lawless who had rebelled against God, seizing the riches of the peoples, thus adding to the guilt of his crimes, and he committed abhorrent deeds in every defiling impurity.[53]

Even though the intended target of the *Commentary on Habakkuk* and the *Psalms of Solomon* are presumably different individuals, the similarity of their complaints is striking.[54] Though off to a good start as 'ruler over Israel,' the high priest eventually went over to the dark side, earning the sobriquet 'the Wicked Priest'. Like the psalmist's Aristobulus, who also allegedly became arrogant and forsook the right path for the sake of financial gain, the Wicked Priest is characterized as practicing extortion and theft as a way of life.[55] The love of money becomes here the root of all kinds of evil.

Yet in the end the high priest's acquisitive ways would come to naught, for the Romans, who the pesherist sees as the fulfillment of Habakkuk's Kittim (Chaldeans), would relieve him of his 'ill-gotten riches'.[56] The pesherist sees this not only as fitting justice for the Wicked Priest's persecution of the Teacher of Righteousness, the venerated leader of the Qumran community, but also as divine retribution for his pilfering the people, for '[s]urely even the stonework from the wall will denounce you ... stones ... laid by tyranny'.[57] The temple itself will testify and revolt against the wicked priesthood that occupies it.

Another text in which the high priest's misdeeds figure prominently is the *Damascus Document* (CD). The author sees the reigning priesthood as standing

---

[53] 1QpHab 8.3–13. This and all subsequent translations are from Abegg, Wise and Cook (2005 [1996]).

[54] The Qumran community's ostensible support for the Sadducee-supported Alexander Jannaeus seems to rule out any direct linkage with the psalmist, who only betrays an 'I-told-you-so' satisfaction at Pompey's slaughtering of the Sadducean priests.

[55] See also 1QpHab 12.7–10.

[56] 1QpHab 9.5–7. I am of course describing time from the pesherist's point of view, who may well have been looking back on Pompey's attack on Jerusalem and describing this – *vaticinium ex eventu* – as a future event.

[57] 1QpHab 9.14—10.1. Apparently, Judaism of this period was not averse to applying Habakkuk's 'talking stone' prophecy (Hab. 2.9–11) against the greedy to a corrupt priesthood and the destruction of the temple. See *Liv. Pro.* 10.10–11: 'And he [Jonah] gave a portent concerning Jerusalem and the whole land, that whenever they should see a stone crying out piteously the end was at hand. And whenever they should see all the gentiles in Jerusalem the entire city would be razed to the ground'; cf. Luke 19.40.

behind the miscarriage of Israel's justice.[58] This and other crimes will be judged by God

> because they did not turn away from traitorous practices; they relished the customs of fornication and wicked lucre. Each of them vengefully bore a grudge against his brother, each hating his fellow; each of them were indifferent to their closest relatives, but drew near to indecency; they vaunted themselves in riches and in ill-gotten gains; each of them did just what he pleased; each chose to follow his own willful heart. They did not separate from the people, but arrogantly threw off all restraint, adopting the customs of the wicked . . .[59]

The similarities to and differences from the 1QpHab are instructive. For both, the complaint of financial malfeasance is a pressing one. But it is not only how the priests obtained the money that was at issue, but what they did with it once they got it: like the wicked priests of 1QpHab (and the *Psalms* for that matter) they are said to flaunt their ill-gotten wealth. Less central but by no means necessarily absent in the pesher is concern over 'customs of fornication', which may refer to anything from spiritual apostasy to consorting with prostitutes, practicing incest, or engaging in marital intercourse during the wife's menstrual period.[60] The practices amount to a kind of apostasy; for all intents and purposes, the high priesthood has collectively converted to paganism.

Facing a corrupt priesthood who has defiled the sanctuary, the Qumran community goes its own way by establishing its own temple organization.[61] Such a temple did not require a building, but only a faithful people. In the community's charter, provisions are laid down for twelve laymen and three priests, who are to 'work truth, righteousness, justice, loving-kindness, and humility, one with another'.[62] These same are 'to preserve faith' by 'atoning for sin by working justice and suffering affliction'.[63] When such a duly constituted body is realized,

> [t]hen shall the party of the *Yahad* truly be established, an 'eternal planting,' a temple for Israel, and – mystery! – a Holy of Holies for Aaron; true witnesses to justice, chosen by God's will to atone for the land to recompense the

---

[58] CD 1.19.

[59] CD 8.4–9.

[60] One interesting point of difference, at least in emphasis, is the charge of internecine strife, which cannot be assumed to apply just to the intense conflict between the brothers Hyrcanus II and Aristobulus II. This accusation comes to be repeated in other sources reflecting on priests of the same period.

[61] The point can hardly be disputed. For studies giving substantive attention to the DSS community self-consciously styling themselves as a kind of new temple, see Gärtner 1965, McKelvey 1969, Klinzing 1971, Dimant 1986, Wentling 1989, Briggs 1999, Brooke 1999, Lee 2001, Swarup 2006, Klawans 2006.

[62] 1QS 8.2.

[63] 1QS 8.3.

wicked their due. They will be 'the tested wall, the precious cornerstone' [Isa. 28.16] whose foundations shall neither be shaken nor swayed, a fortress, a Holy of Holies for Aaron, all of them knowing the Covenant of Justice and thereby offering a sweet savor. They shall be a blameless and true house in Israel, upholding the covenant of eternal statutes. They shall be an acceptable sacrifice, atoning for the land and ringing in the verdict against evil, so that perversity ceases to exist.[64]

A series of observations are in order. First, an 'eternal planting' and 'temple' are mutually interpreting. The former term alludes to the eschatological hope of a renewed Eden, the pristine Adamic reality to which God was directing all of history and creation; the latter refers to the sacred space in which divine and earthly meet. As ancient Judaism envisaged it, this renewed creation would break into earthly reality through the temple. More exactly, where the new temple stood there was new creation – and vice versa.[65] This is confirmed – leading to our second observation – by the fact that the sectarians described themselves in temple-architectural terms, in this case, drawn from Isaiah 28.16 (cf. Ps. 118.22).[66] They themselves would be the fulfillment of Isaiah's vision; they will be the temple's '"tested wall, the precious cornerstone" whose foundations shall neither be shaken nor swayed'.

The temple cornerstone and the temple superstructure pertain, respectively, to the two divisions of the community: the priests and the laity.[67] This implies a high calling indeed for the priests. As the first-laid stone of the temple, the cornerstone was recognized as both a redemptive and creational reality. As a redemptive reality, it was the foundation for the Holy of Holies, the dwelling-place of God and the locus of atonement. As a creational reality, it was the basis undergirding creation itself, for when on the third day God contained the waters by establishing land, the first earthly bulkhead against the forces of primordial chaos, this land was destined to become

---

[64] 1QS 8.4–10.

[65] For the correlation between new Eden and the temple in the Qumran literature, see Gärtner 1965: 27–8, and above all Swarup 2006; for the same connection in Judaism more broadly, Beale 2004.

[66] The text reads as follows: 'Therefore thus says the Lord GOD, See, I am laying in Zion a foundation stone, a tested stone, a precious cornerstone (*'eben bōḥan pinnath*) a sure foundation: "One who trusts will not panic."' The quotation is particularly appropriate because it is drawn from a larger context (Isa. 28.14—29.24) in which Israel's leaders and priests are charged with being drunk and blind (29.1, 9–14). See also 1QHa 14.29 (4Q429) (where 'cornerstone' is the basis of an impregnable temple); *Tg. Isa.* 28.16 (where 'cornerstone' is translated as 'kings'); *Midr. Rab. Esther* 7.10 (where 'cornerstone' is identified as Israel); *T. Sol.* 22.7; *T. Job* 18.14. As to what the author of Isaiah intended by 'cornerstone', whether the temple (Ewald, Childs), the remnant of true believers (Donner, Eichrodt) or something else, may be impossible if not plainly unhelpful to pin down: '[p]erhaps no one identification is correct. The cornerstone may be the whole complex of ideas relating to the Lord's revelation ...' (Oswalt 1986: 518). Also see *TDOT "eben"* 1.48–51.

[67] Gärtner 1965: 26–7, 42–3. This bi-partite division works itself out through various metaphors in the Qumran literature.

the temple cornerstone (*'eben ha-shettiya*).[68] While the temple walls (the Qumran laity) mark out and protect the boundary between the holy and the profane, the cornerstone (the Qumran priesthood) serves as the point at which atonement occurs and creation-threatening forces are contained.

The eschatological tenor of the creational and redemptive symbolism is strongly suggested not only by the eschatological orientation of so much of the Qumran corpus, but also, as it so happens in the cited passage, by the words 'tested' (*bḥn*) and 'precious' (*yqr*) (Isa. 28.16). The latter term refers to the community's elect status; the former, to its destiny as final victors who would prove themselves as 'precious' or elect through the throes of tribulation.[69] After all, much of the purpose of the long-expected messianic tribulation was to separate out those who stood approved by God: that which was not from God would ultimately fall by the wayside, but that which was 'tested' and 'true' would prove undaunted by powerful opposition and unscathed by the fires of trial; that which is 'true' endures to the end of history. The words 'tested' and 'precious' in the *Community Rule* are Isaianic terms redeployed within the sect's theology of tribulation.

All this would seem to have implications for how the Qumran priests would have conceived of their task. Our text in 1QS 8.10 tells us that the priestly community committed themselves to 'atoning for the land' and 'ringing out a verdict against evil'. Like the sect behind the *Psalms of Solomon*, then, the Qumran community took on themselves the priestly role of raising a prophetic voice and atoning for Israel. The community was not simply doing temple works; the community *was* the temple. But in undertaking its tasks, the movement aspired to more than simply re-continuing the redemptive function of a temporally defunct temple cultus. Instead, they saw themselves as performing a unique role that presaged a new start to creation, which required ushering out the corrupted temple and ushering in a newly restored Israel. They saw themselves not merely as part of an *ad hoc* measure until the personnel at Zion could straighten themselves out; rather, the Qumran community envisaged itself as the threshold to a larger and infinitely more glorious temple which could never again be profaned (4Q174 1.1–7; 11Q19 29.8–10). The bridge to that future and perfected temple was the temple constituted by the Qumran community itself.

But that day would have to wait. Meanwhile, the Qumran sectarians sought to do well that which the established temple powers did so poorly:

---

[68] See Morray-Jones 1998: 425, with references. While it is true that this connection is not directly attested in material earlier than the rabbinica, Josephus (*J.W.* 5.4.1–4 §§136–83), in his comparison between the temple areas and creation, seems to be aware of this convention. Indeed, the cornerstone's function in staying the forces of the flood may be discernible in the text of Isaiah itself (Oswalt 1986: 504).

[69] 1QH 14.28–32. On the Qumran conception of messianic woes, see Leaney 1963: 292–4; Elliott 2000: 203–21; Pitre 2005: 91–120.

obey the covenant. Thus the members making up this new temple are said to be 'true witnesses to justice' (1QS 8.5). This justice is not abstract but is to be visibly embodied in the context of community relationships. In contrast to the false priests, whose bickering and hatred for one another sealed their disqualification, this community was to manifest justice through loving-kindness, humility, and self-control.[70] Because the priesthood was in theory considered to be the living and organic extension of the temple, reflecting the weighty glory of heaven and earth's convergence, and because too this glory was being badly marred through the actions of the contemporary priests in Zion, the Qumran community regarded personal righteousness and moral fiber as indispensable for their own calling. The effectiveness of priestly activity depended heavily on the righteousness of the priestly character. The members of Qumran, like many Jews of their day, would have found it impossible to detach the objective claim to be the true temple of God from the more subjective expression of personal character.

In this connection, we consider the Qumran sectarians' identification with the 'poor of the flock' or more simply 'the poor'.[71] For the authors of the DSS, part of what it means to be poor is to insist that those who belong to the true temple eschew the rapaciousness of the temple elite in Jerusalem.[72] Part of what it means, too, at least for those who had been fully admitted to the circle, is the transfer of a sizable portion of one's own resources to a collective pool of wealth.[73] And, finally, part of what this means is a distinctive orientation, involving association and practical care, towards the socio-economically marginalized of Jewish society.[74] While various rationales have been suggested for the sectarians' identification with and ministry to the poor, the most compelling must do justice to the fact that for this community poverty was not just a condition to be endured but an eschatological reality to be embraced: God would honor the righteous who gave freely, and God would deliver and save those who in their poverty 'take upon themselves the period of affliction'.[75] In their determination to allow their own righteousness to throw into dark shade the greed of the Jerusalem priests, and in accordance with the eschatological narrative which required a season of impoverished affliction, the Qumran covenanteers seized on self-identification with 'the poor' as a badge of true priesthood.

---

[70] CD 3.17–21; 1QS 2.24; etc.

[71] CD 19.9 (cf. Zech. 11.7); 1QpHab 12.2–4.

[72] CD 5.14–17; 1QHa 26.31–32.

[73] 1QS 5.1–2, 7.6–8, etc.

[74] See the review of evidence in Capper 1995: 327–50; Murphy 2002.

[75] See 4Q171 3.8–11 ('"The wicked borrow and do not repay; but the righteous give generously, for those whom God blesses will inherit the earth, but those whom He curses will be exterminated" [Ps. 37.21–22]. This refers to the company of the poor, who will get the possessions of all [. . . , who] will inherit the lofty mount of Israel and enjoy his holy place.') and 4Q171 2.9–12 ('Afterwards they {= the company of the poor} will enjoy all the [. . .] of the earth and grow fat on every luxury of the flesh.').

The connection between suffering and the priests' ultimate victory is hardly fortuitous. The Qumran faithful saw the suffering of the messianic woes as having atoning significance, even if that suffering primarily served to render them as more perfect and therefore fitter agents of atonement.[76] Suffering with obedience was preparatory: by virtue of their keeping the Mosaic covenant even in the face of suffering, they 'shall *be* an acceptable sacrifice' (emphasis added). But lest the picture be oversimplified, it should also be said that atonement is also connected with daily or seasonal cultic activities, including perhaps prayer and meals, which may have replicated animal sacrifices.[77] This does not necessarily mean that the DSS community thought of there being various and sundry mechanisms of atonement. But it can at least be said that personal and corporate righteousness, patient suffering, prayer and priestly meals were symbolic expressions of the sectarians' belief that they were in fellowship with Yahweh and his holy ones; such acts were also likely the appointed means by which Israel would be released from exile. That day of release, as in other major streams within Second-Temple Judaism, is closely linked with the coming of the messiah. On the day of the messiah's advent, truth would out and the Qumran community would stand justified, joyfully so to those of their community, painfully so to all of their sworn enemies.[78]

In sum, on perceiving the corrupt priesthood as being the primary source of Israel's problems and on perceiving themselves to be the beleaguered victims of that same cadre of temple officials, the Qumran sectarians deduced that (1) the hour of apostasy and tribulation had arrived, (2) this hour included no small store of suffering and poverty for their community as the righteous remnant, and (3) God would apply this suffering and poverty to Israel's atonement. Meanwhile, the sharper the contrast between, on the one side, the unrestrained wickedness of the ruling priests and, on the other side, the intensified commitment to righteousness within the DSS community, the more the latter came to be convinced that the predicted eschatological woes had arrived and that God in due course would use this antithesis to work out his salvific purposes. Reflecting on their own role within the cosmic drama, the sectarians saw themselves much like actors on the set of an action film whose final scene was just underway. And like the final scene of countless action films, this scene portended a last battle – a protracted, grueling

---

[76] 1QHa 14.11.

[77] See the archaeological argument to this effect in Magnes 2002: 116–26. For further discussion, cf. Schiffmann 1999: 272–6; Klawans 2006: 162.

[78] See, e.g., 1QS 9.10; CD 19.7–11, 33; 1QSa 2.11–22. While I am generally sympathetic to the balanced conclusions of Klawans (2006: 173–4), I disagree with his statement that the Qumran covenanteers 'did not assert that the divine presence dwelled among them' (174). Their expectation that Yahweh would redeem remnant Israel from within the community presupposes that Yahweh is also in some sense present among them. They thought that *they* 'would best bring humans into close contact with God' (Schiffmann 1999: 272).

fight – between the hero and the arch-villain (up to this point, it had only been minor villains getting their just deserts). What is more, the Qumran community expected to come out on top in the end. After all, in action films and scripture alike, it is ultimately in being wounded but nevertheless winning that the real hero proves himself once and for all to be, well, the hero. Setting out to fulfill their priestly calling, the community was confident that it would emerge victorious and set the stage for the final, everlasting, God-made temple.

Summary of *Psalms of Solomon* and Qumran materials

According to the communities behind the *Psalms of Solomon* and the DSS, business-as-usual at the temple had become intolerable to a breaking-point. The catalogue of unrighteous behaviors stemming from the priests' greed, lust, and hatred – all these were more than enough to disqualify the established leaders from office and render Yahweh's temple useless. But this hardly frustrated God's purposes. On the contrary, all this was part of a divine plan, for God had chosen another people and another venue for accomplishing the salvation of Israel and the world. Once it became clear that the great apostasy was underway, it also became clear that the hour of salvation was imminently at hand.

In the minds of both groups, those functions which had previously and under normal circumstances been assigned to the temple were now the remit of the remnant, the true temple of Israel. But both groups also identified themselves as a transitional community, a community marked out as 'the poor' of scripture, who through their faithfulness even in the midst of persecution and poverty would pave the way for the final, eschatological temple. Simultaneously functioning as the new temple and the not-yet temple, both communities saw themselves as straddling two eras: the era of the present age and the era of future glory. The central figure attending the age of future glory was the messiah himself, who would introduce the final temple. Such seem to be the key features of a counter-temple movement.

John the Baptizer and his sect

Also waiting for the turn of an era, several generations after the writings of the *Psalms of Solomon* and a good number of years after the DSS, was a figure by the name of John the Baptizer. John did not, as far as we know, belong to a guild of writers and critics who prophesied with their pen. But he did, as I think it can be demonstrated, belong to a line of dissidents who insisted that the old order was corrupt and rapidly fading. And if the old order was on its way out, that meant that a new order, a new temple, was on its way in.

One would be hard-pressed to think of a New Testament figure – outside perhaps of Jesus himself – who proves to be more puzzling than John the Baptizer. Often portrayed as something akin to a revivalist tent-preacher, and at other times as a well-meaning if not largely self-deceived man, John seems to raise more questions than he answers. In some ways, even though I find both of these characterizations as completely out of keeping with the historical data, full disclosure must confess that there is a frustrating lack of historical data to begin with. The camel-skin clad figure still provokes a good deal of mystery.

In historical-critical research into John, assurance has also been hard to come by because of the perception that the early Church downplayed the significance of John in order to discourage the faithful from elevating the martyred prophet into a cult figure.[79] The extent to which this anti-Baptizer agenda played itself out in the formation of the gospel tradition is another question, and one which cannot be dealt with here to complete satisfaction. But neither will this be entirely necessary. When it comes to determining whether John could be considered as the spearheading figure behind yet another counter-temple movement, it will be enough to begin by calling up a list of assertions which I believe most scholars would assign to the realm of factual history. They are as follows:

John the Baptizer . . .

1   lived an ascetical lifestyle which took him to the desert;
2   preached the necessity of a baptism of repentance in light of Israel's sin;
3   expected the near arrival of eschatological judgment;
4   attracted large crowds;
5   included Jesus among his adherents through baptism until Jesus broke off to start a new movement;
6   was not embraced by the ruling temple authorities of his day;
7   died at the hands of Herod Antipas.

Limiting myself for the sake of argument to these seven propositions, it may be asked whether these brushstrokes invite us to recognize in John's portrait a man who is shouldering responsibility for a counter-temple society. I believe that this very case can be made.

We start with point (1), relating to John's locale and spare lifestyle. As more than a few scholars have noted, the desert was attractive for John's purposes for symbolic reasons.[80] It is true: anyone going into the desert could be motivated by a desire to hide or retreat. But going into the desert *and starting a movement* is to do anything but hide or retreat, especially in first-century Israel.[81] The desert was after all the historical location of Yahweh's

---

[79]   So, classically and seminally, Baldensperger 1898; Bultmann 1968 [1921]: 246–7.
[80]   See, e.g., Meyer 2002 [1979]: 115–17; Horsley 1986; Wright 1996: 160–1; Murphy 2003: 132.
[81]   Josephus recounts a number of first-century, desert-based insurgent movements. These include a large gathering near Mount Gerizim, which was quickly crushed by Pilate (*Ant.* 18.4.1 §§85–87); Theudas, who (in more ways than one) was chopped down by Cuspius Fadus (*Ant.* 20.5.1 §§97–98; Acts 5.36); a Zealot-like movement, quickly put down by Felix (*J.W.* 2.13.4 §§259–60); an Egyptian who modeled himself on Joshua, also ruthlessly repressed by Festus (*J.W.* 2.13.5 §§261–63; *Ant.* 20.9.6 §§169–72); a 'certain impostor', dispatched by Festus (*Ant.* 20.9.10 §188).

greatest redemptive act when he brought Israel out of Egypt and formed a new nation. By creating a following in the desert, John was posing a serious challenge to the religious and political rulers back in Jerusalem, for in effect he was saying, 'Yahweh is beginning again with a new Exodus and a new nation. It is starting under my auspices – here and now.' Well aware of the decisive way in which Israel's first-century leaders tended to deal with desert movements, John knew that his activities could only be interpreted as being politically charged.[82]

This remains true even if John, contrary to the practice of the resident Qumran sectarians, expected his initiates to carry on with their day-to-day existence back in 'the real world', as least as far as their jobs were concerned (Luke 3.13–14).[83] Apparently, in John's mind, the formation of a new Israel did not necessitate a clean break from all aspects of workaday life in Jerusalem nor from, as far as we can tell, regular involvement in the life of the temple. This is an important point: if the Qumran sectarians registered their dissatisfaction by geographical self-removal, while the community behind the *Psalms* was content to express their vexation while remaining a separate worshipping body in Jerusalem, John's approach may have been less radical than both.[84] As the Baptizer saw it, it was not necessary to break from the social fabric of Israel in order to be the new Israel.

This is not to say, however, that John came short of preaching a radical ethic. Radical it was. John apparently had a few things to say about what it meant to be faithful to the covenant, at least judging by Luke 3.10–14, which shows John excoriating his hearers for greed. In John's ideal world, those with two shirts would share with those who had none (Luke 3.11); meanwhile, those who aspired to make more and more money would learn to be content (Luke 3.14). The latter point echoes some of the sentiments already touched on in the *Psalms* and the DSS, but also in Judaism more broadly. More noteworthy is the former instruction. If John seriously expected his followers to heed this teaching (here it will not do to resort to the common hermeneutical maneuver of saying, 'Oh, what John really meant was that people should only be *willing* to share one of their shirts'), then this implies a kind of communal reciprocity in which those with any means committed themselves up-front to ameliorating the lot of those who were impoverished. In this

---

[82] Arguing against the hypothesis of an anti-temple Baptizer, Avemarie (1999: 396–8) does not find the desert a significant point of comparison between John's following and Qumran, at least in their potential capacity as counter-temple movements. But his argument fails to acknowledge either Qumran's anti-priestly polemic or the likelihood that other desert revolutionary movements of the day were also, in their own way, necessarily *contra* temple (one doesn't plan a coup of Jerusalem, unless one is also prepared to take down its temple-based rulers as well).

[83] On the authenticity of the speech material in Luke 3.10–14, see below.

[84] Christiansen's (1995: 200) claim that the Baptizer's immersion had no implications for community boundaries founders on Luke 7.29–30, which clearly presupposes that those who were baptized by John were publicly identifiable as 'in', while those who were not duly baptized were 'out'.

case, John's community and network, like the Qumran sect and perhaps too like the pious poor behind the *Psalms*, must also have seen this *modus vivendi* as a way of distinguishing itself from larger Judaism.

This last point of course depends on whether Luke 3.10–14 should be treated as a typical scene going back to the time of the Baptizer, or merely the handiwork of Luke (or a Lukan source). While the evangelist's obvious interest in themes of 'rich and poor' may incline us to the latter judgment, this seems premature. It would hardly be extraordinary if someone consciously and prominently adopting the lifestyle of the poor also wished to show solidarity with them by speaking out on economic concerns. Moreover, as it is fairly certain that John, like Jesus after him, employed the agricultural metaphor of 'bearing fruit' in his preaching (Luke 3.8–9), then it is only a small step to surmise that John set his prophetic sights on issues like the ones we find flagged up in vv. 10–14. John's socio-economic concern, at any rate, lines up with the consistent direction of 'fruit-bearing' imagery in the prophetic literature.[85] Issues of economic justice, just as they are recorded in Luke 3.10–14, appear to echo the very voice of the Baptizer.

Inevitably, the implicit claim to be reconstituting Israel would have entailed the equally implicit and controversial claim that the temple in Jerusalem was no longer fully operative and that its essential functions were being transferred to John and his community. After all, John does seem on a symbolic level to be starting a new theocracy, and a new theocracy would have been inconceivable apart from a correspondingly new temple. That John was seeking to establish just that begins to become evident on consideration of point (2) above: John's double declaration that Israel had broken the covenant and that re-entry into the covenant required undergoing a personal baptism of repentance.[86] Although the case for an early first-century Jewish practice of baptizing proselytes remains contested, it makes most sense of the data to affirm that, from John's point of view, any attempt to attach oneself to Israel would require a ritual reserved for those entering into Judaism for the first time. Whereas those aspiring to come into Judaism in that day would normally have been directed to seal their 're-conversion' at the temple, here John directs them to himself and to his baptism. Likewise, since in the normal course of things, the temple was the place where one confessed sins and offered the

---

[85] On 'fruit' as a symbol for economic justice see, e.g., Isaiah 5; Jer. 17.3b–8; 21.12–14; Ezek. 16.49—17.10; Hos. 10.12–13; Amos 8.1–6; Hab. 1.1–4; 3.17. On the authenticity of the Baptizer's images on other grounds, see Becker 1972: 109; Meier 1994: 28–32; Webb 1991: 358 n. 16.

[86] I do not view the 'break' as absolute, although it did imply that 'all claims to salvation on the basis of racial solidarity with Abraham were unavailing' (Meyer 2002 [1979]: 121). For examples of warnings (contemporary with the Baptizer) against relying on descent from Abraham, see Hägerland 2006: 179.

prescribed sacrifice, John's invitation to receive forgiveness outside of the temple apparatus essentially rendered the Jerusalem institution redundant.[87] Apparently, like his religious competitors down the road at Qumran, John had come to believe that a new temple was already taking shape.

This judgment is further confirmed by his warning that 'God is able from these stones to raise up children to Abraham' (Luke 3.8) On consideration of this saying, whose authenticity is broadly granted, it bears stating that when Yahweh is described as 'raising up' (LXX: *anistēmi*) something, that something is frequently either his 'offspring/seed' or the 'temple'.[88] Moreover, when people in biblical literature are referred to as 'stones', it is regularly in reference to their capacity either as citizens of Israel or as temple members (if a distinction between these two roles can even be made).[89] The thrust of the Baptizer's pun, borrowed directly from scripture, is obvious: through John, God is raising up new children of Israel, who will also be constitutive of a new temple. Under the Baptizer, Israel is starting afresh, and with this new start comes, as a matter of course, a new temple.

The reconstitution was an urgent one, for John fully expected God to bring imminent judgment on unrepentant Israel. Although some scruple that this could not have been a specifically 'messianic judgment', such arguments seem to be based more on silence than the best reconstruction of the facts. In favor of John's messianic expectations, the Baptizer more than likely equated the 'stronger one' (Mark 1.7//Luke 3.16//Matt. 3.11) with the 'coming one' (Luke 7.19//Matt. 11.3; Luke 19.38//Matt. 21.9), and at least for a time entertained the possibility that both of these designations were appropriate to Jesus (Luke 7.18–23).[90] The expectation of imminent messianic judgment would have also entailed the belief that Yahweh was on the verge of restoring Israel from exile, for that was after all a recurring bullet point with the extant messianic job descriptions. All of this lends credence to the notion that it was not the early Church but John himself who saw his ministry as the fulfillment of Isaiah 40, a passage describing forgiveness of sins and return

---

[87] An able defense of this position is found in Wright 1996: 160–2.

[88] For Yahweh 'raising up' 'offspring/seed' see Gen. 38.8; 2 Sam. 7.12; 1 Chron. 17.11; for 'tabernacle/temple/booth of David', see Exod. 26.30; Num. 1.15; 7.1; Isa. 44.6; 58.12; 61.4; Amos 9.11.

[89] See Jos. 4.6–9; 1 Kings 18.31–38; Isa. 54.12–13, etc. This is also represented by the high priest bearing 'precious *stones*' (*'abnē-šōham*), engraved with the names 'of the *sons* (*benē*) of Israel' (Exod. 28.9; 39.7, etc.), a practice from which the Hebrew 'son'/'stone' word play may have been hewn.

[90] *Pace* Theissen and Merz 1998 [1996]: 211; see Meier 1994: 131–7; Webb 1991: 278–82. Meier's (1994: 132, 199 n. 90) disinclination to attach messianic significance to the epithet of 'the coming one' does not engage with the evidence presented in Strobel 1961: 173–202. However, Meier's convincing arguments for the reliability of Luke 17.18–23 par., together with the passage's obvious raising of Jesus' messianic status (see here the oft-cited parallel from 4Q521 which provides a messianic parallel to Jesus' self-description), speak in favor of John having seriously entertained the notion that Jesus was the anointed one.

from exile. An apocalyptic, oracular prophet, John saw his own moment as a decisive turning-point in Israel's history.[91]

Having discussed the ways in which John's movement fits hand-in-glove into other counter-temple movements, there is to this point a crucial striking difference: the absence of hard evidence that the Baptizer criticized the temple authorities.[92] Obviously, the absence of explicit testimony to this effect does nothing to advance my case, but neither does silence on this score force its retreat. For starters, it almost has to be assumed that the relationship between John and the temple establishment was, at best, a chilly one. In their reaction to John's message, which implied that a few leading folks back in Zion should start looking for a new job, the temple dignitaries were largely dismissive.[93] But this failure to respond would not likely have prompted John to smile and say, 'That's okay. To each his own; they're entitled to their opinion.' The Baptizer was clearly stepping on some priestly toes, and it can only be supposed that these priests, when they were not coyly pulling their feet away, were by fits and starts thrusting their feet right back in his direction. And one way they may have been doing so is by putting in appearances, arms tightly folded and eyebrows firmly arched, at the baptism gatherings.[94] In this light, history's silence on John's explicit views of the temple certainly cannot be construed as evidence against his polemic posture.

At the same time, I believe that John's criticism of the temple can be established even without explicit testimony to that effect. I begin with a seemingly incidental point: the synoptic tradition's attesting that John lived off the land.[95] This odd and attention-drawing habit may well have had more than a few purposes, but it could hardly have gone unnoticed among John's admirers (many of whom wondered whether he was the 'Coming One') that his diet was very similar to that of another messiah-like figure. Those who relived Israel's glory days through storytelling would have known the story of Judas Maccabeus inside and out. In this case, they would have recalled that after Antiochus Epiphanes profaned the temple in 167 BCE by slaughtering a heifer on the altar, Judas together with his followers fled into the wilderness and 'continued to live on what grew wild, so that they might not share in the defilement' of the temple and surrounding city.[96] Once John's observers

---

[91] As summarized by Webb 1991: 381–2.

[92] See Webb 1991: 370–2.

[93] Mark 11.31–32.

[94] While most commentators treat Matthew's (3.7) mention of the Sadducees at the baptism as redactional, Webb (1991: 175–8) provides insightful explanations as to why a Sadducean (and thus a temple) presence may arguably be historically likely.

[95] Matt. 3.4; Mark 1.6.

[96] 2 Macc. 5.27b. So Taylor 1997, 43–4; Kelhoffer 2005. Certainly, when Jesus enters into Jerusalem a few years after the height of John's activity, he is doing so in conscious imitation of Judas Maccabeus. It is no great leap to suppose that John was up to much of the same. As Mr Ron Kneezl points out, a similar anti-priestly posture may be implicit in John's assuming Elijah's garb.

put two and two together, quite apart from his having to say anything explicit and thus risking a premature end to his ministry, they would have drawn their own conclusions. Among their inferences would be that a desecration akin to that of 167 BCE has occurred and that John, invoking the memory of Judas 'the Hammer', was in his own way poised to lead the life of a guerilla warrior until the temple should be restored.

Other rebel movements closer to John's own day seemed to order their steps by a similar logic. In a clear re-enactment of the Exodus and Conquest, Josephus informs us, Theudas had called on a sizable crowd of followers to gather all their earthly possessions and join him in crossing the Jordan River, which he promised to part miraculously.[97] Likewise, when an Egyptian Jew led his massive following to the Mount of Olives, east of Jerusalem and on the cusp of the Judean desert, he anticipated divine intervention similar to that which Joshua experienced in the taking of Jericho.[98] Such New Exodus uprisings seem to have presupposed, on a deeply symbolic level, an equivalency between the land of Judea and historically impure regions. How else could the promised land be impure unless the temple space, the center of purity, had also become impure? Moreover, those recruiting men in the desert must have figured squarely on the likelihood that in their anticipated holy war against the 'powers that be', it would be the temple elite and their forces who would be among the first to launch a pre-emptive strike against them.

There is yet another indication that John was highly critical of the temple. This evidence comes indirectly by way of Jesus' disciples when they ask their master to teach them to pray '*exactly* as John taught his disciples to pray' (Luke 11.1). As is increasingly recognized, Jesus responds to this request with what was likely intended to be a set prayer for the season of tribulation: the Lord's Prayer.[99] If so, then John – having provided a prototype of the *Pater Noster* – must have also given his disciples a prayer by which they could endure the impending trial.[100] That means too that John the Baptizer, again like the psalmist and the Qumran covenanteers, considered his own day as being on the very cusp of messianic tribulation and his own community as a catalyst in bringing about the necessary train of events.[101] Because first-century Jews were by and large convinced that the period of tribulation would be closely attended by apostasy at the highest levels, John's grievances against

---

[97] *Ant.* 20.5.1 §§97–98.
[98] *Ant.* 20.8.6 §170.
[99] See, classically, Brown 1968 [1961]: 314–19. Jeremias 1971b: 201–2.
[100] On the Baptizer as possibly being the source for the Lord's Prayer, see Taylor 1997: 151–3.
[101] So too Allison (1998: 146–7, 193). Pitre (2005: 177–98) rightly makes a case for Jesus having perceived John along these lines, but this hardly would have been plausible unless the Baptizer had maintained beliefs and practices consistent with that perception. Cf. Rothschild 2005: 59–63.

the temple hierarchy are necessarily to be inferred from his conviction that the great affliction was at hand.

Convinced that transgression of Israel's religious leadership had rendered the temple profaned, John had come to conclude through his reading of scriptures that the messianic tribulation had already been set into motion. God *had* to provide a form of temple worship, the Baptizer reasoned, and where else would he begin to do this but through John himself and the following he was to inspire. Thus, those functions which otherwise would fall to the temple, including atonement and prayer, now devolved on the community under his auspices. But John's temple would not be a return to normalcy, but an Edenic return to a deeper, more thoroughgoing righteousness, manifest most clearly in the community's mutual benefaction. This socio-economic ethic was enforced as an interim norm, until the day when God would visit Israel through his messiah. God *had* to act, because where one finds the darkest hour, there soon after one would also find the dawn. The platform of this divine activity would be with the substitute temple community which John had initiated.

Conclusion

On surveying the *Psalms of Solomon* and the Qumran corpus, I have sought to discern certain characteristic features of counter-temple societies in Second-Temple Judaism. After comparing this profile with the discernible facts relating to John the Baptizer, it is possible to make some general observations regarding all three movements, a rough phenomenology of ancient Jewish counter-temple associations. While there are of course important differences between the groups, there are also significant family likenesses. First, like the communities behind the *Psalms of Solomon* and the Qumran writings, John's band found serious fault with the ruling priesthood, so much so that they considered the contemporary temple system defiled. Second, as a result of this conviction, John and his analogues also came to believe that the time of tribulation was underway; moreover, their estrangement from the temple establishment was seen as part and parcel of this tribulation. Third, there is also some evidence that this perception of tribulation led John's people, like the communities behind the DSS and the *Psalms*, to regard themselves as the scriptural fulfillment of 'the poor'; all three groups in some sense embraced a vocation on behalf of the poor. Fourth, again like the first two sects under review, John's disciples took it upon themselves to carry on certain temple functions in response to the failings of the Jerusalem cultus. In each case, this reconstituting of Yahweh's temple was seen as a provisional measure, leading up to the messianic advent and apocalyptic judgment. In light of the crisis, the boundaries and contours of time, space, and Israel itself had been redrawn. I believe a fair-minded reading of the evidence supports my initial hypothesis that John's movement was a counter-temple movement.

Since Jesus launched his own career from within this ministry, this is no insignificant point. It is of course possible that Jesus took sharp exception to his cousin's thinking – as a few scholars believe he eventually did.[102] But in my view this one-sided approach is not the best read of the limited data. Jesus obviously parted ways with John for a reason, but at the same time history never gives us the impression that the former had repudiated all that he had come to embrace under his one-time master. Besides, in the history of sectarianism, new sects are birthed not through an absolute renunciation of the mother movement, but through a decisive swerve. The most promising explanation of Jesus' words and actions then is one which latches on to elements of both continuity and discontinuity between John and Jesus.

But continuity and discontinuity between John and Jesus are not enough to launch my basic hypothesis. There is another side of the river and another pier across from the one I have already described. Before reconstructing the bridge which may have existed between these two piers, before talking about Jesus and his intentions, one more building-block needs to be in place: the early Church. Did the early Church also bear the marks of a counter-temple movement? If so, how does this help us formulate an initial hypothesis in regard to Jesus? While the second of these two questions will have to wait, the first of these questions comes under view in the following chapter.

---

[102] Crossan 1994: 48; Theissen and Merz 1998 [1996]: 208–11.

2

'Don't you know that you yourselves are the temple of God?'

The early Church as a counter-temple movement

Introduction

Propositions may '*tell* it like it is', but images, which can be powerful things, have the rhetorical advantage of '*showing* it like it is'. That is why sometimes the most revealing indications of a group's self-understanding lay not so much in its formal pronouncements but in its favorite word-pictures. Sharing a reservoir of stories and verbal pictures in their sacred scriptures, Second-Temple Jewish interpreters applied these narratives and images to their own situation in such a way that neither the past nor the present could be seen in quite the same way again. If the only meaningful way to draw on the common reservoir was by digging a channel between the generations of old and one's own day, it goes without saying that the channel would have to cut in a particular direction with a particular trajectory. The past speaks into the present so as to inform and transform it, but as it does, the past too is transformed, as is the future. Scriptural interpretation in Second-Temple Judaism thus typically involved, even if only implicitly, not only a retracing of the storyline of Israel, but also the embedding of the interpreter's community within an unfolding story that would not be finally resolved until the eschatological climax. Generally speaking, it is the eschatological scenario – and this is true whether one considers Sirach or Zechariah, the Enochic literature or *Jubilees* – that ultimately defines the trajectory of Israel's history.

It is thus all the more surprising, within scholarly discussion of the early Christian community's co-identification with the temple, that the cultus should so often be treated as an abstract and timeless concept, when early Christian 'temple talk' seems to have presupposed the temple as a redemptive-historical, eschatological reality.[1] More precisely, while a good many commentators have rooted early Christian self-understanding *qua* temple in the established Jerusalem cultus, or in the temple practices of the surrounding Greco-Roman environment, it is seldom countenanced that the most significant

---

[1] Notable exceptions can be found in earlier works: Lohmeyer 1961; McKelvey 1969.

point of comparison and orientation for the early Christians was not any visible temple but the long-awaited eschatological temple. As vitally important as the recent investigations into the relationship between first-century Judaism and early Christianity may be, perhaps this interest, together with a methodologically suspect Comparative Religions approach to the two 'religious systems', has induced us to think of these two movements as parallel lines of religious phenomena. But what if these two movements are not parallel lines at all? What if they are more like two vectors leading up to and converging onto the same culminating vertex point – a final temple wrought not by human hands?

I believe that the best explanation of the evidence points exactly in this direction. In making this case I will be situating myself between, on the one side, the view that the early Christians only saw themselves as being merely *like* the temple without nurturing any serious aspirations of *being* the temple, and, on the other side, the view that the early Christian community saw itself as *directly* usurping the role of the Jerusalem temple without remainder. In my judgment, the former approach generally fails to appreciate the redemptive-historical trajectory (i.e. the storyline) implicit in those passages in which Christ or his followers are compared to the temple; the latter approach typically involves an insufficient grasp of the fact that for the early Christians all earthly temple existence had, as a result of the Christ event, acquired a provisional cast. To put these respective readings of the historical data in theological terms, those who argue that the early Christian community staked no ontological claim in its self-comparison with the temple seem to be reflecting an under-realized eschatology; as for those who argue that the early Christian community claimed to replace the temple in an absolute sense, I suspect there is, correspondingly, a lingering over-realized eschatology.[2] In my view, both positions ultimately fall short either on their not fully appreciating the close connection between corporate self-understanding (ecclesiology) and eschatology in early Christian thought, or on a misunderstanding of the latter. Once it is recognized that Judaism considered the eschatological temple to be operating in tandem with the earthly temple in Jerusalem, and once it is allowed that early Christianity saw itself as the community in which the eschatological temple was taking shape, there should be no difficulty in imagining that the early Christians recognized *both* their own Church and the structure in Zion as temples in a meaningful sense.

---

[2] By 'under-realized eschatology' I mean an underestimation of the degree to which the early Christians saw God's promises as being realized in their own experience; by 'over-realized eschatology' I mean an overestimation of the same. With both of these terms I am referring not so much to a theological imbalance (although this may play a part), as much as a historiographical imbalance in interpreting the corpus of early Christian literature. Taken as a whole, the first-century literature retains a firm tension between the 'already' and the 'not yet'.

Approaching the question from a different angle, one might say that any analysis of the early Christian claim 'to be temple' should involve some consideration of how Judaism as a whole thought about sacred space and functionality. The historical evidence suggests that when there were grave concerns regarding the temple's functioning, those harboring such concerns would sometimes attempt to sustain Israel through a kind of provisional temple service, even if the expedient fell short of implying that the prescribed sacred space had been rendered obsolete altogether. On the other hand, if a provisional temple successfully carried out the functions which the established temple could no longer legitimately sustain, then there was naturally some sense in which the former became the temple. This is because, as John Walton reminds us in his discussion of Jewish ontology (notion of being), existence was predicated of things not simply on the basis of their physical being, but also and even more so on the basis of functionality:

> [I]n the ancient world something came into existence when it was separated out as a distinct entity, given a function, and given a name ... I will label this approach to ontology as 'function-oriented.' This is in stark contrast to modern ontology which is much more interested in what might be called the structure or substance of something along with its properties. In modern popular thinking (as opposed to technical philosophical discussion), the existence of the world is perceived in physical, material terms ... I will designate this approach to ontology as 'substance-oriented.' In the ancient Near East, something did not necessarily exist just because it happened to occupy space.[3]

While the space in which the temple activity occurred was not irrelevant, there is nonetheless good reason to suppose that the notion of sacred function was at least as important. The attempt to carry out temple functions outside the sacred space of the temple did indeed constitute a temple of sorts but did not necessarily carry with it a thorough and irreversible repudiation of the temple for which it sought to compensate. For temple dissidents who were torn between property and propriety, a cultic 'home away from home' seems to have been a deeply ambivalent affair.

My concern in the remainder of this chapter will be to argue that the earliest Christian voices, despite their variegated concerns and rhetorical interests, shared the common conviction that the heavenly temple, the great hope of Judaism, had broken forth in preliminary fashion in the resurrection of Jesus Christ. By providing atonement through his death and taking the right hand seat of God, Jesus Christ had proven himself to be the final high priest. This meant, retrospectively, that the kingdom of God had already reclaimed the realm of this world through Jesus' earthly activity; prospectively, it meant that the kingdom would continue to advance until the climax of history, when the final temple would be completed. In the meantime,

---

[3] Walton 2006: 179–80.

the body of the crucified and risen Lord was the portal through which true worshippers gained access to the heavenly temple (of which Israel's temples heretofore were only a copy); Christ's body, soon identified with the Church itself, was also the ingress through which the heavenly temple would take shape in creation. God's breaking into earthly reality, which amounted to God's establishing the heavenly temple on earth, was signaled by the Spirit's presence. By virtue of their possession of the Spirit, believers deemed themselves to be the true temple of God, but only in an anticipatory sense.

It was not its broad outline of the eschatological narrative (as I have presented it) that set the early Church apart from surrounding Judaism, but rather its specific Christological and pneumatological re-scripting of that narrative. Whereas other Jewish sects had seen the inauguration of the final temple as a wholly future reality, early Christian voices are consistent in asserting that this climactic event has already been anticipated in the present. Persuaded that Jesus Christ was risen and that the Spirit had been poured out on the Church, the first Christians interpreted these events as proof positive that God would indeed complete the final temple at the end of the ages, but – in distinction from surrounding Judaism – that this final rebuilding was now taking place within history.

This, as I see it, is the broad outline of early Christian apocalypticism. In order to sustain this claim, I undertake a brief survey of texts involving early Christian self-identification with the temple. Obviously, the review must be limited in both scope and depth. Despite the fact that Christian temple talk evolved through the first century and well down into the later patristic era, and despite too the fact that a handful of complex exegetical issues confront us along the way, my approach will necessarily be confined to broad strokes and a limited historical period.

There are several sources which I have chosen to bracket from discussion. The first is the *Gospel of Thomas*. Even if *Thomas* first did begin to take shape in the first century (a mighty 'if' in my mind), its relevance here is minimal: the only logion which speaks to the temple (*Gos. Thom.* 66) is so likely to reflect a late stage of redaction that it must be disqualified from consideration.[4] Two sources which lay a considerably better claim to antiquity are Mark and Q. Yet I set these aside as well. Although Mark's understanding of Jesus as temple would otherwise be highly relevant to this survey, the difficulties in ruling out the evangelist's dependence on pre-Markan tradition or reminiscence at key points would require a painstaking, methodologically overwrought discussion that would take us too far afield.[5] The same intricacies would beset

---

[4] I have argued for a late second-century *Gospel of Thomas* elsewhere; see Perrin 2007.

[5] I take up a good deal of Markan material below, at any rate. For illuminating studies on Mark's vision of Jesus as temple, see, e.g., Juel 1977, Heil 1997, Gray 2009.

the use of Q. True, it would perhaps be possible to make recourse to the standard criteria for determining where Jesus' voice ends and where the voice of the Q community picks up, but given the variously proposed strata of Q, serious questions regarding the unity or textuality of Q, and even further questions regarding its existence, the better part of wisdom would seem to be to invest the reader's attention elsewhere.[6] In my judgment, a representative sampling of early Christian reflection can be teased out of the earliest available patristic literature, the Johannine writings, 1 Peter, Hebrews, Matthew, Luke–Acts, and then, finally, certain critically assured letters of Paul.[7]

The temple and temple imagery in early Christianity

Patristic and Johannine literature

We begin with a small collection of texts known as the Apostolic Fathers, written between the later first and mid-second century CE. Following instructions regarding the Eucharist, the author of the *Didache* commends a prayer in which congregants are to recite these words: 'We give you thanks, Holy Father, on account of your holy name which you have caused to pitch a tent in our hearts.'[8] As a eucharistic prayer, this can only be drawing an implicit analogy between the believers' partaking of the Eucharist and the tabernacle high priests' ingesting the Bread of the Presence: like the priests of a prior epoch, Christian believers were sustained in their holy calling through the holy bread.[9] In a different, slightly later text, the author describes Christians not only as priests, but also, collectively, as a temple or, better yet, as a temple in the making: 'Let us become a perfect temple for God.'[10] Likewise, 'a dwelling place of our heart ... is a holy temple for the Lord'; or, as Ignatius puts it, 'you are stones of a temple'.[11] By the opening decades of the second century, there was clearly a firm tradition that believers constituted both a new priesthood and a new temple. Part and parcel of this tradition was

---

[6] Goodacre and Perrin 2004; Dunn 2003: 147–60. Those desiring to persevere despite the haze surrounding Q might consult Han 2002. Here, as elsewhere, the redactional interests of Matthew and Luke are more easily discerned, and so there is no need to omit these texts from the study.

[7] Obviously, in limiting myself to those texts which are indisputably Pauline, I am neglecting several so-called deutero-Pauline texts which serve as important witnesses to the trajectory I am describing (not least in the case of Ephesians). Their exclusion is only a reminder that my discussion makes no claims to being exhaustive.

[8] *Did.* 10.2. The translation of non-biblical material in this chapter is my own.

[9] Barker 2002: 147–50; Milavec 2003: 385; Perrin 2008. The author's choice of verb in *Did.* 10.2 is significant: just as Yahweh had 'pitched a tent' in the midst of Israel in the tabernacle and then in the incarnation (John 1.14), now the divine presence was pitching a tent in the believers' hearts.

[10] *Barn.* 4.11.

[11] *Barn.* 6.15; Ign. *Eph.* 9.1, respectively.

the expectation that this priesthood of believers would be tested through messianic tribulation right up to the parousia.[12]

How this new temple related to institutional Judaism becomes fairly clear, at least in the case of the *Epistle of Barnabas*. For Barnabas, Judaism had already forfeited God's graces through the golden calf incident; so it is no surprise that the author also sees the Solomonic temple and its successor as little more than temptation to idolatry, luring the Jews to 'place their hopes on a building'.[13] The only justifiable temple was a temple of the regenerate human heart (*Barn.* 16.7). While it is true that in *Barnabas* we have one of the earliest and most extreme expressions of replacement theology, together with a rather crude statement of 'temple ecclesiology', this account stands in sharp contrast to earlier Christian writings, which integrate cultic imagery with considerably more theological nuance.

Moving backwards to the close of the first century, we find temple imagery in Revelation but this time without the sharply supercessionist overtones. In the closing chapters of his apocalypse, John the seer declares:

> Then I saw a new heaven and a new earth; for the first heaven and the first earth had passed away, and the sea was no more. And I saw the holy city, the new Jerusalem, coming down out of heaven from God, prepared as a bride adorned for her husband. And I heard a loud voice from the throne saying, 'See, the home of God is among mortals. He will dwell with them; they will be his peoples, and God himself will be with them.'[14]

By this point in the vision sequence, Satan's fate has already been sealed (Rev. 20.7–10), the dead have been judged (vv. 10–13), and death has been eradicated (vv. 14–15); the way is now paved for the establishing of an eschatological temple-city. It is a realm which tolerates neither suffering nor the wicked (21.4–8); only those who have received the 'water of life' (21.6) and have 'overcome' (21.7) are within its walls. On the foundations of these walls are the names of the twelve apostles (21.14), suggesting their unique role not only in the establishment of the eschatological community, but also in circumscribing its limits. Well aware of the challenges facing his seven churches (including persecution from local synagogues [2.9–10; 3.7–10], immorality associated with false teaching [2.14–15, 20–24], and spiritual lethargy [3.1–3, 14–20]), John holds out the eschatological temple as the climactic promise: those who remain faithful to Christ and the apostolic community in the face of divinely ordained tribulation will inherit the eschatological temple.

Earlier in the apocalypse, John recounts a vision of two witnesses. The scene begins as follows:

---

[12] *Didache* 16. For discussion, see Dubis 2002: 80–4.
[13] *Barn.* 4.6–8; 16.1.
[14] Rev. 21.1–3.

Then I was given a measuring rod like a staff, and I was told, 'Come and measure the temple (*naos*) of God and the altar and those who worship there, but do not measure the court outside the temple; leave that out, for it is given over to the nations, and they will trample over the holy city for forty-two months.'[15]

Like many portions of this cryptic book, this passage has its share of interpretive difficulties. Is this temple (*naos*, denoting the inner sanctuary not the temple precincts) which must be measured literal or figurative? If the former, is it one and the same as the Second Temple or is it a future temple? If the temple is figurative, what is meant by the symbolism?

The best answer, I propose, is one which confines John's meaning neither to the purely 'literal' nor to the purely 'figurative'. Given that the seer consistently uses *naos* elsewhere to refer to a not-normally-visible but nonetheless present reality (Rev. 14.15, 17; 15.5–8; 16.1, 17; and possibly 3.12 and 7.15), it appears that John is referring to the heavenly temple which is 'literal' inasmuch as it actually exists, though not necessarily within our own time–space continuum, but is 'figurative' inasmuch as it may only be apprehended through symbolic description. Those who worship in this transcendent sanctuary (*naos*) are the true believers. The act of measuring refers to God's assurance that although his elect may suffer physical harm at the hands of 'Gentiles' (i.e. all those who oppose God's purposes), their salvation is under divine lock and key, safely bound up in the heavenly sanctuary.[16]

But since only priests had the ability to enter into the sanctuary, the worshippers envisaged within the inner sanctuary are also necessarily priests. This is in keeping with the doxology which introduces the book as a whole: 'To him who loves us . . . and [has] made us to be a kingdom and priests to serve his God and Father . . .'[17] The believers' priesthood is analogous to the priesthood of Jesus himself, who has 'freed us from our sins by his blood'.[18] Just as Jesus' suffering and death served priestly goals, so too would the trials and persecutions of the faithful.[19] As such, the 'trampling' which believers must endure in 11.2 is implicitly modeled on the priestly suffering which Jesus had to endure.[20] Those who faithfully endure these sufferings, whether ethnically Jewish or Gentile, will be made into 'a pillar' in the eschatological temple of God (Rev. 3.12). They will also inherit the 'tree of life' (Rev. 2.7; 22.2), the central symbol of the restored Edenic temple, and will walk with Jesus 'dressed in white' (Rev. 3.4), the attire of priests. For Jesus and his followers alike, priesthood works itself out in the context of persecution.

---

[15] Rev. 11.1–3.
[16] See Boring 1989: 143; Bachmann 1994; 478; Beale 2004: 316–17. On measuring as a symbol of divine protection and assurance, see in particular Ezekiel 40—48, cf. *1 En.* 61.1–5.
[17] Rev. 1.5–6; cf. 5.10.
[18] Rev. 1.5.
[19] Rev. 6.9–11.
[20] Krodel 1989: 220; Beale 1999: 566–71.

One might even say that persecution is the necessary condition for effective priestly service; patient endurance of persecution is confirmation of one's final participation in the eschatological temple. The seven seals, trumpets and bowls (Revelation 6—16) are emblematic of this suffering, which is also the messianic woes.[21]

The author of the Fourth Gospel is eager to associate Jesus with the temple, and does so no later than the fourteenth verse: 'the Word became flesh and lived among us, and we have seen his glory'.[22] As is widely recognized, John here programmatically sets forth the incarnation as a recapitulation of the glory cloud pitching its tent among the Sinai generation.[23] On meeting Nathaniel in the same chapter, Jesus promises a vision in which the newly recruited disciple 'will see heaven opened and the angels of God ascending and descending upon the Son of Man'.[24] This is clearly an allusion to Jacob's dream, in which angels ascend and descend on a ladder leading to heaven (Gen. 28.10–22). Whether John's readers would have recognized Jacob's ladder to be a cipher for the temple (being the one place through which one may ascend to heaven) or – as in the targumim – the glory of God contained in the temple, his point is clear enough: Jesus the Son of Man is the glory-filled temple.[25] The same idea is reiterated not much later in the narrative, when Jesus identifies his body with the temple, and his resurrection as a kind of rebuilding of the temple (John 2.19–22).

In John 4, Jesus approaches a Samaritan woman at the place of Jacob's well and says:

> Woman, believe me, the hour is coming when you will worship the Father neither on this mountain nor in Jerusalem. [...] But the hour is coming, and is now here, when the true worshipers will worship the Father in spirit and truth, for the Father seeks such as these to worship him. God is spirit, and those who worship him must worship in spirit and truth.[26]

In the Judaism of the day, Jacob's well was symbolic of Torah (CD 5.20—6.11) and the water of the well, the Spirit (1QS 4.15–23). So when the woman asks Jesus, 'Are you greater than our ancestor Jacob, who gave us the well?' (John 4.12), the evangelist hints that Jesus is indeed greater, the herald of the anticipated new age based on a new covenant, when true worshipers would worship in the spirit which is also the abiding truth.[27]

---

[21] Allison 1985: 70–1; Aune 1998: 2.440–5.

[22] John 1.14.

[23] See, e.g., Hoskyns 1940: 147–8; Brown 1970 [1966] 1.32–4; Coloe 2001: 62; Keener 2003: 416–17. Note also the connection with John 12.39–40, which invokes Isaiah's temple vision (Isa. 6.10).

[24] John 1.51.

[25] Kinzer 1998: 448, with references.

[26] John 4.21, 23–24.

[27] Jer. 31.31–34; Ezek. 36.24–32; 37.26–28. So Hoskyns 1940: 245; Dodd 1953: 317; Brown 1970 [1966] 1.180; Coloe 2001: 99–108.

Jesus' identification with the temple is once again confirmed when on the last day of the Feast of Tabernacles, he cries out: 'Let anyone who is thirsty come to me!'[28] The sense of Jesus' next words is ambiguous in the Greek, but I am persuaded by the merits of the following reading: 'If anyone is thirsty let him come to me; and let him who believes in me drink. As the scripture says: "Out of his navel shall flow rivers of living water".'[29] Jesus' declaration is meant to invoke a ritual, associated with the Feast of Tabernacles and inspired by Zechariah's eschatological vision of 'living water' flowing out from the temple-city (Zech. 14.8, 16–21), whereby the priest would approach the altar and pour out wine and water to either side.[30] Since the temple was considered the navel of creation (Ezek. 38.12; *Jub.* 8.19) and the source of life-giving water (Gen. 2.10; Ezek. 47.1; Ps. 46.4), Jesus' words must be taken as another implicit claim to be the temple.

All this prepares for Jesus' promise that his 'Father's house' had many 'rooms' (*monai*) (John 14.2), a statement which notwithstanding countless funeral homilies should be understood as referring not to heaven or its floor plan, but to the eschatological temple.[31] Next, in saying, 'I am going there to prepare a *place* (*topos*) for you' (John 14.2), Jesus is declaring that he will do exactly what Yahweh would do for Israel: prepare a *place* where Yahweh would establish his name.[32] John's Jesus points to a reality beyond the sphere of human experience, yet paradoxically hovering over and intruding on it. It may be in symbolic preparation for this reality that Jesus washes his disciples' feet (John 13.1–11); after all, priests about to enter the inner space were compelled to wash their feet. This foot-washing scene itself is not only an invitation for the disciples to share in his priestly ministry, but also a prelude to Jesus' high-priestly prayer (John 17) and his atoning death.[33]

Bound up in the disciples' sharing Jesus' priesthood is no small share of suffering. If the world hates and persecutes the disciples, this is only because

---

[28] John 7.37, my own translation.

[29] John 7.37b–38. As closely argued by Kerr 2002: 231–41; similarly, Dodd 1953: 349; Brown 1970 [1966]: 1.307; Yee 1989: 79. Even if one were to opt for the alternative rendering of John 8.38 ('He who believes in me, as the scripture has said, "Out of his heart shall flow rivers of living water."'), it would only mean – as Jones (1997: 15–55) shows – that it is the disciples themselves who are the temple.

[30] So Kerr 2002: 226–7. For the evangelist, Jesus' status as eschatological temple seems to have been first actualized on his death, when blood and water flow from Jesus' side (John 19.34), symbols of the wine and water poured out towards the nations. So Schnackenburg 1971: 367; contra Fuglseth 2005: 277 who, without engaging the evidence, dismisses this reading as being of 'little historical value'.

[31] The only other use of 'Father's house' clearly refers to the temple (2.16); also, like the first temple (1 Chron. 28.11–12), the Ezekielian eschatological temple included many chambers (Ezek. 40.17). On this point, see above all McCaffrey 1988; also, Coloe 2001: 160–2; Kerr 2002: 276–8; Kinzer 1998: 450–1.

[32] Deut. 12.5–11; cf. John 4.20; 11.48.

[33] John 19.28–37; cf. 1.29.

it has already hated and persecuted Jesus himself (15.18–20). The envisaged persecution, even involving the prospect of death (16.2), is the lot of those destined to face the messianic birth-pangs (16.21). During that ordeal it will no longer be necessary for the disciples to ask Jesus anything; it will be theirs to approach the Father directly, and he will grant every request (16.23–24).[34] The concepts of suffering and priestly prayer, for Jesus and disciple alike, are coordinated.

Viewed against the synoptic Gospels, which stridently lay blame for Jesus' death at the feet of the temple elite, John appears only slightly less critical of those in established positions of Jewish leadership.[35] All the same, it is with the persecutions against Jesus that the messianic travails begin. Jesus' disciples will continue to experience these sufferings after him (15.18–25), presumably, until the messiah appears again in order to establish the archetypal heavenly temple (14.1–4), which in the mean time has been inaugurated through the Spirit.[36] The unjust actions of 'the Jews' were no reflection on the temple itself, for the temple was indeed the 'Father's house' (2.16; 14.2), the antitype of that which Jesus and his disciples were ushering in. It is through his resurrection that Jesus fulfills the role of the eschatological temple-builder and indeed becomes the temple, the source of life, light, and truth – God's glory (1.3–14).

1 Peter and Hebrews

The text of 1 Peter provides further description of the believing community as temple-*cum*-priesthood. In exhorting believers to approach Christ, the author writes:

> Come to him, a living stone, though rejected by mortals yet chosen and precious in God's sight, and like living stones, let yourselves be built into a spiritual house, to be a holy priesthood, to offer spiritual sacrifices acceptable to God through Jesus Christ. For it stands in scripture: 'See, I am laying in Zion a stone, a cornerstone chosen and precious; and whoever believes in him will not be put to shame' [Isa. 28.16]. To you then who believe, he is precious; but for those who do not believe, 'The stone that the builders rejected has become the very head of the corner' [Ps. 118.22] and 'A stone that makes them stumble, and a rock that makes them fall' [Isa. 8.14]. They stumble because they disobey the word, as they were destined to do. But you are a chosen race,

---

[34] Allison (1985: 57–8), followed by Pate and Kennard (2003: 276), rightly affirms that the terms employed in John 16.16–22 are associated with messianic tribulation. However, it seems unlikely, as these authors also hold, that Jesus' words here refer only to his immediate sufferings. In that case, Jesus' promise of answered prayer (vv. 23–24) oddly obtains only for the period between the passion and the resurrection.

[35] John 2.18; 7.45–52; 8.48–49. It may be, however, that his constant casting the 'Judeans' in a negative light (2.18, 20; 5.18; 9.18, 22; etc.), is an oblique charge against Jerusalemite powerbrokers.

[36] John 4.23; 7.37–39; 14.15–31.

a royal priesthood, a holy nation, God's own people, in order that you may proclaim the mighty acts of him who called you out of darkness into his marvelous light.[37]

Even through this bewildering collage of metaphors and allusions, it becomes apparent that the author of 1 Peter, like other authors examined so far, found no awkwardness in simultaneously affirming, on the one side, the Christian community as temple and priesthood, and, on the other side, Christ as temple-foundation and high priest. This double correlation is central to Peter's pastoral strategy. Because the chief cornerstone Jesus Christ was rejected yet precious, the believers are to consider themselves likewise. This was especially relevant since Peter himself acknowledges that his audience is enduring the predicted messianic sufferings.[38]

The preciousness of God's elect was no cause for drawing back in self-protection; on the contrary, precisely because Christ was the true and final temple foundation (*themelion*), in realization of Isaiah's promise that God would lay in Zion 'a precious cornerstone' and 'a sure foundation' (Isa. 28.16), those who identify with Christ should take heart and brace themselves for opposition.[39] The comparison between the epitome of righteousness and the temple cornerstone is – as it was for the Qumran community – a theologically rich one.[40] Just as Qumran had assigned the role of 'cornerstone' (that which serves as a bulwark against dark chaos) to its priests, Peter makes the association with Christ. Given Peter's concern to speak to a church which was painfully conscious of the malicious forces arraying themselves against it, Peter's allusion to Christ as cornerstone is hardly surprising.

In a similar vein, Peter's call to holy living in the midst of suffering is closely connected with the priestly role which he assigns to his readers. The believers' salvation unto 'obedience to Jesus Christ' is accompanied by 'sprinkling by his blood' (1 Pet. 1.2), invoking the covenant-making ceremony of Exodus 24 when the people are rendered ritually pure through Moses' sprinkling of blood (vv. 6–7). 'Now that you have purified your souls by your obedience to the truth', Peter writes his hearers, they are free to love one another sincerely (v. 22). Their service, faith, and call to proclaim the gospel in the face of opposition all hinge on their status as priests.[41] The community's priestly calling, a recapitulation of the 'royal priesthood' status of the Sinai generation (1 Pet. 2.9; cf. Exod. 19.6), is bound up with Christ's

---

[37] 1 Pet. 2.4–9.

[38] 1 Pet. 4.12–19. For a thorough argument to this effect, see Dubis 2002.

[39] Peterson 2003: 161.

[40] The association is directly paralleled in the Gospel accounts of Jesus' Parable of the Wicked Tenants (Mark 12.1–12/Matt. 21.33–46/Luke 20.9–19), and probably bears some relation to Christ as 'foundation' in Eph. 2.20 and 1 Cor. 3.10–12. See above Chapter 1, pp. 32–4.

[41] 1 Pet. 2.4–12.

priestly vocation. In exhorting his audience to follow Jesus, Peter is calling them to follow a crucified and risen high priest.[42]

Before leaving 1 Peter, perhaps a few words are in order concerning several unhelpful conclusions that, at one time or another, have been drawn from this text. First, when Peter enjoins his hearers to perform 'spiritual (*pneumatikos*) sacrifice' as part of belonging to a 'spiritual house' (1 Pet. 2.5), this should not be taken as meaning 'spiritual' as opposed to physical. To read the adjective this way is to invest it, anachronistically, with a kind of Platonic dualism utterly foreign to Peter's intended meaning. The term *pneumatikos* has less to do with physical character traits and more to do with the moral quality of what is being described.[43] Thus, Peter's word choice cannot be taken as evidence that he expected his audience to function either as a make-shift (albeit 'spiritual') substitute for the standing structure in Jerusalem or – if the text was penned after the fall of Jerusalem – as the appointed post-70 CE continuation of the temple. There is no sense that Peter is struggling to help his readers come to terms with their relationship to the temple, rather his concern seems but to be on the ethical quality of their service.

Furthermore, I believe it is best to reject readings which see Peter's cultic imagery as little more than the incidental by-product of his rhetorical strategy. It is of course theoretically possible that the author, in deploying temple and priestly imagery, began with a set of ethical ideals and worked his way back to a fitting illustration by which to motivate his audience, making the motif little more than an extended poetic flourish.[44] However, given the intertwining themes of priesthood and suffering (2.4–12; 4.12–19; 5.8–9), it is much more likely that the author of our epistle begins with the well-known narrative of messianic sufferings, which are priestly inasmuch as they are atoning, and builds his ethical edifice from this ground up.[45] He calls his hearers not merely to act like priests in isolated moments, but to realize the fullest extent of their priestly calling by enduring their appointed suffering.

Themes of priesthood, temple, and suffering also figure prominently in the Epistle to the Hebrews. Following a brief allusion to Christ's priesthood in Hebrews 1 (vv. 3–4, 13) and his incomparability when compared to the angels and Moses (2.5—3.6a), the *auctor Hebraeos* turns to a brief discussion of 'God's house' and declares, 'And we are his house if we hold firm the confidence and the pride that belong to hope.'[46] Here, as in certain other

---

[42] 1 Pet. 3.17–22.

[43] See Beare 1970: 122–3; Michaels 1988: 101–2; Senior and Harrington 2008: 54.

[44] In this case, too, 1 Peter must be considered an instance in which the rhetorical tail of a clever illustration wags a theologically very light dog. From personal experience in the pew, I grant that this is not impossible.

[45] See Dubis 2002, passim.

[46] Heb. 3.6.

texts examined so far, there is a direct link between the believers' perseverance and future participation in the eschatological temple. This assurance
is in turn predicated on both Jesus' role as high priest (2.17; 4.14—5.10;
6.19—10.18) and the believers' role as priests, who share a familial link with
Jesus (2.10–12). For the purposes of the writer's argument, the significance
of the correlation between Jesus' high priesthood and the community's priesthood, both of which eventuate in 'perfection' (2.10; 10.14), can hardly be
overestimated.[47]

The engine on this train of thought is Christological. An important passage
is found at the beginning of Hebrews 8:

> Now the main point in what we are saying is this: we have such a high priest,
> one who is seated at the right hand of the throne of the Majesty in the
> heavens, a minister in the sanctuary and the true tent that the Lord, and
> not any mortal, has set up.[48]

As the argument proceeds, Christ's superiority as high priest is made
clear not only on the incomparability of his sacrifice (Heb. 9.11–14), but
also on the relative inadequacy of the Mosaic cultus (8.7). That the Mosaic
temple was imperfect, as the author of Hebrews says, was a claim with which
countless many of his contemporary Jews would have concurred. By common
agreement, the real temple was in heaven, and the pattern which Moses took
down was but a copy of the true heavenly temple.[49] The more contentious
assertion was that Jesus Christ as high priest entered into the heavenly
tabernacle through his death, once for all.[50] For those among his hearers who
had already claimed Jesus as their high priest and were contemplating a return
to Judaism, the *auctor Hebraeos* argues that this in effect would be moving
backwards.

Assuming that Hebrews and its argument were not rejected outright
by its first audiences, it appears that a respectable swathe of first-century
Christianity saw its own 'temple worship' not as a weak replacement for
the Jerusalem cultus (or its vestiges, if we date Hebrews after the fall of the
temple), but as a far preferable alternative. Put differently, the Christians here
did not see themselves as establishing a kind of imitation temple; quite
the opposite, it was the Mosaic temple which was an imperfect copy of the
reality which now had broken through in Christ. Christ's penetration of
the heavenly sanctuary did not make the individual believer's identification
with the eschatological temple absolutely certain, but it did allow the writer
to say: 'we are confident of better things in your case, things that belong to
salvation'.[51] For the author there was a sense in which his audience was the

---

[47] See especially Scholer 1991.
[48] Heb. 8.1–2.
[49] Heb. 8.5; 9.1–10.
[50] Heb. 9.24–28.
[51] Heb. 6.9.

true temple (3.6; 12.22–24); there was also a sense in which the promise was still to be realized (12.25–27). Poised within this eschatological tension, the writer enjoins his audience: 'let us give thanks, by which we offer to God an acceptable worship with reverence and awe'.[52] Not insignificantly, this same exhortation, describing the believers' responsibility in cultic terms, heads up the remainder of the epistle's practical ethics.[53] This is altogether in keeping with the author's grounding his ethical appeal on Christ's role as high priest and the believers' collective role as the already-but-not-yet temple of God.

Hardly incidental in this connection is the notion of suffering, which Pate and Kennard are right to understand as specifically messianic suffering.[54] Given the audience's experience of suffering (10.32–39), and the author's linking this suffering with Jesus' priestly suffering (2.14—3.1), the writer's logic suggests that it was precisely in the addressees' capacity as priests that they were called to suffer. While Christ's death provides expiation for sins (10.1–5), his faithfulness as high priest also provides a model (6.12) for the believer-priests to follow.[55] The author of Hebrews saw the trials of his churches as a condition of exile (3.7—4.10), but also as the necessary context in which believers were to fulfill their priestly calling, just as Jesus had fulfilled his high-priestly calling.

Matthew and Luke–Acts

In the Gospel of Matthew, we see that the temple comes in for mixed reviews. On the one hand, Matthew preserves words of Jesus that attest to a fairly positive view of Zion. In the Sermon on the Mount, Jesus presupposes that gifts at the altar are efficacious.[56] Likewise, when Jesus inveighs against the oath-taking practices of the scribes and Pharisees, he takes for granted the 'greatness' of the temple (Matt. 23.17). For Jesus, the temple altar imparts holiness to the gifts on it (Matt. 23.19), and this because the temple remains the dwelling-place of God (Matt. 23.21). While Jesus' diatribe in Matthew 23 has been taken as evidence that the evangelist's audience was at serious odds with the synagogues of the day, it should not be overlooked that in the midst of this intramural polemic are very clear statements speaking to the on-going validity of the temple.

On the other hand, Matthew's Jesus is obviously quite discontented with the temple. The source of this discontent lies not in the temple *per se*, but in the spiritual condition of Israel, especially its leaders. As Matthew sees it, Israel is in a state of exile and remains liable to judgment so long as it fails to

---

[52] Heb. 12.28.
[53] Heb. 13.7–17. See Gäbel 2006: 435–66, especially 448.
[54] Pate and Kennard 2003: 484–7.
[55] Still 2007: 752–4. Vanhoye (1967: 291–305) and Hamm (1990: 281–2) see Jesus' faithfulness specifically as faithfulness *qua* high priest.
[56] Matt. 5.23–24.

respond to Jesus' summons of restoration.[57] This state of affairs becomes one of the prompting motivations for Jesus' sending out the Twelve to the 'lost sheep of Israel'.[58] The strongly negative reaction which the disciples would provoke within the synagogues was not only another indicator of the temple hierarchy's disobedience (Matt. 10.17), but also a sign that the messianic woes were at hand even in the resistance to their missionary activities (10.18).[59] Yet the intransigence of Israel would finally have its end-result. While the true 'house on the rock' (the one which obeys Jesus' words) would stand, the false house (the one which refused to obey his words) would be shown up for its faulty foundation and come to ruin.[60] This certainty is spelled out further in the Olivet Discourse of Matthew 24, where Jesus very clearly predicts the temple's demise.

Side by side with Matthew's denunciation of the temple leadership (Matthew 10—11) and within the context of the disciples' persecution (12.1–8) is the claim that 'one greater than the temple is here' (v. 6). That 'greater one' is either Jesus' movement or, more likely, Jesus himself.[61] The statement implies not only that the current temple has in some sense been made redundant on his coming, but also that the functions typically predicated of that temple have now been either transcended or devolved onto Jesus himself. Yet in stating that the Church on analogy with Zion would be grounded on 'this rock', which cannot be anything but Peter (Matt. 16.18), and would also be assuming the organizational structure of the synagogue which was bound to the temple (Matt. 18.15–20), Matthew's Jesus is also intimating that his followers are on their way to becoming the temple.

But the goal of this new temple existence cannot be achieved apart from suffering and persecution (Matt. 5.10; 10.5–42; 11.12; 13.21, 57; 16.24–28; etc.), which would reach new levels of intensity in the dissolution of the current order (24.4–31). The eschatological goal required not just a new Exodus but a new conquest of sorts. Just as Moses encouraged Joshua in his mission of conquest in order to establish 'the place' of God's worship, so too must Jesus exhort his fearful disciples to subdue the nations which constitute the new Promised Land of worship.[62] The culminating note, 'I will be with you always' (28.20), marks the climax of God's temple purposes, which have

---

[57] Matt. 10.15; 11.20–24. Wright 1992: 384–90; Charette 1992: 63–82, 121–40; Leske 1994: 897–916; Chae 2006: 244–6, 369–86.

[58] Matt. 10.5–42.

[59] As Pitre (2005: 200) correctly points out, Matthew 10 is 'rich with the standard tribulation-motifs of persecution and strife'.

[60] Matt. 7.24–27. As far as I know, this was first proposed by Wright 1996: 292, 334. Since the obedience (or lack thereof) of the temple-based scribes and Pharisees serves as a baseline at the beginning of the Sermon on the Mount (5.19–20), a thinly veiled allusion to the consequences of the same group's (in)actions at the end of the sermon is appropriate.

[61] Matt. 28.19–20. So Gundry 1982: 223; Davies and Allison 1988–97: 2.314.

[62] On the allusions to Moses' charge to Joshua in Matt. 28.18–20, see Davies and Allison 1988–97: 3.679.

always been to establish an intimate point of contact between the one God and the one God's people.[63]

Because Matthew recognizes his community as a newly reconstituted Israel, a new temple people, his view of the Jerusalem temple is equivocal. This becomes evident on considering Jesus' teachings on the temple tax (Matt. 17.24–27). In this passage, Jesus takes up the issue of the temple tax by comparing earthly kings and their sons to God and Jesus' disciples, respectively (v. 25). Whereas on the logic of this comparison, the sons of God should not have to pay temple tax (vv. 25–26), all the same, Jesus enjoins doing so in order 'that we do not give offense to them' (v. 27). In paying the temple tax, Matthew's Jesus defers to certain deeply embedded sensibilities, and members of Matthew's community, by implication, should follow suit, even if they are not strictly bound to do so. The birth, life, death, and resurrection of 'one greater than the temple' implied for the Matthean community a relative demotion of the Second Temple and an altogether new relationship to it. At the same time, the fact of this new reality did not override the pragmatic necessity of preserving ties with neighboring Jewish communities, which were themselves tied to the temple.

Caught between these two temple-worlds, the Matthean community appears to be working out its faith within the ambiguity of exile. It was an ambiguity and an exile which would ultimately be resolved, but until then, the order of the day was to remain faithful despite opposition. Suffering was only the appointed sign that the 'end was near'; patient endurance of this same suffering was instrumental in bringing about this end. For Matthew, the eschatological temple was in some sense already present in the person of Jesus, but those who attached themselves to this greater temple would not secure a final place of worship until the 'end of the age' (Matt. 28.20).

When we come to the Luke–Acts, we enter into a narrative that also casts the Jerusalem temple in both rose-colored and jaundiced hues, leaving us to puzzle once again as to whether the evangelist's characterization is hopelessly incongruous or, more generously, deeply paradoxical. On the one hand, we find what seems to be ringing endorsement of the cultus both before and after the resurrection. It is in the temple that John's birth is announced (Luke 1.5–25) and that Jesus is circumcised (2.21–40); it is to the temple the young boy Jesus returns, insisting on his need to be at his 'Father's house' (2.49). Later, Jesus sends those he heals to the temple priests (17.14), enjoins temple prayer (18.9–14), and commends temple giving (21.1–4).[64] In Acts, following Pentecost, the Christians continue to meet in the temple (Acts 2.46; 3.11; 5.12), while the leaders of the movement maintain established hours of temple prayer (3.1). In this context, the temple grounds serve as the

---

[63] Exod. 6.6; Lev. 11.45; Deut. 4.20; etc.; cf. Matt. 1.23.

[64] I am assuming with most commentators that Jesus is reflecting positively on the woman's sacrificial giving, not criticizing it; contra A. G. Wright 1982.

primary venue for the Jerusalemite Christians' proclamation (5.17–42). Further on in the narrative, Paul shaves his head as part of a vow that can only be discharged through the temple (18.18); he also pays for the offering of his four companions, as the culmination of purification rites (21.17–26). When asked about his own posture towards the temple, Paul declares, 'I have in no way committed an offense against the law of the Jews, or against the temple.'[65] On the basis of such evidence, it is tempting to agree with the frequently made statement that Luke was 'pro-temple'.[66]

To leave matters stated so baldly, however, is not only to oversimplify but also to obscure the reality. It is also to overlook the numerous indicators in Luke's writing that something is amiss in Zion, while something seismic – as far as the temple is concerned – is afoot in Jesus and in the early Church. There is of course a running polemic against the priesthood, hinted at as early as Luke 3, where Annas and Caiaphas are lumped in with such notorious powerbrokers as Pontius Pilate and Herod (3.1–2). But Luke's vision for change encompasses far more than a change in personnel. According to the evangelist, a salvation-historical shift has taken place in and through Jesus, and this shift implies a reconfiguration of the temple and its traditional functions. This is signaled at an early stage in the narrative, when the glory of God appears to the shepherds as part of the announcement of Jesus' birth (Luke 2.8–12). Joel Green summarizes well the import of the moment:

> Given the respect assigned earlier to the Jerusalem temple and particularly to its sanctuary as the *axis mundi* – the meeting place between the heavenly and the earthly, the divine and the human – this appearance of divine glory is remarkable. God's glory, normally associated with the temple, is now manifest on a farm! At the birth of his son, God has compromised (in a proleptic way) the socio-religious importance of the temple as the culture center of the world of Israel.[67]

The point is corroborated elsewhere in Luke. Jesus' touching a leper without incurring uncleanness (5.12–16), his forgiving sins (5.17–26), his assumption of Davidic priestly status (6.1–10) – all these are symbolic indicators that Luke thought of Jesus as a kind of high priest. In the thinly veiled Parable of the Wicked Tenants, Jesus identifies the current temple regime with those who violently reject God's purposes and then identifies himself with the foundation of a new temple.[68] As with the other synoptic Gospels, this parable demands to be read alongside the so-called Cleansing of the Temple (19.43–48), which on any interpretation serves as a stinging condemnation of the temple personnel. From here the wheels begin to turn more quickly,

---

[65] Acts 25.8.
[66] See, e.g., Lüdemann 1987: 93; Chance 1988: 36.
[67] Green 1997: 131.
[68] Luke 20.9–18.

and following a swift turn of events Jesus is crucified. Luke sees Jesus' death as a result of Jerusalem's wickedness; the rending of the temple veil, a kind of judgment on the temple itself.[69] The Gospel closes and prepares for its sequel with an account of Jesus' ascension, where Jesus takes on a benedictory and therefore high-priestly posture, while his disciples carry out the temple activities of worshipping and blessing God – of all places, *outside* of Jerusalem.[70]

In discussing Acts, I restrict myself to two passages. The first is the episode at Pentecost.[71] It has been convincingly argued elsewhere that Luke's depiction of the disciples' Spirit-filling and speaking in tongues in Acts 2.1–13 is modeled on the Sinai event, a decisive redemptive-historical moment in which God's glory descends so as to make Sinai itself a kind of temple.[72] Seen against this background, the tongues of fire (2.3), reminiscent of descriptions of the heavenly sanctuary in the contemporary literature (*1 En.* 14.8–25; 71.5; 4Q204 6.19–29), are indicative of God's shekinah glory coming to rest on the early Church.[73] Just as Yahweh's glory had 'filled' the tabernacle (Exod. 40.34), and later 'filled the house' of the Lord as built by Solomon (1 Kings 8.10), now the 'sound like the rush of a violent wind . . . filled the house' (Acts 2.2), where the believers were at prayer (which may have been the temple itself). For Luke, then, Pentecost signaled the onset of a new epoch in salvation-history, and the end of the order under the current temple, just as Peter's apocalyptic, textually and symbolically rich, sermon intimates.[74] Even by the second chapter of Acts, Luke's meaning could hardly be clearer: Jesus' ascension to high-priestly status was both the promise of and preparation for a new temple.[75]

The second passage requiring attention is Acts 7, which recounts Stephen's speech. Stephen is brought before the Sanhedrin because he 'never stops saying things against this holy place and the law'.[76] Recounting the story of Israel as part of his defense, Stephen comes to Solomon, the builder of God's house. He continues by quoting Isa. 66.1–2:

---

[69] Luke 23.26–34, 45.

[70] Luke 24.50–53.

[71] Acts 2.1–40.

[72] Important here are the Isaianic references to 'tongues of fire' (Isa. 5.24–25; 30.23–33). In the latter passage, in which Isaiah promises redemption from exile and idol-worship, the focal text reads: 'See, the name of the LORD comes from far away, burning with his anger, and in thick rising smoke; his lips are full of indignation, and his tongue is like a devouring fire' (30.27). In the former text Yahweh employs 'tongues of fire' as judgment against his people (Isa. 5.24). See Fitzmyer 1998: 234; Beale 2004: 205.

[73] Cf. Acts 1.4–8. References cited in Beale 2004: 206; Beale 2005: 76–91.

[74] Acts 2.14–41. N. T. Wright's description of Jesus' predicting the temple's destruction in Mark 13 ('The language – apocalyptic metaphor and symbol, to evoke the full resonances of Old Testament prophecy and to invest the coming events with their full theological significance – is . . . utterly appropriate to the occasion' [1996: 340]) applies equally well to Peter's sermon in Acts 2.

[75] Luke 24.48–49; Acts 1.4–8.

[76] Acts 6.13.

Yet the Most High does not dwell in houses made with human hands; as the prophet says, 'Heaven is my throne, and the earth is my footstool. What kind of house will you build for me, says the Lord, or what is the place of my rest? Did not my hand make all these things?'[77]

It is unwarranted to suppose that Stephen finds fault with Solomon for building the temple. On any reading of the Hebrew scriptures, there is no indication that the intention on the part of David's lineage to build the temple was morally questionable; on the contrary, the burden of the post-exilic prophets centered on the importance of temple-building (Haggai, Zechariah, Ezra). Thus, unless we are prepared to retroject into Luke's Stephen a kind of proto-Marcionite dualism, as we come close to finding in the *Epistle of Barnabas*, we should look for another explanation. Such an explanation is in fact forthcoming in discerning that Stephen intends neither a wholesale criticism of the law nor a rejection of the temple in principle. Rather, Stephen's point is that the fulfillment of Isaiah 66.1–2, in which God promises a temple not made by human hands, is simply the climactic phase of a salvation-historical narrative that began with Abraham.[78] Furthermore, to resist this new temple, which supplants earlier provisional arrangements, would only be to cling to Israel's historical pattern of disobedience. At the end of the day, it is reductionistic to deem Stephen's sermon as either undifferentiatedly 'pro-temple' or flatly 'anti-temple'. The speech reflects eschatological nuance, implying an important role for the Jerusalem temple in its day but asserting the necessity of a new temple order.

So much for Stephen's views. As far as the third evangelist is concerned, it will not do at this point to suggest, following the old Tübingen school, that an ecumenically minded Luke recorded this speech in order to reconcile Stephen's extreme position with more conservative forces in the Church. To be sure, the earliest Christians in Palestine and in the Diaspora must have had varying levels of sympathy for the cult in Jerusalem and, too, must have had different ideas as to how allegiance to the temple should work itself out. At the same time, the fact that Luke makes Stephen out to be an exemplary hero (Acts 6.8; 7.56, 59) and gives him such ample air-time forbids our distancing the author of Luke–Acts from the thrust of Stephen's speech. Whatever the sources behind Luke's account of Stephen's speech (which most scholars take to be authentic), it is a speech which Luke heartily endorses.[79]

---

[77] Acts 7.48–50.

[78] See Dahl 1976: 72–3; Larsson 1993: 387–95.

[79] Contra Dunn (1991: 65), who labors under the unqualified and therefore inaccurate premise that Luke's attitude towards the temple was 'very positive' (65). Likewise, Haenchen's comments (1971: 265), that Luke inserts the account 'only to explain how Stephen ... came to occupy so prominent a position in the community', are oblivious to the evangelist's narratological finesse.

This observation is an important first step towards reconciling Luke's diverse evaluations of the temple, which have been accounted for in a number of ways. Perhaps, it has been said, Luke is too muddled to be aware of his own inconsistencies or, more exactly, the inconsistency between his sources. Perhaps, we have also heard it said, Luke is attempting to sketch out a trajectory, in which the temple begins on a positive note but ends on a sour note. This dynamic becomes part of Luke's larger agenda to show the Church as supplanting Israel. Or perhaps, again, Luke is consciously bringing together the disparate voices within a church struggling to define itself against the temple; perhaps he is doing so to strike a compromise of sorts. Against all these suggestions I venture that Luke's posture is actually remarkably consistent.[80] On the one hand, he hopes to validate Jerusalem as the center and root of all Christian mission; on the other hand, his narrative urges that this same mission must now through the Spirit go beyond the boundaries of the Jerusalem temple. On this reading, Acts can be seen as a storied argument against those who deny either the foundational status of Jerusalem or God's missionary interest in the 'ends of earth'. In this respect, his carefully balanced thinking on the temple is not unlike the approach of Paul, who insists both on an unfettered Gentile mission and, in almost the same breath, on the appropriateness of converts of this mission giving financial honor to the mother–church in Jerusalem.

Paul

When we come to the apostle Paul, we find a corpus of literature permeated with temple imagery. For example, when in his earliest preserved letter he refers to Peter, James, and John as 'pillars' (Gal. 2.9), he is likely referring not simply to the three apostles' status as ecclesiastical powerbrokers, but, much more richly, their central place within the newly constituted temple of God.[81] This prepares for his reproach of Peter: 'But if I build up again the very things that I once tore down, then I demonstrate that I am a transgressor.'[82] On one level it is clear that by 'very things' Paul means the law, but the law here is represented metaphorically by the temple, or as in Ephesians 2.14, the temple wall. Thus in so many words Paul is chiding Peter for 'rebuilding' the Mosaic temple, a temple which has been decisively torn down in Christ.[83]

---

[80] There does seem to be a kind of progression, from the temple to the world outside the temple (somewhat analogous to the ordering of Acts 1.8), but this progression does not terminate with any sense of Israel's being eternally removed from God's good graces.

[81] The pillars were after all the gates to the inner court of the temple. See Bauckham 1995: 441–50; Barrett 1953: 1–19; cf. 4Q164. Later (second-century) Christian tradition gives these same 'pillars' high-priestly status; see Horbury 1984: 277 n. 64.

[82] Gal. 2.18.

[83] Gal. 2.19–20. So, e.g., Dunn 1993: 142. The verb 'build up' (*oikodomeō*) is regularly used in reference to the (re)building of the first (2 Sam. 7.5; 1 Kings 3.2; 5.3; 6.2; 2 Chron. 3.1), second (Isa. 44.28; Ezra 1.2; Hag. 1.2; 1 Macc. 4.47–78; 5.1), and eschatological (Isa. 44.28[?]; Zech. 6.12; Tob. 1.4; 13.11; 14.5) temple.

In the first two chapters of Galatians, then, Paul leaves tantalizingly subtle hints of a clash between two irreconcilable temple economies.

This is teased out much more thoroughly later in the epistle. Whereas in Galatians 1—3, Paul had been interpreting his own controversy with the Judaizers along the lines of a 'faith'/'works of the law' dichotomy, which is roughly coterminous with another contrast between 'spirit' and 'flesh', now in chapter 4 these taxonomies are recast as a matter of temple commitment: the present city of Jerusalem, corresponding to 'works', and the heavenly temple-city 'that is above', corresponding to 'faith'.[84] Whatever divided Paul from his opponents, the apostle reframes the question as if to say, 'With which temple will you identify? The temple of present-day Jerusalem or the eschatological temple which is the Jerusalem above?' However the individual Galatian believer chooses to settle out on this issue, the apostle seems to suggest, is a telling indication of one's (logically prior) temple allegiance and therefore ultimately one's destiny.

In Galatians 4 we find that Paul himself is in the pangs of messianic childbirth until Christ should be fully formed in the believers.[85] This figure of speech, much like the terms 'groans' (*systenazai*) and 'suffer agony' (*synōdinei*) in Romans 8.22, was typical of Jewish ways of talking about catastrophic events leading up to the messiah.[86] It is likely for this reason too that the apostle saw the present age as an 'evil age'.[87] Paul's conviction that he himself participated in and in fact 'filled up' the messianic sufferings (Col. 1.24), so convincingly established elsewhere, need not be belabored here.[88]

Similar such 'temple logic' is operative in 1 Thessalonians. Following mention of Timothy's return, Paul prays for the believers that they might be strengthened to be 'blameless in holiness before God'.[89] The terms 'blameless' (*amemptos*) and 'holiness' (*hagiōsynē*) have cultic connotations; 'before God' is not a vague circumlocution for 'in God's full view' or something of the sort, but refers instead to that particular holy space where atonement was secured.[90] The repeated valorizing of 'continuous prayer' probably reflects the image of the *tamîd* offerings within the temple, a continuous offering without which the temple would cease to function.[91]

In the Corinthian correspondence, cultic imagery rises up at numerous points. This may possibly occur, for example, in Paul's repeated calls to 'build

---

[84] Gal. 4.21–31.
[85] Gal. 4.19. Gaventa 1990: 194; Matera 1992: 161–2; George 1994: 329–30; Martyn 1997: 430; cf. 1 Thess. 2.7–11.
[86] So, e.g., Cranfield 1975: 1.416.
[87] Gal. 1.3.
[88] Allison 1985: 65–6, with references.
[89] 1 Thess. 3.14.
[90] See Exod. 28.12; 29.11; Lev. 10.17; 23.28; etc.
[91] Curiously, the phrase recurs uniquely in 1 Thessalonians (1.2; 2.13; 5.17; cf. Rom. 1.9).

up' (*oikodomeō*) one another. Even if 'to build up' with the sense of 'to edify' has become something of a dead metaphor in contemporary idiom, Paul's usage shows temple imagery lurking none too subtly in the background. Having already noted the connection between this verb and the building of God's temple, I would suggest that this is the apostle's shorthand way of saying, 'Work towards realizing God's goal of building the eschatological temple.'[92] In the Corinthian letters, Paul continues to expand on the metaphor of temple in various places, not least in the following passage which I have touched upon earlier:

> For we are God's servants, working together; you are God's field, God's building. According to the grace of God given to me, like a skilled master builder I laid a foundation, and someone else is building on it. Each builder must choose with care how to build on it.[93]

Although some readers suppose that Paul's analogy between the Corinthian community and 'God's building' was more or less arbitrary, as if 'God's building' could just as easily have been exchanged with, say, 'God's pyramid', with limited difference in meaning, I find this approach unconvincing.[94] After all, had *any* building served Paul's analogy, he could have quite easily omitted the qualifier 'of God', but obviously chose not to do so. Second, the effortless slide from 'God's field' to 'God's building' in v. 9 is not an abrupt mixing of metaphors, but an appeal to two lines of imagery (architectural and horticultural) that in the Jewish literature find their convergence in the temple.[95] Third, the very fact that vv. 16–17 of the same chapter explicitly compare the Corinthian believers to a divinely inhabited temple – and from the Jewish point of view there was only one of these – should further disincline us to think that Paul has anything but the temple in mind here.[96] God's building is not any old house belonging to God; it is God's unique temple.

Granting this point, however, does not solve the problem as to whether Paul is simply using temple imagery as a rhetorical flourish or whether he actually envisages his audience as the temple in some realistic sense. Although the former argument has been put forward, I believe this reading crucially overlooks the way in which Paul's language draws on eschatological expect-ation as articulated in the scriptures. The apostle continues:

> For no one can lay any foundation other than the one that has been laid; that foundation is Jesus Christ. Now if anyone builds on the foundation with *gold, silver, precious stones,* wood, hay, straw – the work of each builder will become visible, for the Day will disclose it, because it will be *revealed with fire,*

---

[92] The idiom occurs in 1 Thess. 5.11; 1 Cor. 8.1, 10; 10.23; 14.4, 17; 2 Cor. 10.8; 12.19; 13.10.
[93] 1 Cor. 3.9–10.
[94] Contra, e.g., Orr and Walther 1976: 174; Collins 1999: 153; Fitzmyer 2008: 196.
[95] See discussion in Chapter 1 above, pp. 32–3.
[96] Cf. 1 Cor. 6.19; 2 Cor. 5.1–2; 6.16.

and the fire will test what sort of work each has done. If what has been built on the foundation survives, the builder will receive a reward. If the work is *burned up*, the builder will suffer loss; the builder will be saved, but only as through fire.[97]

Incorporating such terms as 'gold', 'silver', 'revealed with fire', and 'burned up', the terminology invokes an important passage from Malachi 3—4, where the prophet speaks of the Lord's coming to his temple like a 'refiner's fire': 'he will sit as a refiner and purifier of silver, and he will purify the descendants of Levi and refine them like *gold and silver*, until they present offerings to the LORD in righteousness'.[98] On that day the righteous shall be refined, that is, 'revealed with fire'; moreover, 'all evildoers will be stubble; the day that comes *shall burn them up*'.[99] The end-result of this judgment is a scenario where 'righteous offerings will be presented'.[100] Judging by the highly allusive language, it appears that the eschatological fire of Malachi 3—4 and the fire of 1 Cor. 3.11–15 are one and the same: through this fire the true and final priesthood will be purified and proved. It is then a priesthood so closely identified with the temple that it is represented by the materials that make up the temple.[101] Recourse to this particular sub-text is further supported by the fact that Paul writes these words in a time when traditions regarding Jesus and John the Baptizer, including the tradition that John was the 'prophet like Elijah' and therefore the fulfillment of Malachi's prophecy, would have enjoyed vibrant circulation.[102] Within this fertile interpretive mix, Paul's allusion to Malachi's eschatological temple must have been understood as linking the same temple with the movement to which John and Jesus each in their own way helped give birth. The Corinthians therefore were neither like a temple nor even like *the* temple: as co-participants in the fulfillment of Malachi 3—4, they *were* the temple, at least in an anticipatory sense.

That Paul here should use temple imagery drawn from scripture in order to point to the believers' participation in the eschatological temple comes as little surprise, especially when similar such allusions occur in subsequent correspondence to the same church. Indeed, as Gregory Beale has persuasively argued, scriptural language referring to the eschatological temple (Ezek. 11.17; 20.34, 41; 37.26–27) also underlies Paul's identifying the Corinthian believers

---

[97] 1 Cor. 3.11–15 (emphasis added).

[98] Mal. 3.2–3 (emphasis added).

[99] Mal. 4.1 (emphasis added).

[100] Mal. 3.3.

[101] Thus it is little coincidence, as Beale (2004: 246–7) points out, that the building materials Paul mentions here are the very same ones used to build Solomon's temple, as attested by David's words pertaining to the temple's construction: 'So I have provided for the house of my God, so far as I was able, the gold for the things of gold, the silver for the things of silver . . . besides great quantities of onyx and stones for setting, antimony, colored stones, all sorts of precious stones, and marble in abundance' (1 Chron. 29.2).

[102] Mal. 3.1; 4.5–6; Luke 1.76; 7.27.

as the 'temple of God' in 2 Corinthians 6.14—7.1.[103] In discussing appropriate relationships with those outside the believing community, Paul's turn to Ezekiel's exilic theology would have provided a helpful narrative for a church besieged by various ideologies marshaled by the dominant culture. Seizing on the prophet's vision pertaining to a glorious temple established in connection with the return from exile (Ezekiel 37, 40—48), Paul's argument presupposes that the temple has already been established in Christ and, simultaneously, that it is presently constituted by the believing community.[104] The present Spirit-indwelt temple is both the true temple and the temple in exile.

In Romans one may also detect the occasional expression of a deeply rooted eschatological-temple theology. Following his description of his apostleship as a 'priestly duty' (Rom. 15.16), Paul describes his preaching the gospel as building 'on a foundation' (*themelios*) (Rom. 15.20), a term which in the capital and so-called deutero-Pauline letters consistently denotes the temple foundation.[105] In this context, again, believers are to seek what leads to 'mutual upbuilding' (*oikodōmē*) (Rom. 14.19), while earlier in the letter Paul had exhorted believers to offer themselves as 'living sacrifices to God', an act of 'spiritual worship' (Rom. 12.1). The climactic note of 12.1 is well in keeping with Paul's fundamental notion, namely, that God's presence has now through the Spirit taken up residence in the physical bodies of the believers.[106] In the aftermath of this apocalyptic reality, everyday believers and apostles alike were bound together in their common role of temple-builders and priests, even if those roles worked out practically in different ways. Paradoxically, this state of affairs meant a reconfiguration of Israel (at least on the level of long-held categories), but hardly a complete supplanting of the temple-state.

The last Pauline epistle under examination is Philippians, an epistle which makes ample use of cultic imagery in the context of suffering. Paul calls on the Philippians to do everything without quarrel, 'so that you may be *blameless and innocent (amemptoi kai akeraioi)*'.[107] The latter descriptor, often used to denote pure or unmixed wine, prepares for Philippians 2.17: 'But even if I am being poured out as a libation over the sacrifice and the offering of your faith, I am glad and rejoice with all of you.' In wording reminiscent of Romans 12.1, Paul sees his own life and ministry as a cultic offering, constituting real worship, offered in the Spirit.[108] The same of course applies for

---

[103] Beale 2004: 235—9.

[104] The divine declaration that 'I have been a sanctuary to them for a little while in the countries where they have gone' (Ezek. 11.16b), which I believe stands behind 2 Cor. 6.14—7.1, dovetails well with not only the apostle's Christological monotheism but also his understanding that return from exile is underway in Christ, who in incorporating the believers, serves as a kind of sanctuary (Rom. 3.25; Phil. 3.3).

[105] See 1 Cor. 3.10, 11, 12; Eph. 2.20; 1 Tim. 6.19; 2 Tim. 2.19; cf. Heb. 6.1, 11.10.

[106] Romans 6—8, esp. 8.9—10.

[107] Phil. 2.15.

[108] Phil. 3.3.

his audience, for the gifts which Paul himself has received are to be counted as 'a fragrant offering, a sacrifice acceptable and pleasing to God'.[109] This ties in further with Paul's intention that Christ be exalted in his body either by life or by death.[110] These remarks need to be read against the background of a priestly theology: Paul essentially understands his suffering as a necessary condition of the gospel mission, for through that suffering God's purposes will finally be realized.[111] In Philippians, as in his other letters, the apostle seems to resort to cultic imagery almost reflexively. The Church as the extension of God's temple purposes into the future provides the basis not only for Paul's self-identity and mission, but also for that of the Philippian believers as well.

To summarize, one could hardly do better than agree with Klaus Berger's description of Paul's practical theology as a 'cultic-priestly ethic'.[112] This is not necessarily to assert that the temple is the center of the apostle's thought, if it is even helpful thinking of Paul's thought in those terms. My point rather is that for Paul the redemptive-historical shift has occurred in Christ and as a result those who are of Christ and filled with the Holy Spirit corporately make up the new locus of God's presence. As members of the eschatological temple, these believers are also ordained to priestly suffering, thereby partaking in the messianic sufferings, for the furtherance of the gospel mission. This squares with Paul's own sense that his community is the faithful remnant, seeking to hold their own at every turn against 'false brothers' (Gal. 2.4). When it comes to reflecting on appropriate conduct for those in Christ, it is the fact of the Spirit's new-found presence that becomes the basis for all subsequent rumination. Where the Spirit settles, there one finds the temple. And that for Paul, as for other early Christians, has made all the difference in the world.

Excursus: Paul, the early Church and the poor

Since it was observed that the counter-temple movements under review in Chapter 1 (the Qumran sect, the community behind the *Psalms of Solomon*, and John the Baptizer's movement) share a special, albeit (from our point of view) ill-defined, concern for the poor, it is necessary, before leaving off this study of the early Church, to consider whether a similar pattern obtains in primitive Christianity. I freely grant that the contours of this template are neither neat nor crisp. As far as the sources show, it seems that each of these

---

[109] Phil. 4.18.
[110] Phil. 1.20.
[111] Ware 2005: 201–36. Phil. 1.28–30.
[112] Berger 2006: 160. Similarly, Vahrenhorst (2008: 345–6) writes: 'On the other hand, for Paul "holiness" is not simply a designation. It has its own actuality in the fact that God through the Holy Spirit is realistically present in the communities. On the basis of this presence are grounded ethical implications which are appropriate to sanctified existence. Otherwise the community, precisely in its integrity as the location of God's presence, is at risk.'

protest groups regarded the poor not simply as a category of humanity worthy of charitable attention, but as something more. What that 'something more' is exactly may be hard to say. Clarity is elusive in part because within the primary sources one senses fluid boundaries between the community and the poor: temple dissidents identified themselves with the poor, but also placed a premium on ministry on behalf of the poor. Whether these counter-temple communities saw the experience of the poor as a reflection of their own experience, or whether they saw the poor as being an organic extension of their group, or both, is not clear in each case. It is clear, however, that each community considered the poor to be a segment of society very much worth paying attention to. To put it concisely, for all three dissident groups the poor were at the front and center of their concerns.

In due course I will consider the question as to what degree concern for the poor figured in the thinking of the historical Jesus. As a preliminary point, however, I wish to raise the question as to whether earliest Christianity, as attested by Paul and other writers, also shared this disposition. Did the earliest post-Easter followers of Jesus make a point of attending to the poor? If so, how did those intentions surface in teaching and/or practice?

Despite the paucity of evidence as to how ambient first-century Judaism related to its impoverished, I believe that first-century Christianity was self-conscious of its own posture towards the lower echelons of society.[113] Even if this is not the space in which to offer a full-blown exploration as to why the Church took an interest in the poor, it will be sufficient to observe that it did. And if the Church proves to do so at an early date, this will reinforce the impression that ministry to the poor was for the early Church a basic and fundamental value.

Returning to Galatians, we see that Paul recounts his meeting with the 'pillars' of the church, a meeting which eventually finds the apostles mapping out their joint mission: with James, John, and Cephas focusing on the Jews, and Paul going to the Gentiles (Gal. 2.7–9). Interestingly enough, there is an outstanding condition for the Jerusalem troika: '[t]hey asked only one thing, that we remember the poor, which was actually what I was eager to do'.[114] It is striking that amidst all the things Paul and the Jerusalem-based apostles would have discussed as agreed-upon components of the Church's mission, the 'one thing' asked of Paul was simply this: to remember the poor.

It is certainly a plausible and much-touted interpretation that when Paul uses the phrase 'the poor' here, he refers to the church in Jerusalem and anticipates the collection he would later take up on its behalf. However, I am more compelled by a different interpretation which simply takes 'the

---

[113] I am inclined to agree with Seccombe (1978), who takes Jeremias to task for anachronistically supposing that a highly organized, pro-active effort to care for the poor was in place within temple-based Judaism before the advent of Christianity.

[114] Gal. 2.10.

poor' to mean, quite generically, 'the poor'. After all, given the fact that pagan society in its complete indifference to the plight of the impoverished stood in sharp contrast to Judaism at its best, and given too that the broader Christian community around this time was struggling to settle on defining marks which would set Gentile converts to Christ apart from their erstwhile companions (Acts 15), it makes perfect sense for the apostles to have expressed broad concern on this point.[115] If Paul was to be entrusted with bringing the gospel to the Gentiles, he would also have to be granted the freedom to convey this gospel in a culturally appropriate idiom, that is, without imposing all the details of the law which might have been appropriate for Jewish believers. At the same time, the apostles also wanted to make clear, this relative flexibility in regard to the law did not imply permission for the same Gentile converts to shun the poor. As Paul sought to plant churches throughout the Mediterranean world, he was obliged by his peers to call the fledgling churches to show proper consideration to those who lacked means.[116] Since remembering the poor was the only point on which the three pillars explicitly held Paul's feet to the fire, it would not be unreasonable to suppose that, from their point of view, such remembrance was somehow integral to the gospel-proclamation itself.[117]

This way of understanding Gal. 2.10 is, I believe, supported by the concluding section of the same letter. Here Paul writes:

> So let us not grow weary in *doing what is right* (*to de kalon poiountes*), for we will reap at harvest time, if we do not give up. So then, whenever we have an opportunity, *let us work for the good* (*ergazōmetha agathon*) of all, and especially for those of the family of faith.[118]

It would be mistaken to suppose that 'by doing good (*agathon*)', Paul means engaging in non-specific acts of positive import. The phrase 'doing good' is in fact a technical term for financial benefaction, and in light of Paul's immediately preceding injunction of sharing material 'good' with one's teacher (Gal. 6.6), the same meaning must obtain here.[119] Since it could hardly be argued that the 'good' (*agathon*) of v. 10 is categorically different from the 'right' or 'good' (*kalon*) of v. 9, it appears that 6.6–10 as a whole is taking up the issue of material giving. The exhortation is sustained on an analogy of sowing and reaping, where it is suggested that the allocation of one's resources has direct bearing on one's standing with the Spirit (6.8). Failure to persevere in giving (to teachers of the word, to the poor in

---

[115] On Greco-Roman views of wealth and poverty, which entailed little to no ethical or philosophical impetus for benefaction, see Hands 1968.
[116] So too Longenecker 2007: 58 and now Longenecker 2009.
[117] This may have worked itself out in practice in connection with the Lord's Supper; cf. Reicke 1951.
[118] Gal. 6.9–10.
[119] Winter 1994: 11–40, cited in Longenecker 2007: 52.

general, and above all to the poor within the Church) is to belie one's allegiance to Christ and the people of God.

In 2 Corinthians 8 Paul brings up the matter of the Jerusalem collection and the overwhelmingly positive response which the Macedonian churches showed to it, for 'as I can testify, they voluntarily gave according to their means, and even beyond their means'.[120] In alluding to the Macedonians' generosity, Paul hopes to whip up interest among the Corinthians: 'Now as you excel in everything – in faith, in speech, in knowledge, in utmost eagerness, and in our love for you – so we want you to excel also in this generous undertaking.'[121] The Corinthians' giving is important, the apostle suggests, because their giving is full proof of their love (8.8), not to mention the expression of a spiritual gift.[122] Then follow two further motives for generosity. First, because Jesus Christ himself became poor in order that the Corinthians might become rich, so they too should be willing in imitation of Christ to become poor (2 Cor. 8.9). Second, Paul writes:

> it is a question of a fair balance between your present abundance and their need, so that their abundance may be for your need, in order that there may be a fair balance. As it is written, 'The one who had much did not have too much, and the one who had little did not have too little.'[123]

As for his goals, it appears that Paul is simply trying to achieve a state of equity between the churches in the Mediterranean world. It would not be fair, Paul seems to say, if one church had ample resources, while another went wholly without. While the assumptions undergirding this position are interesting in their own right, equally interesting is the citation of Exodus 16.18, a verse which hearkens back to Moses' injunction that each person receive an omer of manna – no less, no more. In light of this verse, not to mention the considerable evidence that the Exodus served as a significant sub-narrative for Paul's understanding of the Church, it seems that the Exodus-event provided Paul with a starting-point in how he came to understand inter-church economics. Precisely as the recapitulation of the Sinai wilderness generation, the apostle's logic seems to offer, so too should the Corinthians adopt a way of life whereby 'the one who had much did not have too much, and the one who had little did not have too little'. Paul appeals not to traditional Jewish teaching regarding the importance of giving to the poor (although he could have); instead, he points to a specific crisis-moment in Israel's history on the assumption that that same crisis is playing itself out again in the lives of the Corinthian believers. The comparison with Galatians 6 is instructive. Whereas Galatians 6 focuses on the final destiny of those who

---

[120] 2 Cor. 8.3.
[121] 2 Cor. 8.7.
[122] 1 Cor. 1.5–7.
[123] 2 Cor. 8.13–15.

adopt one of two ways, 2 Corinthians 8 approaches the same topic from a different angle by casting the Corinthians within a New Exodus narrative, set in motion by Christ's redemptive act and destined to climax in the final redemption. In both cases, giving no hint that he is exhorting on the basis of some abstract moral principle, Paul firmly establishes his economic ethics within an eschatological framework.

To be sure more could be said in regards to Paul and the poor,[124] but perhaps at this point it should simply be pointed out that what can be reconstructed in regard to the early Church's practices is consistent with Paul's teaching. At least by Luke's record, the first believers held all things in common and provided out of their common purse for all who had need.[125] As a result, the Church as a collectivity was able to alleviate conditions of poverty in their midst.[126] This would have been no small feat, especially since it is likely at this point that the Jerusalem temple had cut ties with the Jesus sectarians, which would have also had dire economic implications.[127] Yet if there be any doubts in regard to the accuracy of Luke's report, it might be countered that given the economic constraints which the temple must have imposed upon the early Church, the very fact that the Jerusalem church survived is evidence enough that a strategy quite like the one Luke describes was employed.

How long the Jerusalem church organized itself in this way, and to what extent this model was replicated in other churches in other regions, is impossible to say. At any rate, the early churches' system of mutual benefaction eventually became strained, thus requiring the implementation of certain policies designed to establish boundaries and safeguard against abuse.[128] This evidence also implies that the practices recorded in the opening chapter of Acts were neither Lukan exaggeration without much basis in fact nor simply a short-term emergency measure: such collectivism did occur, and characterized early Christianity for decades and decades.[129] When believers gave evidence of falling short of this standard, authoritative reproof was swift in coming, as

---

[124] There is, for example, the fact that Luke closes Paul's farewell speech to the Ephesians with specific reference to supporting the weak, that is, those unable to work (Acts 20.35). Its authenticity and significance are corroborated by Paul giving similar instructions at the close of 1 Thessalonians (5.12–14). See also Lindemann 2001.

[125] Acts 2.43–44.

[126] Acts 4.32–34.

[127] In first-century Palestinian society, business transactions were based on and circumscribed by a social network. By opposing the temple authorities (Acts 3), the early Christians had undoubtedly cut themselves off not only from the good graces of the temple, but the good economic graces of those who were attached to the temple.

[128] 1 Tim. 5.3–16; 2 Thess. 3.6–12.

[129] The second-century apologist Justin Martyr famously writes: 'We, out of every tribe of people ... who valued above everything else acquiring wealth and possessions, now bring what we have into a common fund, and share with everyone in need' (*1 Apol.* 61). For more on the second century and beyond, see various essays (Wilhite, Macaskill, Hays, and Kitchen) in Longenecker and Liebengood 2009.

the Epistle of James well attests.[130] The Jerusalem communal model replicated itself in some fashion throughout the known Christian world.

Judging by the sources, one can only conclude that the early Christians did indeed take a pointed interest in the concerns of the poor, particularly the poor in their own midst. This concern worked itself out both in theory and in practice, as attested by Paul's exhortations and the practices of the early Church, as recorded by Luke. Although the historical accuracy of Luke's report has often been discounted, texts such as 2 Thessalonians and the pastoral epistles vouch for some kind of collective arrangement, much like the one described by the author of Acts. Paul gives us some indication, too, that his social ethics were indeed driven by the eschatological moment. This raises the possibility that the early Christian identification with the poor, like that of earlier counter-temple movements, was an ethical posture decisively shaped by the conviction that a redemptive-historical shift was at hand.

Conclusion

On the basis of these representative voices, it does not seem to be the case that the first-century Christians saw themselves either as being merely *like* the temple of God or as supplanting the temple altogether. Against these two extreme options it makes better sense to suppose that these witnesses were united in the common though not necessarily universal conviction that the heavenly temple had begun to break into history through the resurrection of Jesus Christ. Not made by 'human hands', this temple would continue to be built up until the day of redemption, the temple's completion, and the climax of history. In preaching the death and resurrection of Jesus Christ, the Church was in essence issuing a summons to all people everywhere to honor this claim. To accept the Christian hope as one's own was to be incorporated, at least in an anticipatory sense, into the promised eschatological temple; by the same token, rejection of the message constituted – again from the early Church's point of view – a kind of anticipatory apostasy. It is within this framework, which rooted the community's self-understanding (ecclesiology) in its destiny (eschatology), that these writers wished their proclamation to be understood.

What this proclamation implied on a practical level for their communities' relationship to the temple turned out – then as now! – to be a complex and controverted question, as attested, for example, in the apostolic discussion regarding the on-going application of the law. But it is notable that while we have record of discussion revolving around the Gentiles' observance of the law through circumcision (Acts 15), there is no record of anyone

---

[130] See James 1.9–11, 27; 2.1–17; 4.13—5.11.

questioning the appropriateness of Jewish-Christians keeping the same requirements, all connected with temple purity. Nor do we have any indication
among these writers that continued Jewish-Christian participation in the
temple cultus was inherently problematic.[131] The Church's willingness to
exempt Gentiles from the yoke of the law and equal willingness to allow
Jews to pursue the law for themselves, all under the banner of Christ, seems
to reflect a situation in which the Christian community as a whole came to
view the temple through ambivalent eyes.

This ambivalence can be accounted for by the eschatological tension
in which the late-first-century Church found itself. Until more compelling
argumentation can be advanced to the contrary, I am persuaded that when
the above-surveyed writers contemplated the Second Temple (as it existed
in reality and in memory), they thought of it as the house of God, a place
which as long as it remained standing marked out the divine presence in a
special way. If certain swathes of Second-Temple Judaism, critical of the
temple, were skeptical on this point, it does seem to be the case that earliest
Christianity, also critical of the temple, shared in this skepticism.[132] Furthermore,
Luke's attesting to the Church's practice of meeting at the temple well after
Pentecost can hardly have been arbitrary. Unless the first believers were
motivated by purely pragmatic concerns, or unless Luke is attempting to
characterize the practice as futile or wrong-headed (which does not seem to
be the case), both the historian and his heroes must have attributed some
significance to Israel's traditional sacred space. Univocally, from the early
Christian point of view, as long as the temple stood, it remained in some
sense 'God's house'.

At the same time, the Christians had somehow become convinced that
a decisive redemptive-historical shift had occurred. Through Christ and his
resurrection the eschatological temple was finally beginning to break through.
Since Judaism as a whole found no contradiction in regarding both the
Mosaic temple and the eschatological temple as true temples, Christians, who
saw themselves as making up the latter, did not seem to think on the day
after Easter that it was their job to cordon off the gates of Zion with crime-
scene tape. Nonetheless, between the temple's resistance to the gospel and
the in-breaking of God's presence through the Holy Spirit within the Church,
it was clear that the Jerusalem temple was on borrowed time. The heightened
sense of the temple's provisional status, together with the perception that God's

---

[131] The Epistle to the Hebrews is no exception.

[132] Certainly there is textual evidence, mostly from the post-temple era, that certain Jews did not
believe God inhabited the Second Temple (Ezek. 11.22–25; *Tg. Isaiah* 5.5; *Midr. Rab. Numbers*
15.10; *Midr. Rab. Lamentations* 24; *b. Yoma* 21b; cf. Sirach 24.8–34; Josephus, *J.W.* 6.5.3 §299; *m.
Sukkah* 5.4; *Midr. Rab. Exodus* 2.2), but see the cautions of Davies 1991. The testimonium of
Matthew's Jesus stands in contrast: 'So whoever swears by the altar, swears by it and by everything
on it; and whoever swears by the sanctuary, swears by it and by the *one who dwells in it* . . .' (Matt.
23.20–21; emphasis added).

palpable presence had relocated, had paradoxical implications. While the salvation-historical turn of events had in some sense invested the temple with dizzying significance in the broader scope of God's purposes, at the same time, because the institution could no longer claim to be the lasting and unique nexus between heaven and earth, it had been decisively relativized.

If all this had the effect of casting Zion in a jaundiced light in early Christian eyes, the temple's continued failure to embrace Israel's messiah made the aura surrounding the temple only darker with time. The Jewish leadership's resistance to the gospel of course presented a theological problem in its own right, but it was a problem for which the Christians had some ready-made answers. The most important of these comes to surface in the Christian writers' tendency to interpret conflict with the temple-based network, and the resulting social marginalization, as part of the package of redemption-bearing messianic woes. Of course there is nothing distinctively Christian in this response: a similar reaction to perceived intractability at the higher levels of the temple was already anticipated by the communities behind the *Psalms of Solomon* and the Dead Sea Scrolls. Like these other counter-temple sectarians, the Christians interpreted their own suffering as part and parcel of their priestly calling. If suffering was the overture to the final drama, then the heroes were to play out their roles until the curtain should close again to the applause of heaven. The curtain would not come to a close apart from their fulfilling the terms of their assigned script.

There are of course also important points of difference between the early Christians and the sectarians under review in Chapter 1. For example, while the pre-Christian movements under review in this book looked forward to the messiah and his decisive building of the temple as strictly future events, the early Church saw both the messiah's advent and the building of the temple in 'already-but-not-yet' terms. For the Christians, the messiah had come in the person of Jesus, and his resurrection was the first installment of the coming temple reality. The sharp dualism between 'this age' and the 'age to come' so characteristic of Second-Temple Judaism seems to have been assimilated with some revision into early Christian thought. Also unlike these other counter-temple movements, the early Church's criticism of the Jerusalem apparatus, though far from silent, seems nonetheless relatively muted. This may in part have had to do with the sense that some decades after the onset of the messianic sufferings in the life of Jesus, there was no need to belabor the point; moreover, the early Christians' comparatively tame criticism of the temple may also have had to do with the conviction that God would have – or had already – his own way of dealing with Jerusalem's disobedience through the likes of the besieging Roman armies.

Building on the profile set down in Chapter 1, my goal here has been to compare early Christianity with counter-temple movements of an earlier period (the community behind the *Psalms of Solomon*, the Qumran covenanteers, and John the Baptizer's movement). Like these earlier sectarians, the early Christians were convinced (1) that the existent temple leadership had decisively succumbed to moral failure; (2) that this failure signaled the onset of messianic tribulation, which would include intense persecution for the righteous one and the righteous remnant; (3) that this persecution and the remnant's faithfully upholding their priestly role in spite of and through it would serve as a catalyst for the decisive in-breaking of the eschatological temple, which found anticipatory form in the community itself; and (4) until that moment, the remnant was to identify itself both as and for the poor. Despite the obvious differences between early Christianity and other sects, I believe that it can be demonstrated, at least on the basis of these four points, that the early Church subscribed to a general pattern of belief which may be characterized as a 'counter-temple theology', set within an apocalyptic framework.

If this is so, we are in a position to draw a very basic, yet perhaps very controversial, inference. Elsewhere it has been argued that since both John the Baptizer and the early Church were apocalyptic in outlook, it stands to reason that Jesus, who bridges the gap between these two movements, must be presumed to have shared the same stance.[133] Despite some ingenious attempts on the part of those who wish to see Jesus as something other than apocalyptic, there is in my mind simply little getting around the force of this basic argument which, at this point, I would like to take a step forward. If both John the Baptizer's following and the early Church were counter-temple movements, by the definition I have offered, then this grants basic plausibility to the hypothesis that Jesus, who straddled both groups, also saw his own mission and destiny in similar terms. In other words, in light of the evidence it is hardly far-fetched to propose that like John the Baptizer before him and the early Church after him, Jesus found the temple of his day to be corrupt, inferred from this – as did his cousin John – the onset of messianic tribulation, and then finally saw his own calling as a response to this divinely ordained crisis.

Towards specifying the nature of this response, we might think of it as basically having two aspects. First, it fell to Jesus, as it did to his counter-temple predecessors, to call the official leadership of Israel to repentance. Clearly, if Jesus did come to conclude anything like what his dissident predecessors did or his later followers would, he had little choice in the matter. It would be unconscionable for any faithful Second-Temple Jew to regard his or her misgivings in regard to the temple as being merely a privately kept matter. Others had written against the temple in public or semi-public settings: Jesus also felt morally obliged to speak out openly against the temple leaders.

Second, if Jesus saw the hope of Israel as falling to him and his movement, then this would have entailed the carrying on of Israel's temple activities

---

[133] Sanders 1985: 91–5.

outside of the established channels. This does not mean that in addition to whatever concerns and programs preoccupied Jesus, discrete temple practices like prayer and Torah-study would have to be 'add-ons'. Instead we now have some reason to believe that Jesus' counter-temple theology provided the fundamental framework for his understanding of his own role and the role of his movement at that particular crossroads of Israel's history. I also suspect and indeed intend to argue that this same framework informed his defining actions. In short, I suggest *all* the practices which Jesus was to enjoin upon his followers are to be seen essentially as *temple* practices. It is only by situating Jesus within this 'temple context' that we can fully discern the rhyme and reason of what he did.

But towards demonstrating this, it is first necessary in the following chapter to focus on an event taking place during Jesus' last week, one which forced the moment to its crisis. There is, I think, no comparable event, in that there was no other instance in which Jesus' critique of the temple was more forceful or provocative. Were Jesus' opponents alive today to tell the story, I think even they would have to agree. By the reckoning of a good many Jesus scholars, it was this gesture we know as the 'cleansing of the temple' that sealed his death warrant. It is to this gesture we now turn.

3

'Destroy this house!'

Jesus' action in the temple

Introduction

> And he entered the temple and began to drive out those who were selling and those who were buying in the temple, and he overturned the tables of the money changers and the seats of those who sold doves; and he would not allow anyone to carry anything through the temple. He was teaching and saying, 'Is it not written, "My house shall be called a house of prayer for all the nations"? But you have made it a den of robbers.'[1]

Considering the many astounding events attributed to Jesus, it seems little short of remarkable that the eminent Lithuanian scholar Joseph Klausner should deem the cleansing of the temple (Mark 11.15–17) his 'greatest public deed'.[2] Klausner is in venerable company. Some eighteen centuries earlier, the Alexandrian exegete Origen opined that Jesus' overturning of the tables was a feat even greater than his changing water to wine. For the early church father, Jesus' taking the temple court by storm was a Christological revelation of unsurpassed significance, laden with apocalyptic import, bearing both on improprieties within the temple and on its imminent destruction as a result of those abuses. In short, Origen seemed to have been saying, '*all* the dimensions of Jesus' proclamation of the kingdom of God are brought together in the temple-action'.[3] Anyone agreeing with Origen today might say that the temple action was the parable *par excellence*, a deftly orchestrated climactic movement to the symphony that was Jesus' life. Or, to switch metaphors, it was the mountain-top view from which an observer could finally begin to make out the topography of Jesus' ways and days.

There is, however, something in our historiographical instincts, a superego of historical consciousness you might call it, which makes us uneasy about Origen's mountain-top interpretive experience. On meeting a hypothesis which posits explanations on so many different levels, we are instantly

---

[1] Mark 11.15b–17.

[2] Klausner 1925: 312. Although some object to the term 'cleansing of the temple' as being misleading in regard to Jesus' purposes, I retain the phrase simply out of convention.

[3] As summarized by Metzdorf 2003: 67; emphasis added.

suspicious that someone wants to have his cake and eat it too.[4] Surely, when Jesus cleansed the temple, he had something in mind, some*thing* in particular. All things being equal, disciplined historical reasoning prefers 'something' to 'some things', a single cause to a complex of multifarious causes. Like a billiards commentator relishing a game-winning shot by replaying the succession of ball-to-ball impacts, the modern historian is wont to analyze a significant historical moment by working through the chain of events leading up to that moment, with especial attention to the penultimate link, the precipitating motive. This I suspect has something to do with our tendency to think of consciousness and the sense impressions contained by it as discrete *things* – the billiard table and the balls, respectively.

But in the real world consciousness and perceptions are more like a matrix, and the analogy between the hard science of billiards and the soft art of history eventually breaks down. While in billiards it is always possible to trace single-lined trajectories, things are not always so simple in the realm of human decision. Although historians are generally aware of the complexity of human intentionality and therefore must at least in theory reckon on the possibility of there being a convergence of motivating factors for any given course of action, there is a general tendency, especially in post-Enlightenment historiography, to prefer only one explanation, if only one explanation will do. As a result, accounts of human intentionality are often over-simplified.[5]

So if we concede the point as a necessary evil, and with many we say that the cleansing of the temple was in some sense Jesus' final, free act, sealing his death warrant with the temple authorities, it remains to be asked, 'What is the one overriding factor that led Jesus to raise such dangerous havoc in the temple in the first place?' What prompted him to overturn the tables? And what was he hoping to accomplish?

Frustratingly, from Origen's day to our own, there has been no shortage of answers to such questions; that is, no shortage of trails leading up to the mountain-top. This more than likely has to do with the fact that the temple action is not only among Jesus' most ambiguous gestures, but also, paradoxically, among his most self-defining: to grasp the cleansing of the temple is virtually tantamount to grasping the historical Jesus himself.[6]

---

[4] It was undoubtedly Adolf Jülicher who, reflecting late nineteenth-century distaste for allegory, issued the strongest censure of Origen and the like-minded interpreters of previous centuries. But in insisting on one and *only* one meaning for a given parable, Jülicher had merely exchanged a hermeneutic maximalism for a no less artificial minimalism.

[5] On this general point in regard to modern historiography see especially Hughes 2003. I am indebted to Katrina Combs for this reference.

[6] Both points are commonplace in the secondary literature. For example, as Wright (1996: 414) puts it: 'the temple-action is clearly underdetermined' yet 'was closely integrated with, perhaps even climactic to, the rest of his work'. Similarly, Fredriksen (1999: 225): 'the scene at the Temple is the key to the rest of the story'. On this point Wedderburn (2006) is skeptical, but I am skeptical of his skepticism.

It is no wonder then that the event continues to provoke controversy, even as it did in the first instance. Add to this a good measure of complex source-critical and exegetical issues, and we soon find ourselves confronted with a daunting array of divergent scholarly paths. Although at first blush we may despair of blazing our own trail with any confidence, the journey to the peak will be worthwhile, if there we may find the aims of the historical Jesus.

Questions of historicity

Was there a temple action?

'But', some have said, 'that is precisely the question. Do we actually find the cleansing of the temple having anything to do with the historical Jesus or any basis in reality?'[7] Notwithstanding the shared testimony to the event within the four Gospels (five if you include *Thomas*), it has been suggested that these accounts present material that, however useful for the evangelists' theological purposes, remains fundamentally useless for our historical purposes. Because those who hold to this position are reputable scholars, it is important to engage their views; because they are few, my engagement will be brief.

The main sticking points for the historicity of the temple action have been three. First, it is argued, while we can easily imagine either a small unarmed troop or an armed man holding up temple business, it is simply unrealistic to think of Jesus – with or without knotted cords – singlehandedly effecting the kind of disruption that the Gospel writers describe. Second, how is it plausible that one who taught non-resistance and the virtues of turning the other cheek should so suddenly and inexplicably fall into such a tirade? And if Jesus' foray into the temple was controlled and premeditated, the problem becomes even more acute. Third, since it was Passover time and the Roman forces garrisoned at Fortress Antonia must have been on high alert, is it really credible that Jesus could have done such a thing and not incurred swift punishment for it? Since the record shows no such reaction, it follows that the incident could not have occurred in the first place, at least not in the way the evangelists describe it. When it comes to the temple action as history, there are obstacles indeed.

But they are hardly insuperable obstacles.[8] In the first place, the Gospel writers never give the impression that Jesus is in a position of control where he could say to the money-changers something like: 'Drop your coins – I

---

[7] So Miller 1991; Seeley 1993; Becker 1998: 333–45.

[8] Of course, the first objection (which supposes that the operation could not have been sufficiently large-scale to match the evangelists' accounts) cancels out the second and third objections (which suppose that the event could not have been sufficiently small-scale) – and vice versa.

have the place surrounded!' If the evangelists are giving a generally accurate account, neither weapons nor a band of collaborators would have been necessary. As for the judgment that the temple action would have been a violation of Jesus' own ethic of non-violence, this all depends on a very broad definition of violence, if not a rather rigidly narrow application of Jesus' exhortation to 'turn the other cheek'. There is certainly no indication that the money-changers, vendors, or casual onlookers ever felt physically threatened by Jesus' actions. Finally, the lack of Roman response is no strong argument against historicity. The incident is reported to have occurred in the outer court of the temple, an open area providing ample space for lots of activity. If Jesus had moved through the tables very quickly, it is entirely conceivable that the whole event was over before many present had any idea that something out of the ordinary had occurred. It certainly would not have been necessary for Jesus to have carried on at length: as for those intended recipients of the 'message' who had not witnessed it directly, whether friend or foe, they would hear about this demonstration soon enough. On the reasonable assumption that Jesus' intentions were to create a brief but provocative scene and then to move on in order to live another day, we should leave it to his judgment rather than our own, as to how provocative he could be before offending his own sensibilities or those of the nearby-stationed Roman legion. Since none of the objections to the cleansing of the temple's authenticity are compelling, and since (as should soon be clear) it becomes very difficult to explain Jesus' arrest, trial, and crucifixion without at least something like the temple action occurring, it must be allowed to stand.[9]

Did Jesus cite Isaiah 56.7 and Jeremiah 7.11 (Mark 11.17)?

And so we proceed up the mountain in search of the historical Jesus. But we do not move very far before we come to the first point of negotiation, the scriptural quotation ascribed to the temple-cleanser himself:

> He was teaching and saying, 'Is it not written, "My house shall be called a house of prayer for all the nations"? But you have made it a den of robbers (*lēstōn*).'
>
> (Mark 11.17)

Jesus quotes from Isaiah 56.7 and alludes to Jeremiah 7.11. For our part the first order of business is to determine whether the citation, presumably intended to explain the temple action, goes back to the historical Jesus or a later editorializing stage (i.e. as a product of pre-Markan tradition or the evangelist himself). Objections to the authenticity of v. 17 have been raised

---

[9] The demonstration is deemed authentic by most scholars, including not least the Jesus Seminar (Funk 1998: 122).

on various grounds.[10] I demur. I believe it makes far better sense to locate these two quotations smack on the lips of Jesus even as he is cleansing the temple.

This, I think, begins to make sense once we correlate the compositional origins of verse 17 with our best explanation as to how the verse was intended to function. On the one hand, if it was first Mark or an earlier editor who snuck in the prophetic citation, it seems likely that this was done with a view towards providing a self-contained and perspicacious explanation of the event. But in fact if Mark (or the pre-Markan tradent/editor) wished us as hearers to focus narrowly on Isaiah 56.7 and Jeremiah 7.11, we are only marginally better off – if not more baffled – in our understanding of the temple action, for the verses taken together only raise as many questions as they resolve. For example, any attempt to fasten heavy significance to the phrase 'den of *robbers* (*lēstōn*)' seems to lead us in a direction whereby Mark is made to distort the meaning of *lēstōn*, which by itself could not have much at all to do with money-changing, dove-selling, or any matter commercial. Of course this is precisely the point of many of those who take verse 17 as a later addition: it doesn't seem to match the event itself and so Mark must be found out as a tendentious bumbler. This is not impossible. But when facing an apparent disconnect between done deed and explanatory word, like the one we have here between the temple action and scriptural citation, the historian should keep in mind the possibility that the dots' failure to connect properly might be more a result of misunderstanding on our part than on the part of the ancient writer.

That is why I propose that Jeremiah 7.11 and Isaiah 56.7 are not so much self-standing explanations but are the tip of a much larger homiletic iceberg, originating with Jesus and now hidden from the view of history. That the two cited verses are – far from being awkward, late-stage proof-texts – a kind of précis of Jesus' actual message is not only on the face of it a fair surmise (especially given Mark's statement that he 'was teaching' or 'kept teaching'), but is also borne out by the scriptures themselves. This begins to become clear when we consider Jesus' citation of Isaiah 56.7 in its original context:

---

[10] From the form-critical perspective, Bultmann (1968 [1921]: 36) sees the verse as violating the ideal (apophthegmatic) form of the saying and must therefore be counted as a late accretion. From a redaction-critical point of view, the words 'he was teaching and saying' smack too much of Markan style to be assigned to Jesus (see, e.g., Buchanan 1991: 281). Moving on to substantive as opposed to merely formal considerations: if there is indeed a genuine tension between the sense of *lēstōn* ('robbers', 'guerrillas', 'gangsters') and the meaning of Jesus' action by itself (Harvey 1982: 132; Sanders 1985: 66–9; Fredriksen 1999: 207–10), then the citation may have been inserted as the evangelist's attempt to blunt or redirect the thrust of Jesus' intentions. Taking something of a middle ground, Barrett (1975: 18–19) and Murphy-O'Connor (2000: 54) deny the quotation as having been spoken during the temple incident, but regard it nonetheless as being rooted in the Jesus tradition.

[6] And the foreigners who join themselves to the LORD, to minister to him, to love the name of the LORD, and to be his servants, all who keep the sabbath, and do not profane it, and hold fast my covenant – [7] these I will bring to my holy mountain, and make them joyful in my house of prayer; their burnt offerings and their sacrifices will be accepted on my altar; *for my house shall be called a house of prayer for all peoples.* [8] Thus says the Lord GOD, who gathers the outcasts of Israel, I will gather others to them besides those already gathered. [9] All you wild animals, all you wild animals in the forest, come to devour! [10] Israel's sentinels are blind, they are all without knowledge; they are all silent dogs that cannot bark; dreaming, lying down, loving to slumber. [11] The dogs have a mighty appetite; they never have enough. The shepherds also have no understanding; they have all turned to their own way, to their own gain, one and all.[11]

Notably, Isaiah's burden draws together several significant threads from the fabric of salvation-history. First, the prophet holds out the hope of the day when the Gentiles would finally attach themselves to Israel (v. 7). Second, like many others in the prophetic tradition, Isaiah connects this long-awaited event with the end of exile and the restoration of the twelve tribes (v. 8). It is both anachronistic and a distortion of the context to argue, as has often been done, that Jesus is objecting to the temple's exclusion of the Gentiles in principle. It is unlikely that either Isaiah or Jesus would have ever considered the temple 'a house of prayer for all nations' in an absolute and timeless sense, or that either one would have been – along with contemporary western culture – primarily interested in inclusion for inclusion's sake. As Jesus understood perfectly well, Isaiah's text pointed to a future, glorious reality, and in quoting the text he is intimating that the future is now present: the promised pilgrimage of the Gentiles and the eschatological re-gathering of exiled Israel had begun. Since both these expectations have been widely attributed to Jesus in the scholarly literature, tracing Isaiah 56.7 back to Jesus' mouth makes a good deal of sense.[12]

Notwithstanding the hint that salvation was underway, the gist of Jesus' communication does not seem to have been entirely positive, just as Isaiah's message was less than upbeat. In the prophet's context charges are being leveled against 'Israel's sentinels' (v. 10) and 'shepherds' (v. 11), on account of their being blind, ravenous, and greedy for gain. This too is apropos to Jesus' setting. Despite the sometimes overstated case that has been made for disassociating Jesus from his more polemical words only to associate them more stringently with the early Church, it is difficult to deny that Jesus was

---

[11] Isa. 56.6–11.

[12] Although I already assume the point above in the Introduction, it is nevertheless worth noting that a good number of scholars grant Jesus' expectation of return from exile and restoration; see, e.g., Sanders 1985; Wright 1996; Allison 1998; McKnight 1999; Bryan 2002; Pitre 2005. Dunn's (2003: 477) objection to 'the superimposition of a unitary meta-narrative' (*viz.* exile), which itself seems to be based on its own 'unitary meta-narrative', does not directly pertain to my point which sees 'return from exile' as an aspect of Israel's final hope – new temple.

indeed deeply critical of the temple-based leaders of his own day and would have quite likely regarded them as bearing semblance to the sentinels of Isaiah's day.[13] Not only does Isaiah 56.7 ring true in Jesus' mouth as a promise to the expectant faithful (the scriptural fulfillment of Isaiah's remnant), it also serves as a fitting warning against those whom Jesus perceived to be the self-interested leaders of his day (the scriptural fulfillment of Isaiah's false shepherds and sentinels).

In this connection, it seems that Jesus was not the first one solemnly to invoke Isaiah 56.7 on temple grounds. One may recall, as any Jew of Jesus' day would have undoubtedly recalled, a story that has come down to us in 1 Maccabees 7. It is a story which recounts how the wicked Seleucid prince Nicanor, in league with the false priest Alcimus, returns to Mount Zion after a humiliating defeat at the hands of Israel's liberator, Judas Maccabeus.[14] When the temple priests approach Nicanor in good will, he has no intention of returning the favor:

> But he mocked them and derided them and defiled them and spoke arrogantly, and in anger he swore this oath, 'Unless Judas and his army are delivered into my hands this time, then if I return safely I will burn up this house.' And he went out in great anger. At this the priests went in and stood before the altar and the temple; they wept and said, '*You chose this house to be called by your name, and to be for your people a house of prayer and supplication.* Take vengeance on this man and on his army, and let them fall by the sword; remember their blasphemies, and let them live no longer.'[15]

It has already been persuasively argued elsewhere that Jesus in his triumphal entry was consciously modeling himself after the Hasmonean hero Judas Maccabeus.[16] If so, it is hardly a stretch to suppose that Jesus on the next day was again aligning himself with Judas and his supporters, this time by citing the same verse which the righteous priests allusively invoke in their imprecatory prayer against the blasphemous pagan ruler. If Jesus was indeed seeking to rework a familiar story whereby he himself played the role of Judas the liberator and his detractors carried the part of the pagan Nicanor, allied with the regnant wicked high priest, he could have hardly picked a more suitable stage or script.

---

[13] Jesus' entry into Jerusalem, his Parable of the Wicked Tenants (Mark 12.1–10 par.), and his escalating confrontations with the temple leadership during the last week all have decent historical claim and can only be divested of their anti-temple tenor by entirely re-scripting the facts as we have them. There is certainly more to Jesus' counter-temple polemic than these incidents, as I shall make clear, but for now it is enough to rest on these rather than my later-developed case so as to avoid begging the question.

[14] According to 1 Macc. 7.49, Judas' defeat of Nicanor was commemorated annually on Adar 13. The story of that victory together with the chain of events leading up to it were probably rehearsed on at least a yearly basis.

[15] 1 Macc. 7.34–38.

[16] Catchpole 1984: 320; Wright 1996: 492–3.

No less appropriate to the moment of Jesus' entry into the temple was Jeremiah 7. The passage, in which the prophet is speaking the words of Yahweh, also deserves to be quoted at length:

> [5] For if you truly amend your ways and your doings, if you truly act justly one with another, [6] if you do not oppress the alien, the orphan, and the widow, or shed innocent blood in this place, and if you do not go after other gods to your own hurt, [7] then I will dwell with you in this place, in the land that I gave of old to your ancestors forever and ever. [8] Here you are, trusting in deceptive words to no avail. [9] Will you steal, murder, commit adultery, swear falsely, make offerings to Baal, and go after other gods that you have not known, [10] and then come and stand before me in this house, which is called by my name, and say, 'We are safe!' – only to go on doing all these abominations? [11] Has this house, which is called by my name, become a den of robbers in your sight? You know, I too am watching, says the LORD. [12] Go now to my place that was in Shiloh, where I made my name dwell at first, and see what I did to it for the wickedness of my people Israel.[17]

Yahweh's charge through Jeremiah hinges on the accusation that the Jerusalemites of the day had broken the commandments of the Decalogue (v. 8). How so? Well, they had chased 'after other gods'; they had also 'oppressed the alien, the orphan, and the widow' (v. 6). All the while they had carried on with a vacuous religiosity buoyed by an overweening self-confidence. Were they to continue on this path, Jeremiah declared, the end of the first temple would be like that of Shiloh's temple (v. 12) – utter destruction. Inevitably, the brunt of the weight of Jeremiah's message fell on Israel's leaders. These were the ones, after all, who were in the best position to do something about the alleged injustices against aliens, orphans, and widows. Like the prophets before and after him, Jeremiah saw the covenantal faithlessness of the religious leaders as the decisive trigger for exile.[18] Once it became fairly clear that there would be no repentance, Jeremiah preached the imminent doom of the temple not simply as a means of getting the people's attention, but as a symbolic indication that God was about to forsake God's house.

Like Jeremiah, Jesus in his ministry repeatedly appealed to the Decalogue: warnings against stealing, murder, adultery, false witness and idolatry are all part and parcel of the Jesus-tradition.[19] So if the temple act were to be understood as a kind of summative climax of his ethical message, then Jeremiah 7 would be fitting indeed. And if Jesus was particularly interested in taking the Jerusalem leaders to task along similar lines, one might say that Jeremiah 7

---

[17] Jer. 7.5–12.
[18] Isa. 3.12; 9.15; 29.10; Ezek. 13.2–16; Mic. 3.5–12; Zech. 10.3; etc. Cf. Jer. 2.26–30; 4.9–10; 5.13–31.
[19] Mark 3.4 par.; 4.18–19 par.; 7.8–23 par.; 10.1–12 par.; 19–21 par.; 12.1–10 par.; 12.40 par.; etc.

would be an almost obvious text to go to, that is, assuming he wished to mount his verbal attack in the strongest possible terms.[20]

Both Isaiah 56 and Jeremiah 7 inveigh against corrupt leadership; both texts may be considered something between an imprecation and a warning. Both texts are exactly what one might expect of a prophetic figure overturning tables in the temple precinct. Isaiah 56, refracted in Jesus' immediate context through the lens of 1 Maccabees 7, invokes the overthrow of pagan overlords who threaten the temple; Jeremiah 7 ironically intones the destruction of the temple due to unremitting systemic sin.[21] The two texts also make for a natural pair on a formal level in Jesus' setting: conjoined by the shared catchword of 'my house', their combination in an orally presented Jewish homily would fit the genre perfectly. This is not to deny that Mark left his own fingerprints on our text. But that Jesus quoted these very verses and more while standing before stunned temple personnel days before his death – this is easier to believe than to deny.[22]

Jesus' intentions behind the temple action

Surveying the options

Once you have decided that the mountain actually exists, and have come to terms with the scriptural horizon line which oriented Jesus' vista, the next step is to decide the best path forward towards meeting him at the peak. Generally speaking, scholars contemplate one of two approaches: one non-eschatological; the other, eschatological. For those in the former category, the temple action is first and foremost a 'temple cleansing', that is, an attempt to spotlight and ultimately reform some kind of abuse that was occurring within the temple area. On this paradigm, Jesus' aims have little or nothing to do with the temple being destroyed or replaced. Ascending the other face of the mountain are those who regard the temple action as the tremor to an impending seismic shift in Israel's cultic landscape. On this reading, Jesus' aim was not so much to demand any real change in the temple, but to declare that Israel was on the verge of a salvation-historical crisis point, involving

---

[20] Bockmuehl (1996 [1994]: 63–4) rightly flags up the parallel between Jesus' appropriation of Jeremiah 7 and that of Jesus Ben Hananah, who a generation later likewise had an axe to grind with the temple authorities. The point could be extended to a counter-temple text examined earlier, the *Psalms of Solomon*. On multiple allusions to Jeremiah 7 in the *Psalms*, see above p. 23, and Atkinson 2001: 72, 89, 90, 209, 214, 271, 273, 313, 324, and 326.

[21] Thus I find Buchanan (1991: 284) inexplicable when he writes that 'There is no message in Mark 11.17 to suggest that Jesus wanted his hearers to understand that the temple would be destroyed.'

[22] In regard to Mark 11.15–17, Eppstein (1964: 44) aptly concludes: 'Despite a superficial tendential redaction, it is not improbable that in this pericope we have an episode in the life of Jesus for which considerable historicity may justly be claimed'; the remarks apply equally well to v. 17 in particular. So too, e.g., Borg 1984: 173; Crossan 1991: 357–8; Evans 1995 [1993]: 362–3; Wright 1996: 418; Bockmuehl 1996 [1994]: 63–4; Betz 1997: 467–8; Ådna 2000: 267–87.

either the utter redundancy of the temple or its outright destruction. Of course, just as it is possible for a trail to traverse two faces of a mountain on the way to the top, these two broad approaches need not be mutually exclusive. But in such a case it is incumbent on those who pursue such a *via media* to explain how a well-meant call for reform can be reconciled with a proclamation of impending destruction.

In the remainder of the chapter, I intend to do just that. In fact, I will go on to argue that the pitting of an eschatological reading of the temple event against a non-eschatological reading ceases to do full justice to either. Because salvation-historical shifts typically coincide with points where Israel's moral high ground steeply slopes down (as is clear, for example, in the deuteronomic histories), and conversely, because the necessity of restoring the temple's purity implied eschatological renewal, I maintain that the most promising approach is to see the cleansing of the temple as simultaneously 'eschatological', in the sense that it portended God's sovereign and decisive in-breaking into temple affairs, and 'non-eschatological', in the sense that it was meant as a genuine call to repentance. Like so many prophetic pronounce-ments, the temple action holds forth both prediction and prospect: prediction that the fall of the temple was all but sealed, and prospect that if the people did change, such disaster could be averted. While this tension between divine foreclosure and human freedom obviously leaves us with certain questions (Did Jesus think the temple elite had any real hope of repenting? And if they did repent, what might this have meant for Yahweh's purposes for the temple?), it is the kind of tension with which Second-Temple Judaism as a whole seems to have come to terms.[23] Jesus expected God to do something and hoped for human beings to do something as well. Perhaps so much modern scholarship on this incident has gotten off on the wrong foot, happily divor-cing eschatology from ethics, because modernity itself has a low tolerance for tension and mystery – far lower than Jesus and his contemporary Judaism. Perhaps too, were the historical Jesus to read his own press today, he would have deemed the antithesis between 'eschatological' and 'non-eschatological' a false one. I would offer as much. At the end of the day, our common inclin-ation to seal off vertical realities from horizontal realities tells us far more about ourselves than it does about the aims of Jesus.

All the same, the dichotomy of non-eschatological versus eschatological does provide a convenient entry for discussing how others have approached the temple incident. I mention first those who focus on the temple cleansing as a non-eschatological event. By far the most popular path along these lines

---

[23] So, for example, I take exception to Meyer (1992: 261), who in connection with the temple action states that '"the presence of the eschaton" altogether transcends the category of mere reform'. Even if Jesus had little expectation of Israel's repentance, prophetic conditionality always allowed for promises of judgment to be voided on a favorable response. On the tension of divine sovereignty and human freedom in Second-Temple Judaism, see Carson 1981.

is one which sees Jesus as being displeased with shady business practices purportedly occurring in the temple. In recent years this position has been advanced by scholars like Hengel, Bauckham, and Hooker.[24] Given certain historical evidence of profiteering at the temple animal stalls and exorbitant commission rates at the temple exchange,[25] this position maintains that Jesus' basic point bears on the greed of those working at the temple, which is ultimately an extension of the greed of the temple leadership itself. At points this interpretive approach shades over into a second paradigm which emphasizes Jesus' objection to practices which compromised the temple's cultic purity. These violations may have to do with the commercialization of the temple in general (Jeremias, Betz, Casey), the fact that temple coinage bore a blasphemous human image (Richardson) in particular, or, again in particular, the practice of cutting through the temple grounds (Meyer).[26] A third line attends to the term *klētēs*, which traditional Bible translations gloss as 'thief' or 'robber', but which seems more likely to denote something like 'guerrilla', 'bandit', or 'gangster'. Here the point of Jesus' critique is the close connection between an ideology of holiness and Jewish militancy (Buchanan, Borg).[27] More or less opposite of this is the view that Jesus was on the verge of staging a military revolution (Brandon, Horsley).[28] Despite their differences, the common denominator of all these interpretations is their shared insistence that Jesus' criticism be detached from any expectation of a fundamental turn in Israel's salvation-history.

As for more consistently eschatological interpretations, pride of place goes to the view that Jesus had no specific criticism against his contemporaries or their practices, but was merely signifying the removal of the present temple as preliminary to the establishment of a new eschatological temple (Sanders, Fredriksen).[29] A variation of this viewpoint is simply to say that Jesus *was* distressed by improprieties in the temple and in Israel at large, but that this impassioned call to repentance was almost entirely subsumed under the announcement of the kingdom of God and the new temple (Merklein, Meyer, Söding).[30] Closely parallel to this path is the view that

---

[24] Hengel 1971: 15–16; Bauckham 1988; Hooker 1988. See also Bockmuehl 1996 [1994]: 69–71; Tan 1997: 231–32; Herzog 2000: 111–43.

[25] Attested, e.g., in *m. Ker.* 1.7; see also Eppstein 1964.

[26] Jeremias 1971b: 145, 219 n. 92; Betz 1997; Casey 1997; Richardson 1992; Meyer 1992: 263–4.

[27] Buchanan 1991; Borg 1984: 163–70. Earlier Borg (1984) could be assigned to the 'eschatological camp', but later writings (Borg 1995, 2006) render the eschatological horizon relatively moot. Wright (1996: 413–28) is quite close to the 1984 Borg in also emphasizing Jesus' disquiet of Israel's religio-militancy, but nevertheless against Borg sets the critique within a specific eschatological framework.

[28] Brandon 1967: 332–4; Horsley 1987: 297–300. Later Horsley (2008: 197–204) instead comes to emphasize the action as Jesus' attempt to tip his hand, holding cards of a heretofore hidden defiance.

[29] Sanders 1985: 61–70; Fredriksen 1990, 2007.

[30] Merklein 1989: 135–8; Meyer 1992: 262–3; Söding 1992.

Jesus was hoping to communicate his belief that the time of the Gentiles had arrived, and the prophecies relating to their coming to Zion were now being fulfilled (Jeremias, Dunn).[31] Another possibility is to suppose that Jesus was using his action to declare the cessation and imminent transcendence of the present temple cult (Trautmann, Crossan), perhaps by implementing a new basis for atonement and purity (Neusner, Chilton).[32] Finally, some commentators see the act as Jesus' self-declaration of his messiahship, either in fulfillment of scripture (Witherington), or by virtue of implying his authority over the temple (Wright), or on account of his self-designation as the new sin offering (Ådna).[33]

This compressed catalogue of options, not quite exhaustive, is dizzying in its own way. Barring any completely novel angle on the question, how does one proceed to sort through the options? Where does one start?

I suggest we begin by recognizing that Jesus' temple act, like many of his actions and teachings, must have been carefully orchestrated as a *parabolic* gesture. In this case, inasmuch as Jesus' parables were generally characterized by an ambivalence calculated to engender various levels of meaning simultaneously (rather than inviting his hearers to one and only one interpretation, *pace* Jülicher), it is necessary to entertain the possibility that Jesus was intentionally leaving his temple demonstration open to a limited range of interpretations. So long as these elicited responses were mutually compatible and consistent with his purposes, an underdetermined staged event like that of the temple action had the strategic benefit of not only protecting Jesus from immediate arrest but also providing an oblique but nonetheless summative statement as to what he stood for and why. 'The one who has ears to hear, let that one hear.' In this sense, I see the cleansing of the temple as Jesus' last prominently displayed word. It was, as Origen so long ago suggested, a word which comprehended the fullness of his ministry and message.[34]

However, this is not to say that all mountain trails lead to the mountain top; nor are all our interpretive options equally valid. The claim that all these paths lead back to the intentions of the historical Jesus affirms simultaneously too much and too little. If every commentator is equally right, then at the same time no one is really right, and we learn next to nothing about the hero of the story. And even if Jesus executed his carefully

---

[31] Jeremias 1958: 65–6; Dunn 1991: 48. Both authors in their later works (Jeremias 1971b, Dunn 2003) seem to pull back from this position without necessarily recanting it.

[32] Trautmann 1980: 119–28; Neusner 1989; Crossan 1991: 357–8; Chilton 1992: 121–36.

[33] Witherington 1990: 111–15; Wright 1996: 490–3; Ådna 2000: 335–76. Notably, Wright also goes on to argue that the temple action signified the establishment of a new temple (426, 612–53).

[34] My plea is not principally new, even to the modern discussion. Without necessarily saying so explicitly, a number of modern commentators already follow suit with multiple-level patristic interpretation by attaching a manifold significance to the temple incident. See the conclusions of Metzdorf 2003: 254–6.

conceived operation within the temple in order to signify multiple realities (which I believe to be the case), this does not preclude the possibility that he considered only one or two points to be outstanding. There is little heuristic value in the incident unless one is prepared to tease out Jesus' primary concerns.

For now I believe we can do no better than suggest two. In entering the temple that day, Jesus was primarily interested in, first, issuing a prophetic indictment against the regnant temple administration on the grounds of fiscal abuse and, second, indicating his own role of (re)builder of the eschatological temple. Both agenda items speak both to the present and to the future; both are born out of not only cultic concerns, but also an interest in socio-economic-political justice. While assertions like these have already been advanced in one place or another in previous scholarship, and I will certainly be building upon that scholarship here, my final goal will be to demonstrate that Jesus' cleansing of one temple and his introducing another one, far from being stray bullet points within his broader agenda, are inextricably linked. They are, moreover, essential aspects of Jesus' self-understanding as the temple.

The design of the temple action

Sign against the temple

Despite the skepticism of some, it seems beyond doubt that Jesus was deeply interested in shining a light on the darker side of the temple industry. The root source of this darkness was an idolatrous greed, a greed which manifested itself in Israel's temple-based life in different ways. This is borne out by the convergence of three lines of evidence: the focal point of Jesus' actions, the scripture he cites, and the corroborating historical witness to temple greed.

One of the major difficulties of the view that Jesus' action in the temple had nothing to do with financial matters lies in the observation that whereas Jesus could have presumably disrupted temple activity in any number of ways, at any number of locations on temple grounds, for some reason he chose to focus in on those who were on the front line of financial transaction. To put it otherwise, it is hard to conceive of a prophet-like figure suddenly and inexplicably overturning seats and tables, without also giving the distinct impression that he was unhappy with precisely the ones positioned at those seats and tables. Had Jesus only been interested in protesting against the institution or its offices, without wishing to implicate the individuals themselves, we would then also have to suppose that he later issued an apology to those whom he had shamed – human collateral damage from an errant protest-action originally aimed at 'the system'. Jesus clearly targeted those who handled the money, and in order for any explanation of the temple action to be convincing, it must explain why.

I have already noted above how both Isaiah 56 and Jeremiah 7 speak against the leaders of Israel, with whom Jesus in his own day clearly had his own misgivings. Sins of greed figure prominently in both scriptural texts. In Isaiah 56, Israel's sentinels show no understanding because they 'never have enough' and have 'all turned to their own way, their own gain' (v. 11). They are like 'wild animals ... come to devour' (v. 11). Likewise, the rulers of Jeremiah's day are charged with oppressing the socio-economically disenfranchised (v. 6): the alien, the orphan, and the widow. Interestingly, Mark records that Jesus warns the crowds against the scribes who 'devour widows' houses' (12.40), and where else but immediately before his predicting the destruction of the temple (Mark 13). If we allow for the authenticity of Mark 12.40, which stands in admirable continuity both with Jesus' temple action and his prediction, it is only further indication that his interest in these scriptures stemmed in part from their thematizing the evils of greed.

To be sure, Jeremiah 7 touches on a whole range of social-justice issues, of which greed is only one. But judging by the evidence of the Jeremiah targum, which likely reflects interpretive traditions contemporary with Jesus, it seems that there is already an established connection between Jeremiah 7 and sins of avarice in particular. Against the Hebrew text of Jeremiah 7.9, which has 'Will you steal, and murder, commit adultery and perjure?', *Targum Jeremiah* 7.9 reads: *'Thieves (gānōbím), killers of persons, adulterers, men who* swear falsely [...]'.[35] The change from the Hebrew text to the Aramaic rewording is subtle but of certain significance. Whereas in the Hebrew stealing is one offense within a series, in the *Targum* the addressees are specifically defined by their sin of thievery. Meanwhile, instead of the rendering of Jeremiah 23.11 MT ('"Both *prophet* and priest are *ungodly*; even in my house I have found their wickedness," says the LORD') we have in the *Targum*: 'For both *scribe* and priest have *stolen their ways*; also in *the* house of *my sanctuary* their wickedness *is revealed before me*.'[36] The false prophet has been transformed into a temple-based scribe; the charge against him is no longer ungodliness in general, but that he has 'stolen [his] way', presumably referring to bribery. These are representative examples of a general trend within the *Targum Jeremiah*. As a rule, the Aramaic translation reworks the Hebrew mother text in such a way so as both to shift the emphasis from the sins of the people to the sins of the temple-based scribes and priests, and to highlight sins relating to financial improprieties.[37]

The interpretation that Jesus was particularly exercised about the priesthood's greed has not gone unchallenged, especially to the extent it has corralled verse 17's 'den of robbers' to help prove the point. It has been objected, at least since the time of Buchanan's essay of 1959, that the word

---

[35] Hayward 1987: 70; original italics indicate where the Aramaic diverges from the Hebrew.
[36] Hayward 1987: 112, italics original.
[37] See Evans 1995 [1989]: 320; Hayward 1987: 37.

'robber' (*lēstēs*) actually has little do with the notion of an overcharging clerk. Judging by its usage especially in Josephus, the term comes closer to something like 'guerilla' or 'gangster'.[38] This observation in turn has served well those who see Jesus' use of Jeremiah 7.11 as evidence of his exasperation over Jewish militancy.[39] It is well known that during the First Jewish War, the freedom fighters took to the temple as a hideout from the Romans. Jesus' polemic then must have something to do with similar such activity, and certainly similar such ideology, in his own time.

The problem with this approach to Mark 11.17 (Jer. 7.11) is basically two-fold. In the first instance, while the winds of revolution were clearly in the air in the years immediately leading up to the First Jewish War, and these winds blew through the temple as well, the picture we have in the 30s is quite different. The evidence shows that the temple regime of Jesus' day had very self-consciously (and very self-interestedly) come to back the local Roman authorities, a fact which by itself would make the temple an unlikely emblem of militant nationalism and an equally improbable hideout for proto-Zealots.[40] On the face of it, political circumstances of the time do not seem to warrant our supposing that the temple was regarded as a hotbed of revolutionary activity.

Second, in order to argue that Jesus' fundamental issue was with the terrorist-like attitudes of temple adherents, one must lay rather heavy weight on *lēstēs* (i.e. 'nationalist rebel' or 'guerilla'). But just because Mark's Jesus quotes Jeremiah 7.11 ('But you have made it a den of robbers [*lēstōn*]'), this does not necessarily mean that the evangelist meant to hide the interpretive key to the temple action under the mat labeled 'robbers'; even less does it mean that the Greek word *lēstēs* by itself functioned as a kind of one-word summary of the problem. I have suggested that the thematic interests of Jeremiah 7 *as a whole*, brought together with those of Isaiah 56 as a whole, mesh brilliantly with Jesus' conviction that Israel's leaders had gone bad and that restoration was (therefore) also underway. Had Jesus really wished to accuse the money-changers and sellers of being co-conspirators in a militant rebellion, why would he have mentioned Isaiah 56 and Jeremiah 7 at all, since these texts do not even touch on the issue of militant nationalism?

Finally, since so far as we know Jesus did not speak to his fellow Jews in Greek but Aramaic (and in citing scripture he may possibly have referred

---

[38] Buchanan 1959; also, seminally, Barrett 1975: 15–16.

[39] Borg 1984: 185–6; Wright 1996: 417–21.

[40] As Applebaum (1989: 254) writes: 'Politically, the incumbents of the high priesthood were the appointees of the Roman government and, with a few exceptions, subservient to it.' The same basic point is confirmed by Horsley (1986, 1995), whose critique of Smallwood's paradigm of an anti-Roman priesthood serves to modify it substantially. Undoubtedly, the relationship between the priesthood and the Roman authorities was complex, fraught with both self-serving ingra-tiation and fearful hatred, given the fact that both parties were locked in an uneasy alliance of mutual political and economic gain.

to a Hebrew text), any attempt to explain the temple demonstration on the basis of *lēstēs* can credibly do so *only so far as Mark* – not Jesus – is concerned. Were there a conceptual overlap between the Greek *lēstēs* and the Hebrew/Aramaic *pārîsîm* ('thieves'), the term used at Jeremiah 7.11 in Jesus' scriptures, one could perhaps argue that a similar overlap was intended both by Mark and by Jesus. But as Barrett himself concedes, neither the Hebrew *pārîsîm* 'thieves' (Jer. 7.11) nor the Aramaic equivalent convey the sense of 'guerilla' bound up in the Greek *lēstēs*.[41] This means either that Jesus cited Jeremiah 7.11 without any implication that the temple personnel were *lēstēs* ('guerillas') or that he did indeed call them the Aramaic equivalent of *lēstēs* (whatever that might be), but then in the latter case he could have hardly used Jeremiah 7.11. It does not work to hold that the semitic-speaker Jesus cited Jeremiah 7 *and* that he meant to label his opponents guerillas.

The final line of evidence towards proving Jesus' grievances with the economic injustices of the temple is the witness of primary sources. The following quotation from the *Testament of Moses*, dateable to roughly 30 CE (within a few years of Jesus' temple action), provides an excellent example:

> And when the times of exposure come near and punishment arises through kings who (though) sharing their crimes yet punish them, then they themselves will be divided as to the truth. Consequently the word was fulfilled that they will avoid justice and approach iniquity; and they will pollute the house of their worship with the customs of the nations; and they will play the harlot after foreign gods. For they will not follow the truth of God, but certain of them will pollute the high altar by [. . .] the offerings which they place before the Lord. They are not (truly) priests (at all), but slaves, yea sons of slaves. *For those who are the leaders, their teachers, in those times will become admirers of avaricious persons, accepting (polluted) offerings, and they will sell justice by accepting bribes.* Therefore, their city and the full extent of their dwelling places will be filled with crimes and iniquities.[42]

Here the figure of Moses looks into the 'future' and describes the priesthood under the Hasmoneans leading all the way up until the time of Herod the Great (*T. Mos.* 6.1–2). Among the charges brought against this dynasty of priests, the sin of avarice is outstanding: those who oversee the offerings disqualify themselves through their greed and graft.[43] Since the document gives no indication that this scandalous state of affairs had shown any signs of remediation, its 'Moses' must have had as little regard for the moral

---

[41] Barrett 1975: 17.

[42] *T. Mos.* 5.1–6a. Translation from Priest, *OTP* 1.929–30; emphasis added.

[43] The perception of greed among the Hasmonean priesthood was widespread. This is confirmed not only by the *Psalms of Solomon* and certain Qumran texts, surveyed in Chapter 1, but also in such places as *Jub.* 23.21; *T. Levi* 14.1–6; 17.11; *1 Enoch* 89—90.

character of Caiaphas as he had for earlier unsavory priests. This hardly bears stating, for the author of the *Testament* was not interested in Israel's sordid past as a detached historian; such texts were written to make a point about the sordid present.

Some of the most damning evidence for corruption of first-century priests comes down in the rabbinic writings. In Craig Evans's very thorough surveys of post-temple reflection on the priesthood of Jesus' day, we see that charges of greed are virtually a leitmotif.[44] In the *Pesaḥim*, for example, the temple is said to have been defiled by the 'sons of Eli' (alluding to the notorious biblical figures Hophni and Phinehas who pilfered the temple offerings).[45] The rabbinica also intimates that the priestly dynasty of Annas (first-century CE), although already fabulously wealthy, would regularly engage in violent extortion, leaving lower-ranking priests in a state of starvation.[46] Although such reports may appear incredible at first blush, since they are confirmed by Josephus, they can hardly be the stuff of rabbinic legend.[47] On the contrary, it is all but certain that the gangster-style violence of the high-priestly family, employed to maximize the already substantial temple funds (from which the upper-ranking priests freely helped themselves), was a matter of public knowledge. To make matters worse, because the high-priestly family regularly relied on bribery to ensure their remaining firmly ensconced within the larger political machinery of Judea, the dynastic control was impregnable.[48] This too would have been the kind of practice that would eventually be exposed, leaving many in Jerusalem to shake their heads in disgust. It was almost certainly the widespread perception of the high priests' insatiable greed, together with the lower classes' experience of economic deprivation, that led the rebels of the First Jewish War to exact vengeance in such symbolic terms: before executing the high priest himself, they had incinerated the expansive high-priestly mansion as well as the debt records.[49] It is little wonder that post-temple Judaism would look back on the greed of first-century priesthood as being the root of the temple's profanation and the precipitating cause of its destruction.[50]

---

[44] Evans 1989, 1992, 1995 [1989], 1995 [1993].

[45] *B. Pesaḥ.* 57a. The story of Hophni and Phinehas is told in 1 Samuel 2–4.

[46] See references in Evans 1989: 258–9 (*t. Menaḥ.* 13.21F; *t. Zebaḥ.* 11.16–17; *b. Yebam.* 86a–b; *b. Ketub.* 26a; *y. Maʿaś. Š.* 5.15).

[47] *Ant.* 20.8.8 §§180–1; 20.9.2 §§204–7. This history is further corroborated by the fact that during the revolt the lower-ranking priests took part in overthrowing the upper levels of the priesthood.

[48] *Ant.* 20.9.4 §213.

[49] *J.W.* 2.17.6–9 §§425–41.

[50] See *t. Menaḥ.* 13.22B–D: 'As to Jerusalem's first building, on what account was it destroyed? Because of idolatry and licentiousness and bloodshed which was in it. But as to the latter building we know that they devoted themselves to Torah and were meticulous about tithes. On what account did they go into exile? *Because they loved money* and hated one another' (emphasis added).

When we consider Jesus' disruption of business in the outer courts along with his specific charge that the temple personnel have turned God's house into 'a den of robbers', and align these observations with the first-century perception of the high priesthood, who, to use a modern-day analogy, were seen as being a cross between a band of Columbian drug lords and a boardroom of extravagantly overpaid executives, we find that the evidence virtually speaks for itself. The question, it seems to me, is not whether we have sufficient reason to believe that Jesus through his temple action meant to implicate the temple administration for its reprehensible fiscal dealings, profaning as they were. The question rather is whether it would have been possible for any half-informed Jew observing the event *not* to have surmised some reference to priestly corruption.[51] In my opinion, very few if any at all could have failed to make the connection.

In this respect it is altogether appropriate that Jesus' temple action be called a 'temple cleansing', for there is unavoidably a horizontal element to Jesus' aims. By charging the temple elite with being 'a den of robbers' in the Jeremiah-esque sense, Jesus is ineluctably speaking out on behalf of the human wreckage left in the wake of this fiscal abuse, in this case those who would feel the heaviest brunt of their maladministration, the very poor. The problem of embezzlement held especially dire consequences for those living at subsistence levels, since, as has been shown elsewhere, the windfall income that would accrue to the temple leadership through illegal gain could then in turn be quickly turned around for punishingly high-interest-rate loans to the destitute.[52] By being in a position to leverage usurious, high-risk loans, the temple financiers were then able to foreclose quickly and efficiently on landholders struggling to eke out an existence. Increased temple landholdings eventually meant more wealth for the priestly elite, more wealth meant even more high-interest loans, more high-interest loans meant more foreclosures on the land and the cycle went on – crushingly so, for those at the bottom of the economic ladder.[53] Add to this a practice, begun under Herod,

---

[51] As Snodgrass (2009: 460) summarizes after his own list of evidence: 'It would be naive to argue corruption was not a factor.'

[52] Goodman (1982: 418–25) argues that during the first half of the first century the influx of financial capital into the coffers of the upper echelons of Jerusalem society had pernicious effect on the lower classes. Maintaining an oligopoly of credit, the high-ranking priests could control the credit market much to their advantage, which ultimately helped them obtain their goal of foreclosing on land. The effect of this inflow 'should have been beneficial, but in practice it was only the few who benefited: the rich, especially the rich priests, became richer, so did those with Temple monopolies or a function in the service industries ... there was no mechanism for channeling wealth towards the more needy elements of the population except in the form of charity' (419–20).

[53] Goodman 1987: 56–9; Applebaum 1989: 241. While it has been questioned whether the Second Temple could like other temples of antiquity own land, this can hardly be doubted, see Blenkinsopp 2001: 61–8; Buth and Kvasnica 2006: 68 n. 60. Klawans (2006: 222–41) is among the few scholars who (rightly) connect Jesus' temple action with his broader socio-economic ethics, but his finding insufficient evidence of priestly greed is itself a move that fails to convince.

whereby the Roman-backed ruler would forcibly expropriate land and convey it as a favor to members of the Jerusalem aristocracy (which again overlapped considerably with the temple powers), and the spiral of injustice only worsened.[54] By calling out the perpetrators of this unremitting financial scandal, Jesus is inevitably calling attention to the plight of its victims. In the cleansing of the temple, then, we see not only an impassioned protest against the temple elite whose interminable greed drove them to unscrupulous profiteering off the backs of the poor, but also an equally fervent *cri de coeur* for those subject to such oppression. By standing against those victimizing the poor, Jesus was in an important sense standing with the poor.[55]

This state of affairs was particularly vexing, given the deeply shared understanding that the land of Israel was a sacred space belonging to Yahweh the king and that the tribes were his tenants. To own land in Israel was to have a stake in the geographical platform of the temple; thus to own land was to be a full participant in Israel as a political and religious reality. To have been deprived of one's land, however, was in a very real sense to have lost one's inheritance in Israel, to have been estranged from the sacred space of the land, and in some sense to fall outside the purview of Israel. This means that, in addition to whatever economic burdens the disenfranchised would have to bear, the expropriated householder would also have to come to terms with what amounted to the shame of exile on a family level. Exile expressed itself not only in geographical displacement or a subservient political status; it also came to realization through the expropriation of a householder's inheritance. The condition of being 'poor', that is, the condition of being without land or on the verge of insolvency, was simultaneously an economic, social, political, and theological reality. By thrusting those on the economic margins into disinheritance, the priestly rulers were in effect gerrymandering the boundaries of true Israel and forestalling full return from exile.

If with the index finger of one hand Jesus was pointing accusingly at the money-changers and the corrupt system which they helped sustain, with the finger of the other hand he was pointing to the imminent destruction of the temple on account of that corruption. This judgment would have seemed to follow not just on the temple system's impact on the poor, but also on its desecrating toxicity. The historical evidence indicates that the temple regime of Jesus' day had made a practice out of dipping into temple funds, extorting from lower-level priests, soliciting bribes, neglecting tithes, and grossly overcharging faithful Jews requiring temple services.[56] Notwithstanding the varying frequency and seriousness of these offenses, each of the activities

---

[54] Josephus, *J. W.* 1.24.5 §§483–4; 2.6.3 §98.

[55] This practical way in which he does so will be developed further in the next chapter.

[56] On the intriguing possibility that the Parable of the Wicked Tenants was partially aimed at the issue of tithe-evasion, certainly a source of real concern in Jesus' day, see Buth and Kvasnica 2006.

would have undoubtedly been regarded as different counts of one overriding crime: stealing from the temple (*maʿal*). In Jewish thought, to steal from the temple was to profane the temple.[57] More generally, Jesus would have considered the temple on the brink of utter profanation if only because he judged that greed had come to define the priesthood, and greed virtually by definition *was* idolatry.[58] Because a certain deviant attitude towards wealth had become normalized within the temple culture, and because there too certain desecrating activities had also become institutionalized, Jesus came to the conviction that the cult's destruction was right around the corner. In cleansing the temple, he gave symbolic expression to that conviction. It was not in principle that Jesus took exception to the temple, it was on account of certain attitudes and practices. But when it becomes patently clear that the current priesthood has failed, those with eyes fixed on the eschatological horizon could not help but wonder whether a divinely initiated changing of the guards was imminent.

Sign for the temple

If Jesus stood against the temple in its current state, it was with gaze fastened to the future that he also stood for it. By this I mean that the on-going profanation of the temple had somewhere along the line persuaded Jesus that tribulation was at hand and therefore a new era was dawning. It was an era longed for by the prophets, one in which true worship would be restored, the scattered tribes would be re-gathered, the Gentiles would be brought in to Zion, and, most of all, a new temple would be built. He also came to be convinced, somehow, that he himself would be the builder of this new temple, as well as its architect, sponsor and representative. In this sense, Jesus was the temple. He saw himself as its extension into the future. This much is supported by the historical data.

Trial evidence and its tributaries: the testimony of the 'false witnesses'

At this point it bears recalling that the evangelists never intended to provide an exhaustive account of the Jesus story but sought instead to preserve the Church's collective memory of him. The recalling of memories, like history-writing itself, is necessarily a selective process. As much as we would like to have a detailed transcript of all that happened on that day Jesus overturned the tables, it remains to us to fit together the bits and pieces as we have them.

One such 'piece' is likely to be found in the account of Jesus' trial. The second evangelist records the scene as follows:

---

[57] Milgrom 1976: 236–7, 245–7.
[58] The ancient Jewish equation between greed and idolatry is well documented in Rosner 2007.

⁵⁵ Now the chief priests and the whole council were looking for testimony against Jesus to put him to death; but they found none. ⁵⁶ For many gave false testimony against him, and their testimony did not agree. ⁵⁷ Some stood up and gave false testimony against him, saying, ⁵⁸ 'We heard him say, "I will destroy this temple that is made with hands, and in three days I will build another, not made with hands."' ⁵⁹ But even on this point their testimony did not agree. ⁶⁰ Then the high priest stood up before them and asked Jesus, 'Have you no answer? What is it that they testify against you?' ⁶¹ But he was silent and did not answer. Again the high priest asked him, 'Are you the Messiah, the Son of the Blessed One?'⁵⁹

The episode presents several immediate puzzles, the first of which has to do with those giving 'false testimony'. On being questioned, these witnesses claim to have heard Jesus saying that he would destroy the temple 'made with human hands' and then in three days build another, 'not made with human hands'. Perhaps so, but Mark never records Jesus as having said this. Through the temple cleansing, Mark's Jesus may have implied that God was poised to destroy the temple (I have already argued as much), but this is not the same thing as Jesus saying, '*I* will destroy the temple.' Even more mysterious is Jesus' purported claim to build another temple in three days. In light of what Mark has told us, this appears to have been fabricated out of whole cloth. But then again perhaps Mark simply neglected to recount the promise from Jesus' lips, as extraordinary as it must have been. Or perhaps the claim has essentially been recorded by Mark in so many ways, but not necessarily in explicit terms. What may have prompted the witnesses to say such things? Where in particular did the false witnesses get the idea that Jesus would rebuild the temple?

The problem is all the more intriguing on considering the strength of the historical evidence undergirding the accusation (its historicity, not necessarily its truthfulness). Most striking is its broad attestation: Mark 14.58// Matt. 26.61; Mark 15.29–30//Matt. 27.39–40; John 2.19; Acts 6.14; *Gos. Thom.* 71. The saying is further sustained by the criterion of embarrassment, for it would certainly not be in the Christians' best interests – false witnesses or not – to harp on such revolutionary intonations. The taunt, as it is reported at Jesus' crucifixion (Mark 15.29–30//Matt. 27.39–40), has an especially high degree of verisimilitude. Mark's willingness to report events allegedly occurring in a public setting before hostile witnesses, who even years later would be the first in line to refute any inaccuracies, should induce us to think that the evangelist is more likely than not to have gotten it right. That others ascribed to Jesus the claim that he would destroy the temple 'made by human hands' and build another 'not made by human hands' can hardly be denied.

---

⁵⁹ Mark 14.55–61.

Whether Jesus actually said such things is of course another matter. But before turning to this question, a few remarks are in order regarding the significance of the false witnesses' two-part statement. Interestingly enough, both parts of the testimony, one alluding to the destruction of the temple and the other to its rebuilding, consistently appear together. Obviously, from the point of view of those opposed to Jesus, both statements are important, either as highly incriminating evidence or as grist for the mill of ridicule. But it need not be assumed that the two statements would be of equal significance for all audiences. Certainly, the Romans would have probably been exercised about a public figure making open statements relating to the destruction of the temple. Likewise, for those supportive of Caiaphas' regime, any talk about destroying the temple would be seen as nothing less than a direct shot at the high priest, and therefore potential grounds for blasphemy. Had Jesus really spoken about destroying the temple, this would be no light matter either for the Romans or for the Jews. But it is quite another story to imagine the Roman response to someone's claiming to rebuild the temple in three days. As best as we can predict, any Roman magistrate would have probably regarded the claim 'I will rebuild the temple in three days' with bemused indifference; it would have been written off as little more than the ranting of an overly enthusiastic Jew. Therefore, since both statements were clearly designed to implicate Jesus, and since too the second statement would have been no great matter so far as the Roman magistrate was concerned, there must have been something about the second accusation that was particularly scandalous to Jewish sensibilities and roughly on par with the seriousness of the first assertion. Or perhaps, for all we know, the first statement ('I will destroy the temple'), outrageous as it was, was only the lead-up to the second, even more stunning claim ('I will rebuild the temple in three days') – a one–two punch.

Indeed, I believe this is precisely what we have.[60] If the force of the first statement would have provoked a gasp, the drift of the second statement would have left a Jewish audience altogether speechless. For at least a sizable swathe of Second-Temple Judaism, it was the messiah who would rebuild the temple. This conviction was ultimately based on the ancient scriptural association between temple-building and messiah:

> When your days are fulfilled and you lie down with your ancestors, I will raise up your offspring after you, who shall come forth from your body, and I will establish his kingdom. He shall build a house for my name, and I will establish the throne of his kingdom forever.[61]

---

[60] So too Juel 1977: 123.
[61] 2 Sam. 7.12–13.

'He is my shepherd, and he shall carry out all my purpose'; and who says of Jerusalem, 'It shall be rebuilt,' and of the temple, 'Your foundation shall be laid.' Thus says the LORD to his anointed . . .[62]

Thus says the LORD of hosts: Here is a man whose name is Branch: for he shall branch out in his place, and he shall build the temple of the LORD. It is he that shall build the temple of the LORD.[63]

The 'offspring' (2 Samuel 7), the 'shepherd' (Isaiah 44—45), and the 'Branch' (Zechariah 6) were all recognized as intimations of the coming messiah, and, according to these scriptures, where you find the messiah, there you will also find the rebuilding of the temple. To these early traditions one might also add witnesses closer to the time of Jesus: Sirach 50.1–2, 5–6; *T. Dan.* 5.10–12; *1 En.* 53.6; 90.29; *Pss. Sol.* 17.21–23a, 30; *Sib. Or.* 5.414–27, 432–33; *Tg. Isa.* 53.5; and *Tg. Zech.* 4.7; 6.12.[64] Notwithstanding Judaism's intramural disagreement as to what shape the future temple might take, notwithstanding too those texts which may yield the impression that God would rebuild the temple alone, there remained a vibrant tradition which closely identified the expected messianic figure with the task of temple-building.[65] Among the tasks predicated of the messiah, the rebuilding of Israel's holy space was taken for granted by many in Jesus' day. Nor is this any ordinary temple, for Jesus promises – more precisely, is alleged to have promised – to replace the temple 'made by human hands' with one 'not made by human hands'. This is no Hellenistic distinction, but traces itself back to the temple envisaged in Exodus 15.17–18 (also Daniel 2.34), which was understood as pointing ahead to the eschatological temple. Any first-century Jew who said, as Jesus is reported to have said, 'I will destroy this temple and rebuild it in three days', could not have staked a more forcible messianic claim.[66]

This sheds considerable light on why Caiaphas, in the above-cited trial scene, takes what on the surface appears to be an abrupt turn in his line of questioning. At one moment, the high priest is prodding Jesus to defend himself against the charge of destroying and rebuilding the temple (v. 60); at the next, he asks whether Jesus is in fact the messiah (v. 61). This is no *non sequitur*. As the high priest rightly gathered, if Jesus had indeed claimed to be the one to rebuild the temple, he was in effect also claiming to be the

---

[62] Isa. 44.28—45.1a; cf. 2 Chron. 36.22–23.

[63] Zech. 6.12–13a.

[64] On the Enochic texts, which are admittedly less than clear-cut, see Sanders 1985: 81–2; Ådna 2000: 43; Horbury 1991a: 112 n. 12; cf. Gaston 1970: 114. Texts which post-date the time of Jesus include *b. Meg.* 18a; *Lev. Rab.* 9.6; *Amidah* §14.

[65] Of course it is important to be careful here as well. Visions of God single-handedly constructing the eschatological temple should not rule out the possibility of a divine intermediary. The relationship between divine causality and divine agency in ancient Judaism, like the relationship between divine being and divine mediator, can be tricky to delineate.

[66] For further discussion of the messianic temple-builder see Juel 1977: 198–9; Fitzmyer 2007: 62–4; Perrin 2010; also Ådna 2000: 91–100, 382.

messiah. Having heard the incriminating testimony of the witnesses, Caiaphas saw no reason to forestall the cross-examination any longer. An explicit declaration one way or another would settle the import of an implicit claim, not to mention cut short Jesus' career, if not his life.

In light of these considerations, the question as to whether or not Jesus actually spoke of destroying and rebuilding the temple, as the witnesses claimed, becomes all the more significant. Nor is the question rendered moot on Mark's assertion that the witnesses were giving false testimony (Mark 14.56–57). It can hardly be the case that the accusation of the witnesses was completely baseless. If the witnesses were in pre-rehearsed collusion, performing an agreed-upon storyline with no point intersecting in reality, one would in fact expect their stories to line up perfectly. But instead Mark tells us that their stories did not line up (v. 56b). This suggests that, from Mark's point of view, the witnesses were 'false' not because they fabricated the truth, but because they twisted it in competing directions with spiteful intent.

This is confirmed by the data. Even after the cleansing of the temple, there is a good reason to believe that Jesus intimated a thing or two, implicitly or explicitly, relating to the destruction of the temple:

> 'If you say to this mountain, "Be taken up and thrown into the sea,"...it will be done for you.'[67]

> 'What then will the owner of the vineyard do? He will come and destroy the tenants and give the vineyard to others.'[68]

> 'Do you see these great buildings? Not one stone will be left here upon another; all will be thrown down.'[69]

Such statements hardly bode well for Herod's temple. Such statements too would have been a promising start for eager witnesses like these, individuals looking for any opportunity to curry favor with the politically empowered. However, if we stick to the parameters of Mark's account, those testifying against Jesus would still have had to make the leap from the accurate perception that Jesus was predicting the destruction of the temple to the unnecessary inference that Jesus himself was planning on taking an active role in that destruction. Thus the charges were not completely baseless, but neither were they altogether true. Unless the evangelist has grossly distorted the facts, the most the witnesses had to go on was circumstantial surmise.

But then what about Jesus' messianic claim to rebuild the temple? Was that ascription completely out of the blue or, as with the temple-destruction word, was there an element of truth to the charge? I am inclined to believe the latter, if for no other reason than that there are a few points during Jesus'

---

[67] Mark 11.23 par.
[68] Mark 12.9 par.
[69] Mark 13.2 par.

last week at which he may have possibly planted the seeds for this kind of notion. There are a few traces of seed from which the notion of Jesus as temple-builder may have sprouted, or at least a few possibilities.

One possibility may involve Jesus' performing the Parable of the Wicked Tenants, more specifically his affirmation, building on Psalm 118, that the rejected stone *'eben* (= the son *ben*) would become the cornerstone (Mark 12.10 par.). It is quite possible that Jesus' identification with the 'son' constituted a claim to be the founder of the new temple.[70] Certainly, Jesus' enemies recognized that they were not on the winning side of this parable. Perhaps too they saw that Jesus' assigning himself the status of 'cornerstone', especially in conjunction with his claim to be on to something 'much more important than all whole burnt offerings and sacrifices' (Mark 12.33), was all the evidence they needed to infer that Jesus intended to rebuild the temple.

However plausible this explanation may be, a better account is one which explains why Jesus' two alleged provocative statements ('I will destroy the temple' and 'I will rebuild the temple') are consistently paired in the accusations. In other words, whereas Jesus' contra-temple talk throughout his final week may have cemented things in the minds of those preparing their case, the elusive smoking gun can best be traced back to the point at which Jesus would have been perceived as having given grounds for both allegations. In this case, we are best served returning to the temple action, which opens up more than a few options.

For example, on the assumption that Jesus' citation of Isaiah 56.7 (Mark 11.17 par.) is authentic (I have argued as much), it is possible that Jesus' opponents heard him loud and clear and then easily proceeded to read between the lines. If the temple provocateur was implicitly offering himself as the herald of Isaiah 56 and the catalyst for the complex of salvation-historical events described in that passage, then observers might have inferred not just the imminent pilgrimage of the Gentiles, but also – most significantly – *his* rebuilding of the temple. Certainly this chain of reasoning is possible, but hardly provable.

Alternatively, could Jesus' status as temple-builder have been arrived at quite apart from Isaiah 56.7? This is possible if we grant E. P. Sanders's argument that Jesus' prediction of the destruction of the temple necessarily implied the building of a new temple.[71] Perhaps employing the very same reasoning as Sanders, the false witnesses could have taken this logic a step further, inferring that the one who portended the building of the new temple was also the most likely responsible for its rebuilding. This scenario too may plausibly explain why the notion of 'Jesus the temple-builder' came to circulate very quickly.

---

[70] Taking Mark 12.10–11 as reflecting the voice of Jesus, Kim 1987: 134–48 suggests as much.
[71] Sanders 1985: 69–76.

Slightly more compelling than both these proposals, however, is the testimony of John 2.18–19: 'The Jews then said to him, "What sign can you show us for doing this?" Jesus answered them, "Destroy this temple, and in three days I will raise it up."' While it is true that the author of John's Gospel enlists this saying for Christological service, this is no decisive argument against its authenticity. Elsewhere, it has been argued that John's temple-saying, reflecting the earliest of extant traditions, is historically credible as a saying of Jesus, and in my view, it is not only eminently plausible that Jesus spoke along the lines of John's report, it is positively likely.[72] It grants us, at any rate, the missing puzzle piece, with which to make sense of the accusations against Jesus. More than any other bit of evidence, John's account of the temple cleansing provides the best explanation as to why Jesus was both charged and taunted with the claim that he would both destroy *and rebuild* the temple.

An obvious implication of this, given my argument up to this point, is that through the temple cleansing Jesus did indeed insinuate his own messianic status. The one who will rebuild the temple is nothing if not the 'Anointed One'. Of course in some respects this claim would not have been entirely surprising coming when it did. Only a day earlier Jesus was riding a donkey into Jerusalem to the shouts of 'Hosanna!', publicly and prominently giving the crowds every reason to mistake him for the messiah. While the so-called Triumphal Entry certainly raised the question of Jesus' messianic identity (as did other activities which I will cover in succeeding chapters), it did not by itself strictly entail any conclusions. It was the cleansing of the temple, with its twin focus on destroying *and* rebuilding the temple, that forced the issue. Although cleansing the temple may have been regarded as a royal task (inasmuch as temples tended to be built by royalty), Jesus' words and actions lay claim to a status that exceeded anything Judas Maccabaeus or Zerubbabel or even Solomon could aspire to. Previous royal figures had come and gone; previous temples had been built and destroyed, defiled and restored. But Jesus was leading onlookers to believe that he was the unique and destined founder of a temple 'not made by human hands', one that would never be either defiled or destroyed. This is the climactic point, for it is not so much the messiah who would confer greatness on the eschatological temple, rather it was the glory of the temple that granted significance to the messianic temple-builder.[73]

---

[72] The Johannine saying is regarded as reliable by Meyer 2002 [1979]: 180–1; Sanders 1985: 72–3.

[73] Among the interpretive paths, Snodgrass (2009: 471–2) judges the temple action as a 'prophetic protest that pointed to future eschatological hope' to be 'the most compelling option'; it involves 'the expectation that the Messiah would be a temple builder, but the focus of the evidence is less on *who* would build than on the fact *that* a future, glorious temple would be built' (emphasis added).

The new temple: a three-day project

Jesus claimed not just that he would build the final temple, for according to the Fourth Gospel and Mark's 'false witnesses', he would do it 'in three days'! At first glance it might be tempting to regard this component of the testimony as the meddling of the post-Easter community. But in this case it would be rather sloppy meddling, for, as Scot McKnight points out in his matter-of-fact style, 'Jesus was not raised after three days.'[74] Paul, the earliest witness to the 'three-day' formula, says that Jesus was raised 'on the third day' (1 Cor. 15.4; cf. Luke 18.33), conceivably so by ancient practices of counting inclusively. But the earliest tradition has the less chronologically precise 'after three days' (Mark 8.31; 9.31; 10.34; Matt. 27.63). Had this phrase been the by-product of some clever early believers putting words into Jesus' mouth, one wonders why they were not also clever enough to have Jesus predict the time of his own arrival more accurately. Exhibiting anything but ecclesial theologizing, the tag 'after three days' probably pre-dates Paul, certainly pre-dates Mark, and by all means shows the stamp of the most primitive tradition.[75]

Jesus' claim, recorded in John 2.19, to build the temple 'after three days' finds further historical footing on the three passion predictions recorded in Mark (8.31; 9.31; 10.32–34). In this connection, four observations are in order. First, the exact phrase 'after three days' is embedded in all three of Mark's passion predictions. The phrase therefore rises or falls historically with the predictions themselves. Second, given the high-risk stakes raised in his ministry (climactically so in the temple incident), it is *a priori* more likely than not that Jesus considered a premature death a strong possibility and also shared his presentiments with his disciples. Third, inasmuch as Jesus saw his own calling as having divine backing, while his opposition remained unjust, he may well have interpreted his impending demise as integral to his appointed role as 'righteous sufferer' or fated prophet.[76] Fourth, as Jeremias points out, the phrase 'three days' may well represent an underlying Semitic construction by which Jesus meant to say, 'in a short time'.[77] Corroborated by the entirely credible passion predictions, John's report that Jesus publicly spoke of raising up the temple *and* publicly promised to do so in three days holds solid historical claim.

But what are we to make of this mysterious if not rather fantastic assertion? To repeat myself, I believe our quest for Jesus' meaning here

---

[74] McKnight 2005: 233. Perhaps more to the point than the actual number of days between Friday and Sunday is the question as to whether either John or Mark makes any effort towards fitting the passion–resurrection narrative within this window. As far as can be seen, they do not.

[75] So too Patsch 1972: 187; Strecker 1979: 60–1.

[76] Classically, Steck 1967, Ruppert 1972, Kleinknecht 1984.

[77] Jeremias 1971b. In Israel today if your cab driver tells you that he will be at your place 'in ten minutes', he likely means nothing specific; it is a circumlocution for a short but indefinite period of time.

goes amiss if we too quickly home in on Jesus' words as a statement of chronology. Given the widely circulating Jewish notion that God's righteous will not suffer the plots of outrageous evildoers for more than three days, it is somewhat more likely that Jesus is anticipating on a general level his passing through the dark tunnel of suffering and even death only to be finally vindicated at the tunnel's end.[78] More specific still, and not incompatible with the last point, is the possibility that Jesus has a specific scriptural background in mind. In connection with the background of the 'three days', McKnight writes:

> I continue to be amazed by scholars who refuse to think Daniel 7 could be the context for a suffering Son of man. Daniel predicts suffering in the following words: 'He shall speak words against the Most High, shall wear out the holy ones of the Most High, and shall attempt to change the sacred seasons and the law; and they shall be given into his power for *a time, two times, and a half a time*. The Son of man of Daniel 8 is vindicated precisely because the Son of man, a figure for the saints of the Most High, has suffered.[79]

While this is not the place to enter – with bee suit firmly fastened – into the hornets' nest of scholarly discussion on the Son of Man, it should be noted that McKnight's explanation for Jesus' three-day formula does not presume any particular position on the Son of Man debate (Was the Son of Man someone Jesus expected? Jesus himself? A circumlocution for a generic pronoun?).[80] The suggestion is attractive *prima facie*, not least because those who 'shall attempt to change ... the law' would in Jesus' eyes likely fit the description of the priesthood. Meanwhile, the three days which precede the building of the temple would be a dark time when the holy ones 'shall be given into his power for a time, two times' and beyond. It may indeed be that Jesus is drawing on Daniel's vision in order to describe in recognizable terms his own vision of a transition in temple power structures. The remainder of the passage also bears eerie parallel to Jesus' read of the situation:

> Then the court shall sit in judgment, and his dominion shall be taken away, to be consumed and totally destroyed. The kingship and dominion and the greatness of the kingdoms under the whole heaven shall be given to the people of the holy ones of the Most High; their kingdom shall be an everlasting kingdom, and all dominions shall serve and obey them.[81]

In the passage the heavenly court determines to wrest dominion from the evil 'fourth beast' in order to grant the kingdom to the 'people of the holy ones of the Most High'. So the plot of Daniel 7 draws to a close by

---

[78] So Jeremias 1971a: 228; Bayer 1986: 206–7.
[79] McKnight 2005: 234; italics original. The quoted scripture is Dan. 7.25.
[80] On the never-ending debate, see Burkett 1999; Reynolds 2008: 1–36.
[81] Dan. 7.26–27.

mirroring the impending circumstances as Jesus seems to have seen them: the removal of priestly authorities who oppose God's purposes in order that the true and lasting kingdom might be granted to the remnant. This is in fact also identical with the narrative logic of a text encountered earlier in this study, for according to *Psalms of Solomon* 17, the messiah will come – in language highly reminiscent of Daniel 7 – to expose the wicked temple officials and establish a new kingdom under God, and as a constitutive component of that kingdom, a new stone (Dan. 2.44–45), that is, a new temple.[82] In this light, I think that McKnight's adducing the Danielic Son of Man makes excellent sense of the 'method' behind Jesus' madness in the temple cleansing.

The Danielic inspiration for Jesus' action receives further confirmation on our considering those portions of Daniel which predict the 'abomination of desolation' (Dan. 9.27; 11.31; 12.11), that is, the profanation of the temple and the cessation of sacrifice.[83] Just as Daniel 9.26 points to the future destruction of the temple, so too does Jesus' overturning the tables. Just as Daniel's predicted destruction is precipitated by the desecration of the temple (Dan. 9.27), Jesus is laying the same basis by citing two texts (Isaiah 56 and Jeremiah 7) which allude to profanation.[84] But that is not the end of the story – either for Daniel or, presumably, for Jesus. According to the prophecy, the goal of all this, the climax of the appointed 70 weeks, is 'to finish the transgression, to put an end to sin, and to atone for iniquity, to bring in everlasting righteousness, to seal both vision and prophet, and to anoint a most holy place' (Dan. 9.24). If the '*after* three days' leading up to Jesus' alleged building of the temple is one and the same as Daniel's 'times', we might then take seriously the possibility that Jesus interpreted his act as the dramatic announcement of a new, properly atoned-for and anointed holy place. Furthermore, because Daniel closely associates the destruction of the temple (9.27) with an especially severe period of tribulation (vv. 25–27, see also 8.11–17), Jesus' temple action might well have prompted the conclusion that an intensified tribulation was at hand. One might even go so far as to say that Jesus' overturning the tables inaugurated the expected tribulation *after* the tribulation, that is, the final and darkest hour of the messianic woes.[85] If so, then as much as Jeremiah 7 and Isaiah 56 lay beneath Jesus' temple action, at even deeper level stood the text of Daniel. In this case, too, Jesus recognized

---

[82] Vv. 3, 16.

[83] Jesus is recorded as mentioning the same 'abomination of desolation' in Mark 13.14. The connections between Daniel and Mark 13 are not insignificant, but for lack of space cannot be explored here. See especially Wright 1996: 348–52, 358–65; Pitre 2005: 303–9.

[84] Although I remain mildly skeptical of Pitre's suggestion that Jesus or any first-century reader would have understood the temple-destroying 'prince' of Daniel 9 to be a messianic figure (Dan. 9.26–27), he is right that such 'a hypothesis would not only explain the action and words of Jesus, but it would even aid in understanding the rise of the traditions claiming that Jesus had said *he* would destroy the Temple' (2005: 374 n. 364, italics original).

[85] See Pitre 2005: 373–4.

in his opponents a manifestation of a false kingdom which would be supplanted by the kingdom of God. The present temple, hijacked by a corrupt priesthood, would give way to the temple rock 'not made by human hands'. Jesus' status as the not-made-by-human-hands temple, he seems to intimate, would become clear enough on the other side of tribulation.

Conclusion

Having surveyed the two piers on either side of our river in Chapters 1 and 2, it is now time to compare this with what, according to my hypothesis, lies in between. Given what we know of John the Baptizer and the early Church as counter-temple movements, do we have grounds for affirming that Jesus and his disciples can be usefully situated between? In short, I believe we do. Like John before him and the early Church after him, Jesus was persuaded that the temple had incurred profaning corruption, a sure sign that the tribulation was at hand. Also like the Baptizer before him and primitive Christianity after him, Jesus responded to this state of affairs by identifying himself and his followers as somehow integral to the divinely appointed transition leading up to the arrival of the true temple. This was not to be an idle wait, for again like John and the early Church, Jesus saw his own trials on behalf of the true temple as ushering in God's enduring kingdom: '*I* will rebuild it in three days'. The Baptizer's exceptional interest in the poor on the one end and that of the early Church on the other lay along the same trajectory of Jesus' temple action, triggered as it was by indignation over socio-economic injustices against the disempowered. Finally, in declaring the current temple regime redundant, Jesus also implicitly made the political move of reconfiguring continuing Israel and a new cosmic timetable around himself. His predecessor and followers also reconceived of Israel, appointed times, and sacred space. In all these respects, Jesus as the founder of a counter-temple movement (as I have defined such movements) stands in continuity with both his inheritance and his legacy. As the fog on the water between the two piers begins to rise, we begin to make out a bridge which is clearly constructed with the same materials: the bricks of an apocalyptic counter-temple movement.

As we might expect, the bridge and two piers also have their own distinctive shape and structure. After all, if John looked forward to the decisive eschatological climax, it was Jesus who proclaimed that the fulfillment of Isaiah 56 was at hand, that now was the time for the re-gathering of Israel and the convergence of the Gentiles. Later on the early Christians, in keeping with their priestly role, would actively take up their own mission to the Gentiles. The early Christians had a post-Easter vantage point from which at a very early stage they correlated Jesus' messiahship and resurrection. Retrospective reflection on Jesus' messianic claim to rebuild the temple, followed by sightings of the risen Jesus and the empty tomb, must have quickly led the post-Easter community to conclude that Jesus' self-representation as the final temple-builder were now vindicated by his rising from the dead. The risen Jesus had proven himself to be the true and everlasting cornerstone for the true and everlasting temple. In attaching themselves to the risen Christ, the early Christians had declared their union with the unfolding eschatological temple; in regarding themselves as the sons of God through Jesus, these same early Christians saw themselves as fellow priests working alongside the risen high priest Jesus, participating in his sufferings. Even though the Baptizer's following, the Jesus movement, and the early Church all shared a roughly similar framework and disposition to the temple, because they occupied different places in the sequence of redemptive-historical events, the way in which each group worked out its temple calling naturally differed.

Having laid out the trajectory in this way, we now have some basis for supposing that Jesus himself was a counter-temple leader, especially as we seek to understand the scope and nature of his ministry as well as, for now, his intentions in cleansing the temple. In getting to the gist of the temple action I believe we are getting to a clearing; from here it is possible to look in so many directions at once and find a rather large panorama unfolding before us. As the quintessential counter-temple act, the cleansing embodies a microcosm of all that Jesus stood for and focused on.

Quite obviously, he focused on the present state of the cultus and the disenfranchised poor. Against commentators who take Jesus' public demonstration strictly as an eschatological gesture with little reference to the daily hum of temple life, I maintain that he was in fact directing his criticism to current priestly practices, more exactly, the ineradicable greed of Israel's religious leaders. This greed expressed itself in all kinds of ways but culminated in a systematic embezzlement of temple funds. Not only did this abomination along with greed itself disqualify the priests, it also rendered the sacred space impure (as either actual or materializing fact) and therefore vulnerable to destruction. On top of all this, the priests' financially predatory practices served to consign an increasing number of Israel's poor to grinding poverty and alienation from the land. This estrangement ultimately had political implications, as only those who had land in Israel could be considered to belong to Israel. Whereas the prophetic corpus consistently demands socio-economic justice and political righteousness from the priests, the temple personnel's failure to render either proved them unfit. There were plenty of reasons to be distressed by both the vertical and horizontal ramifications of the priestly greed.

Jesus kept his eye on not only the dire present situation but also the brighter future horizon. And so, against scholars on the other side who recognize only the immediate critique contained within the temple cleansing, I also beg to differ. Inspired by Isaiah 56 and Jeremiah 7, as well as the scriptures relating to the Danielic vision of the 'abomination of desolation', the temple action held deeply apocalyptic significance. If the triumphal entry into Jerusalem carried strong overtones of messianism, Jesus' prediction of both the destruction of the temple and its eventual rebuilding removed all doubt. In accordance with the scriptural storyline, the profanation and fall of the temple would occur as part and parcel of the most severe stage of messianic woes, which was also marked by apostasy and persecution of the righteous. Its eventual rebuilding would occur at the climax of those woes and as the inauguration of a new era of unparalleled blessing, marked by the restoration of the twelve tribes and the in-gathering of the Gentiles – the coming of the kingdom. Anyone with the slightest insight who had witnessed the cleansing of the temple would have recognized the enacted parable as a sign of the temple's destruction and its eschatological rebuilding: a sign against the present temple and a sign for the future temple. As much as Jesus was concerned with the oppression of the poor, he was equally keen to spotlight the imminent action of Israel's sovereign God. While certain modern historians may balk at interpreting the temple action as both 'non-eschatological' and 'eschatological', theologians have been comfortable with such compatibilism for centuries. I suspect Jesus, much like his counter-temple forerunners, was comfortable as well, and it is after all his mindset and not our own that matters.

The forceful thrust of the temple cleansing did not go unnoticed by those in charge. As Jesus fully intended, the action constituted a decisive clash between the standing cultic regime and an upstart community proclaiming another temple to come. Calling out the former and insinuating himself within the latter, Jesus was essentially claiming to be the temple, just as his followers were in another sense also the temple. Jesus as the temple and Jesus' community as the temple: the two notions held together without contradiction; in fact, they required each other.

Retrospectively, the connection between Jesus' death-sentence and the temple cleansing underscores the climactic nature of his action. By driving out the vendors and money-changers, Jesus was saying in so many words, 'This temple which you see here today has been profaned by its greedy stewards. Therefore I hereby announce, in accordance with scripture, that the tribulation is at hand and the temple will be destroyed. As for me, after "three days" of tribulation, I will build a new temple, one unlike any other temple, one not made by human hands.' In announcing the near demise of Herod's temple and the messianic foundation of a new temple aligned with his move-ment, Jesus was essentially throwing down a gauntlet – decisively reframing the long-awaited eschatological turn as a very much present existential crisis. On the one side, those who believed in the unimpeachable legitimacy of the regnant temple guardians, despite Jesus' protests, would have to agree that Jesus' message was subversive and even downright dangerous. If Jesus was wrong, he was very wrong indeed. On the other side, if Jesus was right, then this would require coming into line with his movement, one which he identified with the Danielic 'kingdom' and had been in fact proclaiming all along. If Jesus was right, he was very right indeed. In this sense, the temple action was Jesus' way of 'calling the question' as to the legitimacy or illegitimacy of his claims.

And the stakes involved could not have been much greater, particularly since, as Jesus' demonstration implied, all things would become clear through the tribulation. Since God always fought on behalf of his faithful ones and always removed those who were false, the final proof of his authority would be tied up with both temples' respective futures. The temple which remained standing in the face of intense opposition – this was the one which was marked by God's abiding presence and approval. Whichever temple should be destroyed, this would prove to be the one to have been forsaken by the divine presence.[86] By taking the temple by storm, Jesus was not provoking an abstract theological debate; rather he was casting all those who would hear about the event onto the horns of a dilemma. As Jesus saw it, those who had eyes to see and ears to hear would recognize the truth of this counter-temple movement with increasing clarity. For those who did not have such eyes and ears, there would be either insufficient sustaining interest or growing animosity.

In the mean time, the stunned witnesses stood by the overturned tables. Casting their memory back to what Jesus had been doing all along and directing their imagination forward to what Jesus seemed to be promising, they in an instant found themselves caught up with Jesus at his own mountain top. They too were at a watershed point. Whether they would embrace or refuse this new temple reality was something which they as individuals had to decide. There was no room for half-measures: those who witnessed the temple action would be forced to respond, either to oppose Jesus and all he stood for, or to stand courageously with him and his movement until the end. But woe, Jesus intimates, to the one who chooses poorly.

In the end it all came down to two basic questions: 'Who legitimately speaks for the temple?' and 'What does it mean to be the temple?' The two of course are closely related. It would have been impossible to dissociate the true high priest from the true priestly life. The religious leaders of Jerusalem had through their public behavior already demonstrated their vision of their calling, a vision inevitably fraught with socio-economic and political implications. Of course Jesus also had his own vision; it too was a vision which pertained to socio-economic and political realities. Who legitimately speaks for the temple? What does it mean to be the temple? Jesus did as much to *show* his answers to both these questions as he did to speak them. In fact, it is no overstatement to say that both these questions drove all that he did. Positioning himself against the failed priesthood and the ethos it represented, Jesus expected that those who recognized the true temple through

---

[86] This logic undergirds various texts, including Jeremiah 7; Ezekiel 8—10; *1 Enoch* 90; *Apocalypse of Abraham* 27; *4 Baruch* 1—4; 4Q174.

what he did would come in due time. Such a platform, if it was to be meaningful at all, would necessarily have to include its own vision as to how Israel was to conduct itself as a people. And so what was Jesus' vision? What were his socio-economic and political ideals and how, if at all, did these relate to his self-identification with the temple?

Within these looming questions arise a number of more immediate ones. Among them two stand out for now. First, what hope, if any, did Jesus hold forth for the dispossessed? Were there any prospects for the victims of the priestly oppressors? What hope did they or their children or their children's children have for the future? Was there any vision for their being delivered from the prison of their circumstances? Second, what about the oppressive priests? Was Jesus merely shaking a reproving finger at them with a helpless shrug? What, if anything, could be done towards dealing with these false priests and setting the cultic office back on its proper course? So many questions, so few answers – at least for now.

4

'Forgive us our debts'

Announcing the kingdom among the poor

Introduction

The Father's house, Jesus said, was supposed to have been a 'house of prayer'. Apparently, from Jesus' point of view, whatever activities marked daily life in the temple, prayer was not one of them. This is not to say that people didn't pray at the temple – pray they did. But Jesus' denunciation of the temple, far-reaching as it was, seemed to have implied that if the cultus had turned its back on the poor, this would undermine its functioning as a house of prayer. In Second-Temple Judaism, prayer and care for the poor (usually expressed through almsgiving) went hand-in-hand.[1] This is not surprising since ancient Judaism never considered prayer in magical or mechanical terms. Communication between Yahweh and the appointed kingdom of priests, between God and God's people, was only possible within the context of a covenantal relationship. Should God's people fall afoul of the terms of the covenant, which very expressly included care for the poor, then they might as well forget about prayer. While it is true that the scriptures repeatedly insist on the graciousness and mercy of Israel's God, the God who longs to hear prayers, it is equally true that Israel's God has been known to imitate those who shut both ears to the cries of the poor and needy.[2] The same principle applies *a fortiori* to the priests.[3]

Of course it is not as though Israel's demise was rigidly tied to the nation's treatment of the poor. Rather, hardened attitudes were symptomatic of a radical condition – a 'heart of stone', to put it in Ezekielian terms (36.26). Looking back on its history, Jewish tradition regarded Israel's attitude to the disenfranchised as a kind of covenantal barometer needle, and in this respect Jesus' viewpoint was little different from that of the prophets or, closer to his own time, fellow temple dissidents at Qumran. As he and others saw it, temple robbery and oppression of the poor had been occurring in top-down

---

[1] See, e.g., Tob. 12.8–9a: 'Prayer with fasting is good, but better than both is almsgiving with righteousness. A little with righteousness is better than wealth with wrongdoing. It is better to give alms than to lay up gold. For almsgiving saves from death and purges away every sin'; cf. also, e.g., Dan. 4.27; Tob. 4.7–11; Sir. 7.10; *'Abot* 1.2; *b. Bat.* 10a.

[2] The concept is very ancient: Isa. 1.11–17; Ps. 66.18.

[3] Mal. 2.1–9; Jer. 2.8–9; 6.13–20; Ezek. 22.25–31; etc.

fashion, and lacking a critical mass of faithful believers who might positively influence the upper levels of the temple hierarchy, the high priesthood had become – or was on its way to becoming – functionally obsolete. What was desperately needed now was a new, divinely initiated basis on which Israel could carry out its vocation: a new righteousness.

The locus of this new righteousness could hardly be in doubt. If we consider Jesus' convictions (as I have argued them to be) (1) that the current temple had become nigh irreversibly corrupt, (2) that Jesus himself was the founder of a new temple order, then it virtually follows (3) that he also thought of the future priestly life of Israel already resting on him and his community. So while neither the initial formation of the Jesus movement nor the subsequent proclamation of resurrection marked the immediate redundancy of the Second Temple, both events did in their own way harbinger the beginning of the end of temple business as usual. As far as we can tell, the Galilean saw himself and his community as the one and only bridge from one temple, despoiled by idolatry and systemic injustice, to another, exhibiting true worship and righteousness. The more that bridge came into focus through the course of his ministry, the sharper became the tones – both bright and dark – of Jesus' message.

The advocates of this new and radicalized righteousness were not unaware of where the 'old righteousness' had failed. If the current priests had disqualified themselves most conspicuously on their mishandling of entrusted wealth and exploitation of the poor, then one might expect Jesus – like other counter-temple sectarians before him – to have self-consciously exemplified a markedly different approach in both these areas. As a pious Jew he would have done so not as a public relations strategy, but out of an effort to be the true temple before God and God's people. Towards this end, one might further expect, Jesus would do everything he could to ensure that his movement would be the living embodiment of the righteous temple community. Unless we commit ourselves ahead of time to a Gnostic-style Jesus who was blithely indifferent to what other religious leaders of his day were doing, it can hardly be doubted then that Jesus' approach to wealth was in part calculated to be a public critique of current practices.

Yet there also seems to have been another side to Jesus' strategy, a vertical dimension. I have been maintaining that Jesus, standing in continuity with the apocalyptic John the Baptist on the one side and the equally apocalyptic early Church on the other, preached and embodied a message that was also radically apocalyptic in character. And the apocalypse was now. Like others who had gone before, Jesus believed that the plight of the temple had already signaled the hour of tribulation and impending eschatological crisis. Among other things this meant, as it did for previous temple dissidents, that Herod's temple was fading fast and a new temple, the grand focal point of all of Israel's prophetic promises, was on its way. Until the arrival of this temple, a temporary dwelling-place of God would have to be carried along on the shoulders of the suffering faithful, whose unwavering resolution in the face of the official opposition only galvanized their sense of calling.

But in the case of Jesus, as this heaven-sent temple came into realization, it would exhibit a distinctive characteristic. Instead of being introduced abruptly at the end of history, this temple would begin to take shape in the flow of the present. In so doing, it stood in paradoxical relationship to the status quo. On the one hand, by pointing to a future glorious state, the new temple movement would transcend and remain impervious to the toxic ideologies – the socio-economic and political habits of the surrounding pagan culture – that had infiltrated the current cultus. On the other hand, inasmuch as the current true temple society was the present realization of that future order, it posed a stern challenge to those same dark ideologies, as well as any structures bound up with and sustained by them. Because in Jewish thought vertical realities could never finally be separated from horizontal realities, or, to put it in theological terms, because proper worship of the Creator God presupposed a worshipping community whose members stood in right(eous) relationship with creation and with one another, the in-breaking heavenly temple necessarily required that social relations within Israel be set in their proper order. Nothing less would do.

This, I suggest, is the framework within which Jesus understood his entire ministry and its goals. His ministry? To *be* the temple – not simply a 'religious' institution with a 'religious' task, but a movement that set itself to reshaping Israel's corporate matrix. For Jesus to be the temple meant conducting life as an ideal high priest, who not only reflected the character of God in relation to humanity, but also, as the recapitulation of a priestly Adam, represented humanity by taking on the role of true humanity.[4] For Jesus' followers, who were fellow reflectors of God's character and co-participants in this repristinated humanity, to be the temple was to embody an ideal society characterized by righteous relationships. His goals? Well, the goals of the priesthood were fairly clear: bring justice where there was injustice, purity where there was impurity, proclaim the will of God, and maintain the divine–human relationship through sacrifice. While Jesus' understanding of the 'will of God' had both eschatological and ethical aspects, respectively answering the questions, 'What is the God of Israel doing at this point in history?' and 'How then shall we live?', it was the former that served as his fundamental point of departure. God's redemptive acts logically determined the appropriate response of the faithful. Again this 'response' was not religious (in the sense that we tend to think of 'religious'), but a whole-life response, pertaining to every area of human existence, individual and corporate.

Like the other counter-temple voices heard in Chapter 1, Jesus was keen to proclaim that Yahweh was at work even amidst the travesties of Israel's

---

[4] Fletcher-Louis 2002: 92–103; Beale 2004: 66–70.

national life. Throughout his ministry he consistently took it upon himself to declare, as the cleansing of the temple at the end of his life would so powerfully do, that time was expiring on Herod's profaned temple (Jeremiah 7) and that the final stainless temple was being ushered in (Isaiah 56). This was no longer an event safely sequestered away in the sweet by-and-by. No! This heavenly temple-court, the true temple on which the temple 'made by human hands' was based, was now poised to interrupt earthly power structures and thrust itself into the sphere of earthly existence (Daniel 7). As this in-breaking moved to its climax, Israel would finally and thoroughly be ransomed from exile, the tribes of Israel would be re-gathered, and the true worship of Yahweh would be restored. Just as the whole point of the first Exodus and Conquest was to occupy 'the place' which Yahweh would prepare for worship, so too now for Jesus this train of eschatological events presupposed and found its decisive terminus in the true and lasting temple.[5]

But all efforts towards establishing this temple economy would be misdirected if there was not also a corresponding attempt to mend the tear in Israel's socio-economic fabric. Something was rotten in the theocratic state of Israel: the poor were being dispossessed and separated from their ancestral lands; meanwhile, an increasing amount of land was being concentrated into the grip of relatively few landholders.[6] Jesus knew this full well, and all this was a compelling factor in his decision to cleanse the temple. As the temple incident itself makes clear, he apparently did *not* consider it an option to say something like: 'My, it *is* a shame what is happening with the poor these days. Oh well, we better wish them well and get on with our own spiritual business of worshipping Yahweh aright.' On the contrary, his point was that acceptable worship was pre-empted by the failure of God's people to redress systemic injustice within. Along the same lines, in what follows I will suggest that reversing this socio-economic state of affairs, beginning with his own community, was paramount on Jesus' high-priestly agenda. Put otherwise, Jesus' oft-noted 'preference for the poor' finds its ultimate rationale in his calling to introduce the new temple.

Of course, it might be readily objected that, quite apart from all this 'temple business', Jesus' concern for the poor could be explained as an extension of his imperative to love.[7] On one level this is undeniably true. If love of God and of neighbor are the greatest commandments (Mark 11.31b par.), then surely Jesus' heart for the economically and socially destitute must have something to do with the two-fold injunction. Indeed, surely it must.

---

[5] On the building of the temple as the climax of the Exodus and Conquest, see a classical statement in Clements 1965: 50–1.

[6] On the land distribution of the time and its economic effects, see Oakman 1986; Freyne 1988; Fiensy 1999; Pastor 1997. For a brief review of secondary literature, see Harland 2002: 520–1.

[7] Mark 12.28–34 par.; Matt. 7.12; John 13.34–35; etc.

In asking ourselves, 'What has love got to do with it?', the answer can hardly be: 'Nothing at all.'[8]

At the same time, if love *per se* was Jesus' fundamental grounds for his ministry to the destitute, this leaves certain questions unanswered. Why, for example, did Jesus himself assume an impoverished status? 'Was it really necessary,' one might wonder, 'for Jesus to become like the poor if he was to love them?' If one says 'Yes' here, then this only makes more acute the question of the rich: if Jesus came to the poor as the poor because he loved the poor, does this mean that he did not equally love the rich who as far as we can tell are *relatively* overlooked?[9] Positing love as the driving motivation simultaneously answers too much and too little; it is problematic on a historical level.[10]

The problematic remains despite Jesus' emphasis on the two great commandments, focusing on love for God and love for neighbor. To be sure, when the historical Jesus spoke about love, he spoke about it as an overarching principle, 'more important than all burnt offerings and sacrifices' (Mark 11.33). But in prioritizing the dual commandment over 'all burnt offerings and sacrifices', he was not rendering the temple irrelevant, as if what counted was only 'inward' and not 'outward' religion. On the contrary, quite along the lines of Jewish eschatological expectation, he was both granting the relevance of the Mosaic economy as a concrete and visible expression of what was to come, and underscoring the relevance of 'what was to come' itself; that is, the eschatological temple and its attendant realities.[11]

In this case, Jesus' two-fold love command may quite easily be situated within a larger narrative which recounts the on-going, temple-mediated self-revelation of God. This in turn would mean that for Jesus, love was not a perspicuous principle standing on its own feet (however much this option might resonate with our own cultural inclination to validate choices on the basis of what feels like love at any given moment); much less was it a free-floating abstraction, severed in some proto-Marcionite fashion from

---

[8] The view that Jesus' social ethic was comprehensively determined by the principle of love is well entrenched in modern scholarship. After Harnack, its most important advocates include Wernle 1916, Headlam 1923, Scott 1924, Manson 1943.

[9] Jesus' 'preference for the poor' should not eclipse the fact that he also associated with the wealthy (as rightly noted by Buchanan [1964]). At the same time, as I will argue below, he did not maintain these connections apart from at least some interest in his acting as a broker on behalf of the poor.

[10] I suspect the endurance of this paradigm in modern studies of Jesus has something to do with our tendency to project a 'God of the attributes' theology (which Platonistically defines God by essences rather than what God does) onto our Christology.

[11] Likewise, when the rabbis said, 'Greater is the study of the Torah than the rebuilding of the temple' (*Meg.* 16b), this was not meant to nullify the importance of temples past or future, but – just as Klawans (2006: 172) remarks in relation to Qumran – 'by describing its activities in cultic terms, the group is at the same time asserting the significance of the cult'.

Yahweh's prior dealings with Israel. I believe that to leave off with love, as if it were the point of departure for the whole track of Jesus' ethics, is to get off at the wrong station. At the end of the day, as much as this explanation resonates with our romanticist instincts, it fails to take Jesus seriously as a first-century, Torah-reading Jew.

Other explanations for Jesus' consorting with the poor take his historically conditioned aims more seriously. One such view holds that the self-imposed poverty of the Jesus movement was an attempt to model trust in God for the sake of onlookers (Theissen); another agrees with this in principle but includes in the notion of trust the repudiation of self-protection (Hoffmann).[12] Another possibility is that Jesus' distinctive vocation was connected to his notion of the kingdom, for in being with the poor Jesus was 'claiming that God takes the part of the poor ... simply because they are poor, deprived, and despised' (Schottroff and Stegemann).[13] This may not ultimately be far removed from the older position that it was the poor who were eminently open to the graciousness of God (Bultmann).[14] Other interpreters of Jesus and the poor have tended to adopt a more political reading. More exactly, a number have seen Jesus' identification with the poor as his supporting a class struggle which closely overlapped with another conflict falling across regional (Galilee/Judea) and demographic (rural/urban) lines (Crossan, Herzog, Arnal, Horsley).[15] The common denominator of all these approaches lies in the shared presumption that Jesus' presence among the poor was prompted not so much by principle but by certain considerations that were specific to the setting.

Towards answering the question, 'Why did Jesus minister among the poor?', I suggest that the best solution *a priori* is one which relates this activity both to his personal ethic of love, amply witnessed in the tradition as Jesus' timeless summation of Torah, and his specific role within the unfolding eschatological purposes of the God of Israel (as he saw them). I further suggest that both lines come together in Jesus' assumed identity as Yahweh's high priest and eschatological temple-builder. As the duly appointed representative of Yahweh on earth, Jesus took it upon himself to embody all that the divine signified in relation to humanity, including not least the virtue of love, which would naturally direct itself to those in greatest need. As the messianic temple-builder, Jesus took responsibility for restoring the socio-economic equilibrium within Israel by establishing it anew in a freshly reconstituted people. If much interpretation has struggled to correlate Jesus' Torah-based (sapiential) ethics to his eschatology, Jesus-as-temple is an

---

[12] Theissen 1978, 2004; Hoffmann 1994.
[13] Schottroff and Stegemann 2009 [1986]: 36.
[14] Bultmann 1934 [1926].
[15] Crossan 1991, Herzog 2000, Arnal 2001: 203; Horsley 2008.

explanatory model that integrates both equally well.[16] When Jesus came to the poor, he came both as the priestly representative, whose character embodied the love and righteousness of Yahweh, *and* as the priestly warrior, whose quiet campaign promised to clear a new space for the final temple.

Towards establishing this two-fold point I wish first to stake the uncontroversial claim that Jesus, as evidenced by certain historically recoverable encounters (semi-private conversations) and practices, took an especial interest in the poor. Second, I wish to explore the nature of this interest. In a society like that of first-century Palestine, where self-identity was almost entirely predicated on one's kith and kin, to be with the poor was in an important sense to be the poor. In other words, Jesus neither taught about the poor as an abstraction nor gave to them as from a distance: he was socially enmeshed with them as a class. This is not only an important observation in its own right, but also serves to set the agenda for the ensuing discussion. For any account of 'Jesus and the poor' to be convincing, it must explain not only why Jesus stood *for* the poor but also why he stood *as* the poor. Both of these aspects, the 'for' and the 'as', again, are best explained with reference to his priestly calling.

I admit that narrowing my study to encounters and practices may seem to do an injustice to a hefty trove of relevant materials, but it almost goes without saying that, so far as the preserved tradition goes, Jesus had as much to say on fiscal matters as he had to say about anything. In this respect, his consciousness of wealth and poverty finds ubiquitous expression in the gospel tradition.[17] But since an exhaustive treatment of these materials would take us too far afield, I have limited myself. Their significance is amplified by their being widely acknowledged as presenting the voice of Jesus.

A rich man (Mark 10.17–22)

The tradition passes down an encounter preserved in the triple tradition relating to a man who approaches Jesus with a question not uncommonly posed of rabbis of the day.[18] As so often happens in the Gospels, the conversation takes an unexpected turn:

> As he was setting out on a journey, a man ran up and knelt before him, and asked him, 'Good Teacher, what must I do to inherit eternal life?' Jesus said to

---

[16] As Theissen and Merz (1998 [1996]: 379) put it: 'scholars often want to seek the nucleus of Jesus' ethic *either* in wisdom, which is potentially independent of the Torah, *or* in eschatology, which points beyond the Torah. But here in particular it is easy to succumb to false judgments' (emphasis added).

[17] Studies along these lines are not hard to find. See, *inter alia*, Esler 1987, Moxnes 1988, Petracca 2003, Oakman 2008. For a review of earlier studies, see Donahue 1989; more recently, Phillips 2003.

[18] Par. Luke 18.18–23//Matt. 19.16–22.

him, 'Why do you call me good? No one is good but God alone. You know the commandments: "You shall not murder; You shall not commit adultery; You shall not steal; You shall not bear false witness; You shall not defraud; Honor your father and mother."' He said to him, 'Teacher, I have kept all these since my youth.' Jesus, looking at him, loved him and said, 'You lack one thing; go, sell what you own, and give the money to the poor, and you will have treasure in heaven; then come, follow me.' When he heard this, he was shocked and went away grieving, for he had many possessions.[19]

The passage has all the marks of authenticity. Neither Jesus' implicit denial of being good ('No one is good but God alone') nor his distancing himself from divinity would seem to reflect the theological instincts of the early Church. Moreover, both the initial question and the enumeration of core commandments were something like stock forms in rabbinic dialogues. On the face of it, then, the scene reflects realistically on the world in which Jesus did business.

Defining key terms

The account of the exchange, differing only marginally in Matthew and Luke, raises two immediate questions. First, quite simply, who are 'the poor' to whom the man is meant to give? Whereas some have tended to answer this question in purely theological terms (poor in spirit only), and others have seen the poor in strictly social terms (poor in social standing only), and still others have described the category in economic terms (just plain, old poor), the truth of the matter must fully allow for all these categories without destroying the notional distinction between them.[20] On the one hand, the 'poor' were those of 'extreme want and even of destitution' who were materially dependent on the beneficence of others; in Jesus' day, these mostly consisted of peasant tenant farmers and the landless.[21] Poverty in this sense was not simply an economic reality, but also inevitably entailed significant social implications.[22] On the other hand, the 'poor' were the righteous remnant within Israel (e.g. Isa. 61.1–3; Ps. 18.27), those afflicted by the powerful wicked (Pss. 9.18; 10.2; 12.5), or righteous figures who represented Israel (Zech. 9.9). It is primarily in this sense that the Qumran sectarians and the *Psalms of Solomon* community identified themselves as

---

[19] Mark 10.17–22.

[20] For the 'poor' as the pious poor, see Lohse 1981 and Dietrich 1985; as a social description, Sabourin 1981 and Green 1994; as economic, Bammel 1968 and Albertz 1983.

[21] Schottroff and Stegemann 2009 [1986]: 16. Similarly, Hengel 1974: 15–19; Karris 1978: 112–13; Kvalbein 1987; Berges and Hoppe, 2009: 60. Jeremias's (1969: 110) distinction between 'the poor who earned their own living, and those who lived, either partly or wholly, on relief' may not have been a significant one in practice.

[22] As forcefully and rightly stressed in Green 1994. Green's insistence that terminology of 'poor' *primarily* pertains to social status may well be right. This need not stand against the 'poor' as being equally a theological construct.

'poor'.[23] This latter theological sense could and did overlap with the socio-economic denotation, but again to collapse the notions of poverty and righteousness (as if to imply that poverty itself were a virtue) would not only be to ignore the range of semantic connotations inherent in the term, but also to militate against the clear Jewish teaching that material deprivation was an evil to be avoided.[24] Although wealth certainly had its hidden snares, Judaism never taught that poverty was intrinsically beneficial – neither did Jesus. In the case of our pericope, while it is impossible to excise its latent theological connotations, here the term 'poor' refers primarily to those who are the envisaged recipients of the almsgiving. As receivers of alms, these poor are half-starved indigents who are clinging to the margins of society.

The second issue requiring attention is this: what exactly does Jesus mean by the offer of 'treasure (*thēsauros*) in heaven' (v. 21)? Towards answering this question, we first note that the man's driving interest lay in obtaining 'eternal life', that is, attainment of the resurrected state.[25] Unless Jesus is intending to give a stone in response to his inquirer's request for bread, 'treasure in heaven' must refer to something closely associated with salvation culminating in resurrection. For Jesus, then, to possess 'treasure in heaven' was to have secured a place in the general resurrection, a resurrection which he and a sizeable swathe of Judaism fully expected.

There is an important background here: in making reference to 'treasure in heaven', Jesus is alluding to a well-established tradition attested in such texts as the second-century BCE Sirach:

> Help the poor for the commandment's sake, and in their need do not send them away empty-handed. Lose your silver for the sake of a brother or a friend, and do not let it rust under a stone and be lost. Lay up your treasure (*thēsauron*) according to the commandments of the Most High, and it will profit you more than gold. Store up almsgiving in your treasury (*tameiois*), and it will rescue you from every disaster.[26]

Quite clearly, Jesus' instruction finds its roots in the widespread correlation between almsgiving and soteriological merit.[27] But with Jesus there is a twist on several levels. Fully aware of the commonly held notion that almsgiving in the present paved the way for heavenly reward in the future, Jesus doesn't necessarily discount this linkage but moves beyond it by implying an

---

[23] See 4Q171 2.9–10; 1QM 11.8–9, 13; *Pss. Sol.* 5.2, 11; 10.6. The same interchange is commonly detected in the teachings of the historical Jesus: a 'review of the preaching of Jesus has shown that the "social question" is for him simultaneously a "theological question"' (Berges and Hoppe 2009: 79).

[24] See, among countless examples, Prov. 6.11; 10.4; 30.8; Tob. 4.14; Sir. 11.14; for more similar sentiments in the rabbinica see Str.–B. 1.818–26.

[25] For 'eternal life' as the resurrected state, see *Pss. Sol.* 3.16; *1 En.* 37.4; 40.9; 58.3; *T. Asher* 5.2.

[26] Sir. 29.9–12.

[27] See Posner 2007 [1970–1]; Anderson 2007: 51–2.

indissoluble connection between 'treasure in heaven' and joining his movement. Moreover, while by the first century certain rabbis had imposed a ceiling on almsgiving, Jesus is demanding almsgiving without limits.[28] Jesus makes clear that at least in this case signing on with his movement would not be an option apart from the man's willingness to transfer his assets to the poor. As presented, it is an absolute dilemma without a hint of middle ground, or any option of picking and choosing from among the proscribed paths. Both the totalizing nature of the call and its implicitly conjoining of these three cords – complete economic liquidation, treasure in heaven and participation in the Jesus movement – suggest that the Good Teacher is not simply reiterating a standard Jewish response to a standard Jewish question.[29] On the contrary, Jesus' handling of the question is anything but standard.

This raises the possibility – indeed, perhaps even requires it – that the phrase 'treasure in heaven' is being strangely reinvented. In this connection it is all the more interesting that *thēsauros* does not properly mean 'treasure', but rather 'treasure room' or 'storehouse for treasures'. While there is some truth to the statement that Jesus often communicated with homely similes and everyday metaphors that could strike a chord with the common folk, here we encounter an exception to the rule. Given that the vast majority of first-century Palestinian families lived in a space not much larger than a modern walk-in closet, a personal 'treasure room' cannot be counted among one of those 'everyday metaphors'. While some families within Palestine seem to have had a closet which may have doubled as a treasure room (*tameion*), this is not quite the same thing as that which would have been invoked by Jesus' mention of '*thēsauros* in heaven', which would have struck hearers as out of the ordinary. Indeed, even a reference to a personal *thēsauros* in the home would have been odd, for those with surplus did not generally keep their wealth at home, but instead kept it on deposit at the temple.[30] Indeed, in all but a handful of the roughly seven dozen instances of the term in the scriptures, *thēsauros* (Heb: *'ōcar*) refers to the temple treasury: typically the temple in Zion, but also in a few cases the temple which is God's cosmic storehouse, that is, the temple which is in heaven.[31] This storehouse is the

---

[28] Purportedly handing down judgments rendered at the second-century BCE Council of Usha, *b. Ketub.* 50a (cf. also *m.'Arak.* 8.4) stipulates that a householder was not allowed to give more than 20 per cent of his or her wealth. See Hengel 1974: 20–1.

[29] Jesus' reframing of the discussion is summarized well by Sanders (1993: 237): '[h]e regarded his own mission as what really counted. If the most important thing that people could do was to accept him, the importance of other demands was reduced, even though Jesus did not say that those demands were invalid.'

[30] Hamilton 1964: 365–70; Stevens 2006: 136–66. The amount of money kept in the temple was exorbitant. According to Josephus (*Ant.* 14.4.4 §72; *J.W.* 1.7.6 §152; 1.8.8 §179), the sacred monies amounted to 2,000 talents, the equivalent of about 700 million dollars by today's working-wage. See Binder 1999: 427.

[31] Deut. 28.12; Jer. 10.13; cf. Hauck 1965: 136–8.

source of all wisdom and righteousness, essentially the hiding place of true Torah.[32] It is also of course the storehouse which apocalyptic Judaism longed to see established on earth as it was in heaven.

When we read this incident in anticipation of the temple cleansing, where Jesus signals the demise of one temple and promises the construction of *the* other, one must seriously consider the possibility that 'treasure in heaven' refers not so much to some individualized heavenly reward or spiritual benefit, but carries heavy-duty eschatological freight. In other words, we should be prepared to think that here, as in so many places elsewhere, Jesus is speaking parabolically with reference to the kingdom. As such, the phrase would be alluding to, on one level, the soteriological benefit of almsgiving and, on another less obvious level, present participation in the heavenly temple as it was being provisionally revealed through Jesus' ministry. For Jesus, to tender 'treasure in heaven' was to offer a stake in the eschatological temple that was coming and has now come.

The present-time, this-worldly aspect of 'treasure in heaven' is corroborated by what may be another version of the same saying preserved in Matthew (6.19–20) and Luke (12.32–34). Here we find Jesus issuing the following two-part command, which was likely fairly close to our best reconstruction of the presumed Q source:[33]

> 'Do not store up for yourselves treasures on earth, where moth and rust consume and where thieves break in and steal; but store up for yourselves treasures in heaven, where neither moth nor rust consumes and where thieves do not break in and steal.'[34]

Like the words spoken to the wealthy interlocutor, this passage is also reminiscent of Sirach 29 – more so in Matthew than in Luke, who loosens the connection by dropping the mention of corroding 'rust' (cf. Sir. 29.10) – with its nod towards the fleetingness of material wealth. But we should not conclude too hastily that this philosophical observation, a stock motif in Jewish wisdom literature, exhausts the point. In fact the *tertium comparationis* shared by the one treasury (or set of 'treasuries', if we prefer Luke), where thieves break in and steal, and the other treasury 'in heaven', where such things do not happen, suggests that Jesus' drift is not just metaphysical but has an equally compelling reference point within Israel's own recent history.[35] Indeed, had his mention of temple robbery prompted the collective memory

---

[32] Prov. 8.1–21.

[33] See Johnson 2007: 2, along with extended discussion in what follows.

[34] Q 12.32–34.

[35] While Jesus may be voicing sentiments similar to those found in popular Greek philosophy or Cynicism (see Desmond 2006), this hardly speaks to a genealogical relationship. The comparisons between Jesus and Cynic philosophers of the day have, I think, now been shown to be threadbare; see, e.g., Betz 1994; Wright 1996: 66–74.

of his hearers on any point, it would have been the painful fact that their temple had been compromised by numerous and notorious break-ins, usually at the hands of foreign rulers and magistrates.[36] At the same time, as I have argued in the previous chapter, Jesus' audience well knew that the high priesthood was systematically perpetrating its own kind of temple robbery right down into the present. I suggest, then, that with his inimitable obliqueness Jesus is here implicating the temple elite as belonging to a long, sordid trajectory of temple violation.[37] In the earthly treasure room, Jesus seems to say, the order of the day has been metaphysical *and* moral corruption.

Thus the phrase 'treasure in heaven' operates on two planes. On a patent level, Jesus is making the observation, commonplace in Judaism, that there is value in laying up treasure through generous giving. But on another level he is directing a thinly veiled barb against the corruptibility of the current temple economy. Most importantly, he is offering an alternative. This is not a choice between Herod's temple and some ethereal temple of a far-off place and time (which would not really be an 'alternative' at all, at least not any more than dessert would normally be considered an alternative for some-one sitting down to dinner). Just as he would later do more explicitly in the cleansing of the temple, Jesus is calling his hearers to decision in the present moment and forcing a crisis of temple allegiance. 'In Jerusalem,' Jesus seems to say to the rich man before him, 'you have a temple made by human hands (and therefore perishable) and tainted by human sin (and therefore profaned). But I am offering you a temple storehouse in the well-known heavenly temple. This eschatological temple-in-the-making requires not just your acknowledgment, but your very being – your heart and your wealth. Choose you must.' Clearly, offering a better temple treasure and with it a better temple was not something Jesus or anyone could do openly, not at least if he wished to retain a hearing among the temple-affiliated synagogues. Discrete ambiguity was a necessity.

---

[36] Here we might for example think of the pilfering of Antiochus IV (2 Maccabees 3), Crassus (*Ant.* 14.7.1 §105; *J.W.* 1.8.8 §179), Sabinus (*Ant.* 17.10.2 §264; *J.W.* 2.3.3 §50) or, closer to the time, Pilate (*Ant.* 18.3.2 §60; *J.W.* 2.9.4 §175). Schaper (1997: 203–5) also demonstrates that at least from the early post-exilic period, the treasure storage room (*'ōçar*) received not only the tithes but also the 'secular' taxes. If this practice continued into the Herodian period, which is presumably the case, one can hardly resist wondering whether Jesus' words in Matt. 6.19–20 were also meant as a jab at the well-oiled Roman taxation machine.

[37] He may well be implicating the wealthy man himself, especially if Jesus indeed said, 'Do not defraud (*apostereses*)' (v. 19). Certain weighty manuscripts lack the phrase, but it does fit well both on a historical level (Jesus' major complaint against the priestly authorities was in their defraud-ing the poor) and on a narratival level (*apostereo* occurs in Mal. 3.5 in a passage of especial interest to Jesus and his biographer Mark). Interestingly enough, the verb in earlier classical Greek referred to the refusal to return money which had been deposited for safe keeping; see Lane 1974: 362 n. 31.

The socio-economic nature of Jesus' call

To what extent the rich man understood all this, we will never know. But one thing remains clear for both us and him in the first-century moment: there was a clear hurdle. Until this inquirer was willing to liquidate his resources, in particular his real estate holdings, and give the proceeds to the poor, it would be impossible for him to join Jesus' movement.[38] And if that was not disappointing enough for a man attached to his things, it is clear that only in joining Jesus' movement would there be assurance of eternal life, that is, one's place in the now-present eschatological temple. Eternal life, obedient self-divestiture, and discipleship – he couldn't have one without the others.

Perhaps this is not entirely surprising, given what we know about the other counter-temple movements under review here, whether one thinks of the *Psalms of Solomon* sectarians, who clearly embraced poverty as integral to their priestly calling, or the Qumran community, whose initiates were required to turn over the bulk of their possessions to the common purse. Nevertheless, there is no softening the shock that Jesus is here enjoining poverty as a necessary condition for taking part in the new temple, that is, salvation. For someone like Jesus who – if we believe what we have been told by countless writers since Ernest Renan – went about the Palestinian countryside preaching a warm ethic of brotherly love, this seems neither particularly warm nor particularly brotherly. What are we to make of this severe ultimatum, and how does this square with the rest of what we know about the historical Jesus?

Commentators down through the centuries have wrestled with this passage and provided their own answers to such questions, not all of which are equally satisfying.[39] On one level, there is certainly some truth to the traditional explanation that Jesus took it upon himself to diagnose the idolatrous condition of the man's heart and through his challenge sought to prescribe the one and only cure. This is not just Mark's take: this account is entirely plausible in the original setting. Nor does this necessarily require any supernatural insight on the part of Jesus, as some insightful discernment would suffice. Because his stipulations seem to have been specifically suited to his interlocutor, the incident cannot be seen (or appropriated) as Jesus' one-size-fits-all pattern for conversion and discipleship. The movement he led seems to have included a number of members in good standing

---

[38] In Mark 10.22 the evangelist editorializes that the man went away sad on account of his having *ktēmata polla* ('many possessions'). The word *ktēma* typically has reference to landed property.

[39] For example, when Clement of Alexandria (*Strom.* 3.6) says that Jesus ultimately deprives the man of his goal for his failure to keep the Golden Rule, I am not sure whether such an interpretive move actually leaves us with a kinder, gentler Jesus. For other patristic interpretation, see Hays 2009: 261–2; Oden and Hall 1998: 136–7. Cranfield 1951 provides good interaction with interpreters from various periods.

from various socio-economic strata, including sympathizers who had the means to support Jesus (Luke 8.2–3). Thus it was not the man's wealth *per se* but his attitude towards his wealth which helped to separate him from eternal life and proper temple allegiance. The traditional interpretation is not mistaken so far as it goes.

Yet it does not go far enough, for it neither touches on the socio-political implications of the dilemma nor pays sufficient consideration to what Jesus is calling the man *to*. Lest we neglect the latter point, we should heed Meyer's succinct observation on this passage: 'detachment is for the sake of attachment'.[40] Unless we are to imagine an odd scenario in which the man is being asked to do something which the Good Teacher himself was not prepared to do, it is all but certain that Jesus, in calling the man to give up his possessions, was enjoining a way of life which both he and his core followers had already adopted. Again, this is not to say that all of Jesus' followers had taken up voluntary poverty: to repeat, a good number of Jesus-supporters had not, and do not seem to have been esteemed any the less for their choices. But in order to make any sense as history, the incident necessarily presupposes that the heart of Jesus' movement was characterized by an arresting asceticism, one which marked itself off from surrounding society by living life on its simplest terms and showing at least some concern for the poor. In this case, the call on the man to renounce his possessions would not simply entail his relinquishing various comforts afforded by material possession, but perhaps more significantly his social status. In a world of scant resources, where land was leverage and possessions were power, to choose insolvency for the sake of joining Jesus' movement was to choose a kind of social death – at least so far as the socio-economic hierarchy of Palestinian society was concerned. Social identity would then necessarily have to be defined not by external socio-economic factors but according to Jesus himself and his fictive, classless society.

This is not all, for there would have also been political ramifications in joining up with Jesus. To be sure, we know precious little about this man, except that he was affluent and considered himself a faithful Jew. But precisely because he belonged to the upper economic class, there is more than a reasonable chance that he was an aristocrat of sorts who also had solid connections with the wider Roman-backed aristocracy of Judea.[41] No doubt, as he contemplated Jesus' challenge, he could not have escaped the conclusion that crossing the proffered line in the sand would have been akin to Caesar leading his armies across the Rubicon into Italy – an act of political defiance against 'the establishment'. To have eschewed his wealth would also have been to forsake any political advantages that might have accrued to a man of his status – and these would have been considerable. His aligning with

---

[40] Meyer 2002 [1979]: 145.
[41] This is confirmed by Luke's report that the man was a 'ruler' (*archōn*).

a counter-temple movement such as Jesus' would have also raised all kinds of questions for the man's aristocratic peers, who would be forced to conclude that their friend had jettisoned not only his possessions (along with his mind), but also any interest in maintaining ties with the political status quo and those who stood for it.[42] While it is not entirely clear (at this point in my argument) what converting to Jesus' movement would imply in terms of a reinvented political outlook, it is certainly clear that certain options were ruled out by the cutting of social-political ties. Barring the possibility of Jesus and his inquirer being incredibly shortsighted, one must imagine that both men were fully aware that the extended call, if accepted, would exert a crowbar-like force, irreversibly separating the man from all prior allegiances. Ever conscious of the agenda of his own movement, Jesus quickly judged that it would have been impossible for the man to share this agenda without such a decisive extraction taking place. The existential crisis which this dilemma provoked was not just about property holdings, for it related to even more fundamental investments of self-identity. Jesus would tolerate no compromise. Either one must make a clean break and enter into the newly forming world of Jesus, a society which had self-consciously toppled any mental totem poles correlating wealth and status, or remain ever wedded to the current world-system.

If all this is true, this only brings into sharper relief the problem of Jesus' so-called 'economic double-standard'. Even if the disciples did not completely abandon *all* their possessions (which seems to be the case, given the report in John 21 that certain disciples returned to the fishing business after Jesus' death), the weight of evidence confirms that Jesus and his disciples had embraced an itinerant lifestyle of voluntary poverty.[43] On the other hand, other followers outside of the master's close-knit circle seemed to have retained both their wealth and their status – at least in the eyes of the evangelists – as model disciples. Apparently, there were not one but two sets of expectations. Even on the theory that Jesus was interested in constructing a society that was socio-economically egalitarian, we are still left to puzzle why Jesus did not apply his ascetic standard consistently across the board.

The answer, I suspect, comes in the wake of a properly nuanced understanding of Jesus' aims for his community. In my view, this egalitarian ideal of the community – however staggered – was not an end in itself,

---

[42] In this respect, by adopting the ethos of Jesus, the man would have been implicitly rejecting the ethos of the dominant culture. On this point, it is worth quoting Freyne (1992: 88) at length: 'The wealth-distribution mechanisms of Jewish law, such as the poor man's tithe, did not ultimately challenge the inequalities that Herodian-Roman rule perpetuated through lifestyle, apparel or buildings; the value system of the Jesus movement, had it been adopted, would have proposed an ideal in the name of the God of Israel that was the antithesis of prevailing norms ... both Herodian and Jerusalem values were under attack and both were regarded as distorting and alienating.' Cf. also Herzog 2000, Horsley 2008.

[43] As argued, quintessentially, by Theissen 1978.

but integral to another, more fundamental rationale which finds analogy in the counter-temple movement at Qumran. As is widely acknowledged, the Dead Sea community not only pooled their resources, but did so according to hierarchy which presupposed two tiers of membership: the priests and the laity. As some see it, the communal practices of the former class at Qumran were grounded in the priestly practice of living off shared temple offerings, which was itself necessitated by the Levites having no inheritance among Israel; they were to be landless (Deut. 18.1–8).[44] Assuming their priestly role, the 'sons of Aaron' at Qumran contrived an arrangement in which they were – at least in theory – dependent on the offerings of others. On analogy, I suggest that while all the adherents to Jesus' movement were priestly in the sense that their common body politic fulfilled a priestly function, his closest followers seem to have taken on an intensified priestly role. The core disciples self-divested and threw themselves on the beneficence of others in order to mimic the ideal Levitical priest, as representative of the community. For the Twelve, and perhaps some others close to Jesus as well, renunciation and poverty were simply signs of their priestly calling.[45]

Just how this two-tiered economic ordering within Jesus' community squares with the social egalitarianism which I have been describing requires some nuance. To be sure, the Jesus movement was characterized by an egalitarianism of sorts. But we must be careful not to overstate the point, for unless the gospel tradition has completely deceived us, Jesus' society was also characterized by a kind of hierarchy, involving various tiers: the broad following, the inner circle of the twelve, and perhaps, within this circle, the still tighter circle of Peter, James and John. Despite the fashionable trend of painting Jesus as the great egalitarian, there is no indication that he disapproved of the notion of office in principle or that he was interested in

---

[44] So too Gärtner (1965: 10): '[t]he Custom of having common property, as practiced in the community, was more than a mere expression of ascetic piety; it probably had to do with an ideal of cultic purity and may have originated in the distribution among the various priests of the temple income, which took place within the temple itself'. Cf. Rost 1955: 6–7. Likewise, at the conclusion of her massive study, Murphy (2002: 455) states: '[t]he sectarians saw themselves as a priestly people sharing goods as a witness both to divine munificence and to the possibility that humanity, or at least a remnant of it, could be redeemed'.

[45] Undoubtedly with Aquinas in mind, Yoder (1994: 75) frames the question as to whether such self-divestiture 'was for all Christians in all times and in all places or whether it was just a "counsel of perfection" directed to the saints'. But the medieval distinction of *consilia evangelica* (what holds for a spiritual elite) over and against *praecepta* (what holds for everybody) presumed and reinforced a rigid dichotomy which seems alien to earliest Christian experience. When Paul argues, on the analogy of Levitical practices, that those who preach the gospel should make their living on contributions (1 Cor. 9.13–14), this did not prevent him from commending lay believers for giving to the point of poverty (2 Cor. 8.1–5). If early Christians distinguished a special remuneration-bearing office for 'those who preach the gospel', this role does not seem to have been either, on the one extreme, radically different from the lifestyle of a lay believer, or, on the other extreme, virtually indistinguishable from it.

(what we mean by) egalitarianism in the absolute sense. The movement was in fact characterized by both egalitarianism *and* hierarchy.[46]

Perhaps on analogy with the temple building itself, an analogy which the Qumran community explicitly exploited, all members of the Jesus community stood on equal footing in that they were equally constitutive of the temple; at the same time, certain members within that temple structure bore a special priestly role with unique access and responsibilities. Situated within the landscape of first-century Judaism, the Jesus movement would have been conspicuous on account of the former. In principle, Jesus saw the social relations within his community as a function of the imminent in-breaking of the new temple, where all were called to shun the idolatrous worship of mammon (which amounted to a shared refusal to be socially defined by it) and to embrace the worship of the one God with all their strength (which amounted to dedicating one's personal property to the temple cause). While Jesus' vision of the priestly calling did not rule out hierarchy in principle, it did preclude the imposition of extraneous social-ordering principles; more than that, it ensured, at least in theory, that all legitimate hierarchies would be tempered by the awe-inspiring conviction that the divine presence was now present to all in a new way.[47]

Summary

Bearing all the marks of historical verisimilitude, the Gospel accounts of Jesus and the Rich Man shed considerable light on his aims. When Jesus asks the kneeling man to transfer his net worth to the un-landed poor, this does not seem to have been a standing policy for those seeking admission into the movement. Nevertheless, his injunction as recorded history sheds light on the movement's self-consciousness as a counter-temple movement and its related project involving the voluntary redistribution of wealth. Precisely as the in-breaking new temple, the community regarded the poor as an especial focal point of its attention, energies and resources.

Of course, it is not entirely clear to what extent the man before Jesus understood this, but had he done so, he would have recognized the stakes as considerable. It was one thing to be called from one's associations in high society; it was another to be called into the ranks of low society. Inasmuch

---

[46] The hierarchy inherent in the leadership structure of the Jesus' movement seems to be variously overlooked, e.g., by Theissen 1978, Schüssler Fiorenza 1984, Crossan 1991.

[47] Murphy's (2002: 449) findings in regard to the Qumran community are apropos to Jesus' counter-temple movement: 'Through the sharing of wealth, the community becomes a single entity, a *yahad*, united in fidelity and purpose, no longer torn by the greed and violence that characterize the external economy. By virtue of their covenant fidelity, they become an appropriate sanctuary for the holy spirit.'

as an individual is defined by one's kinship group (and this dynamic certainly obtained in antiquity), this also essentially meant *becoming* the poor. Much to the man's dismay, Jesus insisted on both – unconditionally. The goal of Jesus' redistribution of social and economic power had little to do with either some romantic ennobling of the poor or some celebration of simplicity for its own sake: on a practical level, his followers sought not only to identify with the dependent poor, which signified their priestly status, but also to abstain from mammon-driven social structures, which signified the kind of single-hearted devotion required of Yahweh's priests. In light of the recoverable historical data, this seems to be what Jesus and his movement stood for. This also seems to be what the man we meet in Mark 10.17–22 could not finally abide. If participation in Jesus' eschatological temple depended on one's willingness to align with the radical demands of that same temple in present time, perhaps, the man must have reasoned, a better offer was waiting for him down the road.

The woman at Bethany (Mark 14.3–7)

Behind-the-scenes practices on behalf of the poor

There is another historically reliable lens through which to view Jesus' ways with the poor. Returning to his final week, we find further clues of the whys and wherefores of the movement's ministry. The following episode is related, purportedly taking place two days before the Passover:

> While he was at Bethany in the house of Simon the leper, as he sat at the table, a woman came with an alabaster jar of very costly ointment of nard, and she broke open the jar and poured the ointment on his head. But some were there who said to one another in anger, 'Why was the ointment wasted in this way? For this ointment could have been sold for more than three hundred denarii, and the money given to the poor.' And they scolded her. But Jesus said, 'Let her alone; why do you trouble her? She has performed a good service for me. For you always have the poor with you, and you can show kindness to them whenever you wish; but you will not always have me.'[48]

This well-known scene of a woman anointing Jesus possesses the qualities of a realistic account. Whether or not this story speaks to the same event as recorded in Luke 7.36–50 (judgments vary on this), the parallels in Matthew 26.6–13 and John 12.1–12 meet the criterion of multiple attestation. On the criterion of embarrassment, whereby materials reflecting negatively on Jesus or the early Church lay relatively strong claim to authenticity, the pericope comes in for high marks. After all, the 'some who were there' are presumably

---

[48] Mark 14.3–7.

Jesus' disciples, who after rebuking her are in short order themselves rebuked.[49] The story is also connected with an actual witness, Simon the Leper of Bethany, no inconsequential point especially if we grant the force of Bauckham's interesting and provocative thesis that Mark seems to have vouched for the factuality of such accounts through mention of these witnesses.[50] Finally, the event fits well into the chronology that Mark provides. Following Jesus' triumphal entry and cleansing of the temple, the crowds are described as being astir with messianic speculation (Mark 14.1), and on the judgment that the woman intends her actions to be a token of Jesus' newly proclaimed priestly-messianic status, the anointing would simply be an individual instance of this fervor.[51] At the same time, Jesus seems to have reinterpreted the gesture as an anticipatory act of burial anointing (14.8). This too fits the historical situation. Clearly by this point in the train of events, Jesus' fate is all but sealed and this poignant scene, in which he forebodingly contemplates his imminent death with no intimation of resurrection, does not seem to have been the stuff of post-Easter legend. If we have already admitted the possibility of Jesus' anticipating his death, there is certainly no reason why this episode should be assigned to the early church rather than to the recollection of witnesses.

Accepting the incident as historically reliable, our inquiry finds helpful clues in the disciples' grievance against the woman and the reasons offered for it. Noting her extravagance, 'some' present with Jesus are offended, for they realize through a very quick mental calculation that the ointment which the woman used could have been dedicated to the poor. Whereas Mark in part intends this incident to throw into relief the woman's understanding against the disciples' dullness, the recorded details provide incidental but important witness to the ethos of the Jesus movement. The point is this: the disciples all seem to assume that in the normal course of things such a precious commodity would be cashed out on behalf of the poor. This is a significant detail. The disciples' objection implies that up to this point they had made a practice of obtaining material goods, selling them off, and then

---

[49] Mark's highlighting the foolhardiness of the disciples is no argument in favor of the passage being a Markan fiction. Since all the Gospels are at various points more than willing to take the apostles to task, it seems rather dubious to fall back on redaction-critical mirror readings which root every unbecoming word or deed of the disciples in a later church-based polemic. This point applies *a fortiori* here, as the evangelist is softening the punch by the circumlocution 'some who were there' instead of 'the disciples'.

[50] Bauckham 2006; similarly, Schenk 1974: 70. Caveats in regard to Bauckham's thesis have been registered by Schröter 2008, Patterson 2009.

[51] The view that the anointing was messianic, though variously supported (e.g. Schüssler Fiorenza 1984: xiii–xv), has sometimes been disputed. For Collins (2007: 642) the use of ointment (*myron*) rather than olive oil renders the putative messianic aspect problematic. The objection is not compelling. Since the same material was reserved for the Aaronic priesthood and was explicitly forbidden for other usages (Exod. 30.23–33), it is entirely plausible that the woman was signaling her own belief in Jesus' messianic-priestly status.

donating the purchase value to the needy. The only other possible way of making historical sense of the text is to imagine that the disciples, without informing Jesus or the woman, quite spontaneously and inexplicably came up with a plan to convert the perfume into cash for the sake of the destitute. But in this case their reproach would border on the absurd. The much more likely scenario is that the band of disciples were genuinely displeased because the act of pouring out the costly perfume violated their *modus operandi*; apparently, they were accustomed to functioning as a kind of mediator, funneling wealth from the 'haves' to the 'have-nots'.

That the Jesus movement took on such a role on behalf of the impoverished is further corroborated through a stray detail in John's passion narrative. During the last scene in which the Fourth Gospel finds Judas Iscariot with Jesus on friendly terms, the soon-to-be betrayed prompts the would-be betrayer:

> Jesus said to him, 'Do quickly what you are going to do.' Now no one at the table knew why he said this to him. Some thought that, because Judas had the common purse, Jesus was telling him, 'Buy what we need for the festival'; or, that he should give something to the poor.[52]

Earlier in the narrative, the evangelist had already mentioned that Judas was the keeper of the common money box (and that he had helped himself freely to its contents) (John 12.6). Now, the author reports, the disciples are under the mistaken impression that Jesus is asking Judas to dispense some of its contents, either for something in connection with Passover or for the poor. The casual mention of the money box in the narrative does not strike me as reflecting a fictive detail. Rather, given the communal nature of the movement, such an item is precisely the kind of thing one would expect Jesus' band to possess. And if we grant that a common fund existed among the disciples, then there should be no objection to the veracity of John's detail that it was administered on behalf of the poor.

This is further corroborated – returning to Mark 13.3–7 – by the master's statement, spoken in defense of the woman's extravagance: 'You always have the poor with you.'[53] In the first place, it is important to do full justice to the fact that Jesus' words are not intended as an observation regarding life in general, as if to remark almost blandly, 'As long as the sun rises and sets, there will always be poor people.' The thrust of the saying applies to the specific mission of his followers. Looking ahead to the future life of his community, Jesus presumes aloud that the disciples will always find themselves in the company of the poor, only then to point out that they will not always have him. This only reinforces our impression, already palpable in the earlier analysis of the pericope of the Rich Man, that Jesus' followers did not carry

---

[52] John 13.27–29.
[53] Jesus' statement is preserved in all three accounts (Mark 14.7//Matt. 26.11//John 12.8).

out their ministry from a safe and socially detached distance but instead maintained regular, close contact with the poor.[54] As far as Jesus was concerned, it was not enough to give to the poor: *being* 'with the poor' seemed to have been the group's standard practice; he assumed as a matter of course that his disciples would carry on no differently after his death. For the historical Jesus and his movement, association with the poor was a defining feature, or what we might today call 'a core value'.

Priesthood and the eschatological jubilee

It is not enough for history to describe practices; we are also interested in theory. Towards proposing one, I offer the following observation: namely, that in bringing resources to the poor, Jesus' followers seem to have had institutionalized among themselves a practice that bears striking resemblance to a custom that up to that point had been associated with the temple. At least from the time of the third century BCE, temple-based Judaism had implemented a charitable system, depending on the so-called 'third tithe', which provided funds for widows and orphans. As far as we can tell, it was the temple priests (and in post-temple Judaism the synagogue elders) who were responsible for collecting funds and distributing them to the poor. This role seems to have evolved from the principle that the temple was to be the focal point of Israel's resources and the starting-point of its enacted righteousness. By receiving offerings and directing the proceeds to the poor, Jesus and his disciples were essentially taking on a function of the temple.

But straddling John's movement and the early Church, Jesus' following would have more than likely understood this priestly calling in apocalyptic terms. Returning to the words of Mark 14.7, we see that the words shed light not only on the nature of his ministry, that is, what it would look like on a day-to-day basis, but also on the master rationale. For when Jesus says, 'You always have the poor with you', he is patently alluding to Deuteronomy 15.1–11, a passage in which Moses enjoins the seventh year as the year of canceling (*shemittah*) debts.[55]

The section of Deuteronomy is remarkable in its blend of idealism, realism, and pessimism. '*There will be* no one in need among you,' so the text promises, 'if only you will obey the LORD your God by diligently observing this entire commandment that I command you today' (vv. 4–5). But '*if* there is among you anyone in need', the scripture continues on a less confident note, 'do not be hard-hearted or tight-fisted toward your needy neighbor' (v. 7).

---

[54] This point is perhaps already obvious enough given the fact that Jesus and his disciples are being hosted by Simon the Leper, whose sobriquet would have marked him off as 'poor', at least in the social sense. In this connection, perhaps we ought to give credence to Capper's (1995, 2006) intriguing hypothesis that Bethany was quite literally a 'house of the poor', which provided space for those made outcasts by their skin ailments ('leprosy').

[55] While some interpreters hold that *shemittah* here refers to the deferment of debt, this seems improbable; see Cardellini 1981: 270; Chirichigno 1993: 272–5.

Finally, somewhat ominously we read: '*Since* there will never cease to be some in need on the earth, I therefore command you, "Open your hand to the poor and needy neighbor in your land"' (v. 11). Apparently, long before we come to Moses' anticipation of Israel's rebellion in Deuteronomy 29—32, Torah predicts the presence of the poor in the land, an evil associated with covenantal disobedience and directly linked to Israel's failure to remit debt on a septennial cycle (vv. 1–6). According to the scriptures, which Jesus knew so well, the health of Israel's political economy was bound up with the willingness of its individual creditors to forgo due loan payments. By the same token, in saying, 'You always have the poor with you', Jesus is venting an inward conviction which elsewhere has been teased out by other routes, namely, that Israel remained in a state of exile.

The root cause of this exile, his citation of the same text suggests, was economic injustice. This falls in line with the burden of the prophetic witness which closely links exile with Israel's failure to observe the 'seventh seven', that is, the radical program of debt remission laid out in the jubilee requirements, contained in Leviticus 25. Although this chapter of scripture may not seem central to our own understanding of biblical theology, jubilee was in the forefront for apocalyptic strands of Judaism. While on the seventh year the land was to lay fallow (Exod. 23.10–11), and on the seventh year the enslaved Hebrew was to go free (Exod. 21.2–6), and on every seventh year on the 'national calendar' debts were to be canceled (Deut. 15.1–11); on every forty-ninth year

> you shall have the trumpet sounded loud; on the tenth day of the seventh month – on the day of atonement – you shall have the trumpet sounded throughout all your land. And you shall hallow the fiftieth year and you shall proclaim liberty throughout the land to all its inhabitants. It shall be a jubilee for you: you shall return, every one of you, to your property and every one of you to your family.[56]

Overriding all other obligations, the law of jubilee ensured that debt would be forgiven, those in bondage would be released, and most importantly of all, the dispossessed would be restored to their landed inheritance (Lev. 25.39–55). All this was to occur on every forty-ninth (or fiftieth) Day of Atonement.

The slating of jubilee for this day, the highest of all Jewish days, was hardly arbitrary, for the redemption of land and the sin-atonement of *yom kippur* met in the foundational Jewish doctrine of creation. If on the annual Day of Atonement the high priest would enter the Holy of Holies to procure atonement and thereby reinstate the cosmos to its proper order, so too on the day of jubilee the high priest would see to it that true humanity's

---

[56] Lev. 25.9–10.

relationship to the land would be restored to its creational equilibrium.[57] Like the Sabbath year (Exod. 23.10–11), jubilee was supposed to have been a year without sowing or reaping; as in its primordial Adamic state, Israel was only to eat directly from the fields (Lev. 25.11–12). Like the Day of Atonement on which it fell, the jubilee was a temple-centered glimpse into eschatological new creation, at least in theory.

To repeat: 'at least in theory'. Israel's actual track record in keeping jubilee was abysmal and according to at least certain post-exilic reflection, it was this failure – as indicative of a national pandemic of greed – that led to Israel's removal from the land. The connection between exile and jubilee comes into sharp focus in the Chronicler's interpretation of history:

> He took into exile in Babylon those who had escaped from the sword, and they became servants to him and to his sons until the establishment of the kingdom of Persia, to fulfill the word of the LORD by the mouth of Jeremiah [Jer. 25.11–12; 29.10], until the land had made up for its sabbaths. All the days that it lay desolate it kept sabbath, to fulfill seventy years.[58]

Apparently, Israel had transgressed seventy land-sabbaths over the course of 490 years, or ten jubilees. But according to the Chronicler, the nation would get and indeed had already begun to obtain its long overdue release. This is exactly why the Chronicler models the royal emancipator's kingdom-spanning voice on the jubilee horn which was to course over the land (2 Chron. 36.22; cf. Lev. 25.10) and frames the exile as the fiftieth generation from Adam (1 Chron. 1.1—9.1). More interesting still is jubilee's connection with two other momentous events:

> In the first year of King Cyrus of Persia, in fulfillment of the word of the LORD spoken by Jeremiah, the LORD stirred up the spirit of King Cyrus of Persia so that he sent a herald throughout all his kingdom and also declared in a written edict: 'Thus says King Cyrus of Persia: The LORD, the God of heaven, has given me all the kingdoms of the earth, and he has charged me to build him a house at Jerusalem, which is in Judah. Whoever is among you of all his people, may the LORD his God be with him! Let him go up.'[59]

Within the text, as has been argued elsewhere, we find an implicit association between Cyrus' edict calling for a return from exile (537 BCE), the re-building of the temple, and jubilee.[60] This does not seem to be idiosyncratic, as we find a similar juxtaposing of these ideas in so-called Second Isaiah (Isaiah 44—45, 61). Return from exile coincided with the release of estranged

---

[57] The high priest's responsibility for sounding the jubilee trumpet may be inferred from not only Lev. 27.16–25 (which proscribes the priestly task of assessing the relative value of land and labor with reference to jubilee), but also Isa. 61.1–2 (which envisages an anointed royal-priestly figure proclaiming the jubilee 'year of the Lord's favor'). See also 11Q13.

[58] 2 Chron. 36.20–21.

[59] 2 Chron. 36.22–23.

[60] See Johnstone 2000: 311; Bergsma 2007: 210–11.

land; both of these in turn prepared for the climactic event, the realization of Israel's reason for being, the building of the temple. In the Second-Temple Jewish mind one thing was clear: return from exile, implementation of jubilee, and – the point of it all – rebuilding of the temple were inseparably conjoined.

The story does not end there, for although the rebuilding of the temple signaled the end to Jeremiah's prophesied seventy years of exile (Jer. 29.10–14), it appears through the lens of Daniel 9.24–27 that this fulfillment was only partial. Corresponding to the ten jubilees prior to the seventy-year exile, there would also have to be ten jubilees following the completion of this exile. At the end of that period, following a time of desolation, Daniel promises (9.24), there would be an 'end to sin' and the inception of everlasting righteousness. However one dates the beginning of the ten-jubilee period (and there have been differences of opinion among both modern-day and ancient exegetes), when we count off ten jubilees (490 years) from the beginning of the post-exilic period, we come right up to the time of Jesus' day. It is all the more understandable, then, that we also find in that era intense speculation into the fulfillment of the ten-jubilee period.[61]

One of the most interesting documents reflecting such speculation close to Jesus' day is the Qumran document 11Q13. The text appears to be an interpretive *pesher* on Leviticus 25 with its jubilee legislation; like other Qumran writings, drawing together distinct but correlated biblical notions, it is concerned pre-eminently with the actualization of jubilee and *shemittah* ('release').[62] The most relevant portion reads as follows:

> [the interpretation] is that it applies [to the L]ast Days and concerns the captives, just as [Isaiah said: 'To proclaim the jubilee to the captives' (Isa. 61.1) ...] and whose teachers have been hidden and kept secr[et], even from the inheritance of Melchizedek, f[or ...] and they are the inherit[ance of Melchize]dek, who will return to them what is rightfully theirs. He will proclaim to them the jubilee, thereby releasing th[em from the debt of a]ll their sins.[63]

A handful of observations are in order. First, it appears that the envisaged jubilee is eschatological, pertaining to 'the Last Days'. This suggests that the author of the text saw this climactic moment not as one jubilee among many but as a final and definitive jubilee, one in which his community was apparently expected to participate. Second, the driver behind this eschatological release is the priest Melchizedek, the shadowy figure of

---

[61] With an eye to Beckwith (1981), Wright (1992: 313) remarks: 'It has been cogently argued that, according to one way of computing the figures involved, the "seventy weeks of years" mentioned in Daniel 9.24–27 as being the time between the exile, on the one hand, and the rebuilding of Jerusalem and the coming of "an anointed prince", on the other, would be entering upon their last "week" in the mid-60s AD.' It is clear that this countdown into the first century is not just a modern construct; see the survey of Second-Temple texts in Beckwith 1996: 217–75.

[62] 11Q13 2.2–4; see also 1Q22; 1QS 10.6–8.

[63] 11Q13 2.4–5.

Genesis 14 and Psalm 110, who receives this role perhaps on account of his office (Psalm 110) and his association with Abraham's recouping that which was his (Genesis 14). Seeing that the Qumran writer modifies the 'year of grace of the Lord' to the 'year of grace of Melchizedek' (l. 9), we need no further evidence that this Melchizedek is a highly exalted figure: for all intents and purposes, he *is* the Lord! Interestingly, he is also identified both with the servant figure of Isaiah 52.7 and the anointed prince of Daniel 9.25 (11Q13 15, 18). This same Melchizedek will proclaim the final jubilee and thereby – as I come to my third point – will release the inheritance of their sins. Perhaps this is less surprising, as the interchange of forgiveness of sins and return to the land seems to have been a matter of assumption in the Dead Sea Scroll community.[64] As a counter-temple movement, the Qumran community saw Israel's basic problem as the problem of exile which in turn resulted in fruitless worship. The pivotal figure in redressing that problem would be a new high priest, declaring a once-and-for-all jubilee, implying forgiveness of sins and restoration to the land.

While various sects might have had their own distinctive way of working out the details of the jubilee calendar, it is clear that in its broad outline the ten-jubilee cycle was of immense importance for Jewish apocalypticism. Imbued with the spirit of this same outlook, so much of first-century Judaism saw itself as being on the brink of a monumental turn; fervent expectation of Yahweh's bringing about the great release was in the air. This was the air that the Qumran covenanteers breathed. Jubilee-tinged apocalyptic was also, it seems, the air that John the Baptist breathed. Finally, if we were to regard Jesus as one who sought to fulfill the final release, this would be extraordinary in its own way, but it would certainly not in any sense put him 'off the map' of Jewish expectation.

On the basis of such comparisons, we can see Jesus' allusion to Deuteronomy 15 (Mark 14.7) in new light. The phrase, 'The poor you will always have with you', is not just the reiteration of the group's mission, even less an expression of resigned realism. On the contrary, it is the strident assertion of an apocalyptic vision. Bound up in this saying, supported by a good number of other traditions handed down in the synoptic texts, is the driving impetus behind Jesus' mission to the poor: in a word, jubilee.[65] This means too that although the movement's efforts on behalf of the poor were priestly in their own right, they were not ordinary priestly duties. Nor did Jesus consider his followers to be functioning as priests in a static sense. Jesus' counter-temple project must be understood in dynamic terms, within a divinely appointed timetable. Painfully aware of the presence of the landless poor in Israel, which was only added confirmation of the national curse (Deut. 15.6; 28.44), Jesus seems to have reasoned that the curse was about to be reversed through an

---

[64] See, e.g., 1Q22 3.5–11.
[65] Matt. 5.5; 18.21–35; Luke 4.18–19; 11.4; etc.

imminent act of God, and therefore the only appropriate response would be a concentrated effort towards open-handed almsgiving and the redemption of the indebted (Deut. 15.1—3, 11). This would have to occur not simply on an individual and haphazard basis (such giving was already a matter of prescribed duty), but on a corporate and systematic level. In anticipating the imminent return from exile and a rolling back of the law's curse, Jesus saw his own movement as embodying a returned-from-exile Israel, whose task was to initiate among its own numbers a public reversal of the presenting symptoms of exile: expropriation and indebtedness.

This may shed further light on the socio-economic leveling we have already observed within the Jesus movement. Such egalitarianism now makes sense, not as an expression of any doctrine of human rights (which in its modern articulation would have been completely foreign to Jesus), but as the symbolic embodiment of the release of Leviticus 25. After all, jubilee was the one day (out of every 18,000 plus!) on which there would have been a complete absence of debt, servitude, and wealth-based hierarchicalism. It was the one day in which the playing field was guaranteed to be level. If the socio-economic egalitarianism of Jesus' movement had something to do with the disciples' shared priestly status, it may also have served to express, even more emphatically through the praxis of radical redistribution, his aims of restoring the land. This is nothing entirely new: the same principles seem to have been applied by Jesus' counter-temple predecessors at Qumran.[66]

In this connection it may also be suggested that Jesus' abstention from gainful employment and marital sexual intercourse, along with his calling others to follow suit (Matt. 19.10—12), were likewise meant to be an emblem of this sabbatical Day of Atonement.[67] For if jubilee had arrived, then so too had the Day of Atonement, as the former only fell on this most sacred of days (Lev. 25.9). According to Torah, the Day of Atonement was itself a day to be set apart by asceticism: 'Now, the tenth day of this seventh month is the day of atonement; it shall be a holy convocation for you: you shall deny yourselves' (Lev. 23.27; cf. Num. 29.7). There was to be neither work nor sexual activity on the Day of Atonement because the day symbolized the sabbatical completion of work and a return to primordial creation in its Adamic state. (Likewise, return to creation is more or less what takes place when the High Priest, representing both Adam and Israel, enters into God's direct presence in the Holy of Holies.) Perhaps, in setting down such

---

[66] Murphy (2002: 448—9) states that Dead Sea covenanters sought through their communalism to 'realize the sabbatical and jubilee vision on a daily basis'. Thus in 'creating an alternative economy grounded in a radical interpretation of the law, the sectarians propose that they can supplant the Temple as the intermediary of sanctification and thus secure atonement and prosperity for the land'.

[67] As suggested, e.g., by Levine 2005: 520—2. Allison (1998: 172—210) allows for a broader array of motivations, but rounds off his discussion by suggesting that Jesus' celibacy was part of his 'attempt to regain the *Urzeit* in the face of the *Endzeit*' (210).

distinctives, Jesus was seeking to represent himself and his followers as the heralds of jubilee atonement.

The movement's commitment to the principle of jubilee also puts into fresh light the indications in the Gospels that Jesus forgave sin.[68] When Jesus is described as granting forgiveness of sins, this should not be chalked up to some editorial voice within the early Church, superimposing either its atonement theology ('Personal forgiveness comes only through Jesus') or its Christology ('Jesus forgives, no one can forgive but God alone, therefore Jesus must be God'). Although later ecclesial tradition may have come to read Jesus in just this way, this does not seem to have been Jesus' first intention. Because expulsion from the land was a sign of Yahweh's wrath, the full issuance of forgiveness would have been inconceivable apart from at least the prospect of debt cancelation and a corresponding restitution of one's land. Forgiveness betokened not just a heart set right with Yahweh but a fresh start on one's ancestral lands – and vice versa. That Jesus, like John the Baptizer, forgave sins outside the temple apparatus signals his own sense of temple calling. Yet the constitution of a new temple was itself a sign that something truly monumental was at hand: full return from exile and the reuniting of true Israelites with their land. Again, these were but necessary steps for the restoration of Israel's final purpose, which was to worship.

But all this raises the question as to how such an astounding transfer of real estate might come about. How could the poor hope to throw off the fetters of their debt and come back to that which they had forfeited through a society-wide debt crisis? Did Jesus have a strategy for the remnant's return to the land or was the promise of forgiveness akin to hopeful well-wishing?

Certainly one strategy wide open to Jesus, and one which he may well have been tempted to employ at numerous points, was the path of violent revolution. Historically, this certainly had proved to be the strategy of choice, at least so far as the wider Roman world was concerned. In the centuries and decades leading up to Jesus' day, peasant-based revolt movements were usually but not always abortive undertakings; when they did succeed, such movements typically secured redistribution of land, freedom for slaves, and debt remission by force.[69] This historical pattern alone would have certainly caused the Palestinian aristocracy to have kept a nervous and watchful eye on Jesus and his activities, especially since, like earlier mass-movement leaders, he would sometimes find himself surrounded by crowds in remote places.[70] There would have been some substance to the aristocrats' fears, for these

---

[68] Mark 2.1–12 par.; 4.12 par.; Luke 7.47–48; John 20.23.

[69] Plutarch (*Life of Cleomenes*) records one of the more famous of such revolts, occurring under Agis IV in 244 BCE. The end result forced Agis' successor to cancel debts and redistribute land. For further examples and discussion see de Ste Croix 1981: 608–9; Oakman 2008: 13–15.

[70] Restive crowds and out-of-the-way places are regarded as dangerous combinations in the ancient sources: (Tacitus) *Ann.* 15.44; (Josephus) *Ant.* 18.5.2 §118. See Crossan 1994: vii.

gatherings were not innocent events through and through, that is, if we believe John's statement that at one point the crowds sought to make him king (John 6.15). Although uncorroborated as a datum, the evangelist's statement certainly fits well with a picture of a disgruntled peasant class who were ready for a change and who furthermore looked to Jesus as the hoped-for agent of change.[71]

Because someone in Jesus' *de facto* position of leadership might well be expected to level the economic playing field through bloody revolt, his steadfast refusal to entertain this option remains all the more remarkable. The tensions between the unique nature of Jesus' call for land redistribution and the commonly used strategies for effecting such redistribution provide important background to his ethics of non-violence.[72] If Jesus had to make himself clear on any point, it was here. Forcible redistribution of land and debt was exactly *not* the way he was willing to go.

At this juncture it is commonly suggested that while Jesus does indeed envisage a jubilee whereby the land would be restored to the twelve tribes, he redefines both the twelve tribes and the land in such a way so as to transcend both. According to this widely touted interpretation, Jesus spiritualizes the meaning of Israel and land with the result that he could simultaneously affirm a 'real' jubilee for Israel all the while the land remained securely deeded to those who had no long-term claim to it. I find this option unconvincing. In the first place, such spiritualizing can only be leveraged on a kind of dualism which finds little resonance in Jesus' teachings. Second, while we have plenty of evidence of pious first-century Jews looking for an actual redistribution of land brought about by God, we find negligible evidence that Palestinian Jews had somehow transformed the meaning of 'land' so that it came to mean something intangible.[73] Traditional suggestions that Jesus reconstrued land, so that it came to mean either 'heaven' or something similar, does not fit the historical milieu. Since first-century Judaism as a rule expected the restoration of the land, the burden of evidence is on anyone wishing to argue that a different view obtained in the case of Jesus.

In my view, Jesus did indeed expect God to inaugurate a true jubilee, the conveyance of actual plots of dirt and rock to the remnant. Admittedly, there

---

[71] Fiensy (1999) demonstrates how Jesus' association with the crowds would have, on the basis of prior peasant uprisings, exhibited all the makings of a perfect storm. Such economically driven uprisings were not uncommon and were certainly a major factor in the First Jewish Revolt; cf. Hengel 1968; 1974: 16.

[72] As is paradigmatically expressed in the Sermon on the Mount: 'But I say to you, Do not resist an evildoer. But if anyone strikes you on the right cheek, turn the other also; and if anyone wants to sue you and take your coat, give your cloak as well' (Matt. 5.39–40).

[73] This is, for example, even true of the rich man in Mark 10.17–22. Whereas 'the language of inheritance refers "originally and almost exclusively to the possession of the land"' (see Collins 2007: 476, citing Hermann 1965: 774), we must interpret the man's query ('What must I do to *inherit* eternal life') as tantamount to asking, 'What must I do to ensure that the real estate I now have will carry over with me into the life to come?'

is precious little indication as to precisely when he expected this to take place. Conclusively and during his lifetime? Hardly. Why else would he say virtually on the eve of his arrest, 'The poor you will always have with you'? At some distant and detached point in the future? This seems equally unlikely, for why in that case would Jesus be intimating the imminent appearing of jubilee realities in his own day?

For further insight, we might return to Jesus' cleansing of the temple. It is to be recalled that at least for a good proportion of Second-Temple Judaism, the future events of restoration and jubilee would coincide with the building of the temple. If, as argued in the last chapter, Jesus saw himself as the long-awaited temple-builder, it was a temple that embraced both a future and present aspect. It was 'future' in that it looked forward to the decisive in-breaking of the heavenly temple into spatio-temporal reality; it was 'present' in that his followers were to carry out a priestly calling in sustaining that temple, while Jesus was alive and even after his death.

The same fusing of present and future categories appears to obtain in Jesus' understanding of jubilee. This means that while this self-proclaimed temple-builder anticipated Yahweh's restoration of the land in symbolic terms, he certainly did not see the present applicability of jubilee as moot. His efforts were as much practical as they were symbolic.[74] There are indications that he envisaged the prospect of real change and real debt relief in his own day. Such may be adduced from the third Gospel, where Jesus is recorded as saying:

> When you give a luncheon or a dinner, do not invite your friends or your brothers or your relatives or rich neighbors, in case they may invite you in return, and you would be repaid. But when you give a banquet, invite the poor, the crippled, the lame, and the blind. And you will be blessed, because they cannot repay you, for you will be repaid at the resurrection of the righteous.[75]

While Luke's impress can certainly be detected in this passage, it remains patently unlikely that the extended saying is wholesale invention on the part of either Luke or his sources. It is widely acknowledged that keeping varied and questionable company at dinner was one of the distinctive features of Jesus' life. Because we would expect there to have been some pressure on Jesus to provide an explanation for this strange social behavior, when we do find such explanation in the sources we would do well to think twice before dismissing its historical worth. At least a few indicators point in the opposite direction. First, Jesus' list of 'the poor, the crippled, the lame, and the blind' resembles a similar sequence in another scene, typically deemed authentic,

---

[74] Yoder (1994: 76) is on-target when he writes: 'It was a jubilee ordinance which was to be put into practice here and now, once, in A.D. 26, as a "refreshment," prefiguring the "reestablishment of all things".'

[75] Luke 14.12–14.

where Jesus sends back his answer to his doubting cousin John.[76] Second, the passage has close thematic and terminological links with the subsequent Lukan section alleged to have originated in Q (Luke 14.15–24//Matt. 22.1–14) and one which 'is accepted by many as a parable of the historical Jesus'.[77] Finally, the close association here between the resurrection and handling of wealth matches well with Jesus bringing the same together in Mark 10.17–22. The core of the passage must be allowed to stand in Jesus' setting. From all this we may draw a fairly straightforward inference: as part of his program, Jesus encouraged those with means to host those who could never play the host themselves: the poor.

And he seems to have done so regularly. Were this a stray pronouncement or an unrepeated, off-the-cuff idea broached in the company of a few random dinner guests, it is unlikely to have found its way into the tradition. I find it much more probable that this teaching, like so many of Jesus' teachings, was no 'one-off', but something closer to a recurring stump speech. If so, then Jesus also probably expected this strategy of non-reciprocity to be taken up not on an individualized basis but as something integral to the movement's mission. Assuming too that his followers took him at his word and believed that they as hosts to the poor would be rewarded at the resurrection, one must imagine that the entire community worked collaboratively in this direction.

At this point we modern-day interpreters must be careful lest we senti-mentalize Jesus' words or otherwise reduce them to homespun moralism. While it may be tempting to translate such teaching here into our own western idiom by thinking that Jesus was basically asking his hearers to consider (the first-century equivalent of) volunteering at the homeless shel-ter next Christmas, it is unlikely that any of his original hearers would have understood him in this way. The vision was much more programmatic. Calling on his disciples to shed the shackles of reciprocity, involving at every turn an 'I give that you might give' calculation, Jesus enjoins a collective but voluntary trickle-down of resources. Nor would this have necessarily been a small trickle. In a subsistence economy where surplus was unheard-of and the vast majority of the poor householder's income was expended on food, any plan of providing meals to the poor on a regular basis would have made it possible, at least in theory, for these same poor to accrue savings. And where you have accrued savings, there you also have the one thing that the poor lacked: capital. And where there is capital, there is the possibility of economic freedom and reinvestiture within Israel. If this was indeed the final design of Jesus' teaching, then the goal was no haphazard or patronizing benevolence, but economic liberation on a local scale. Judging by the

---

[76] Luke 7.22//Matt. 11.5. See discussion above, p. 41 n. 90.
[77] Meier 1994: 376. Included among such 'many' are, e.g., Crossan 1991: 261–2; Dunn 2003: 235–6; Horsley 2003: 91.

practices of early Christianity, it seems that this is exactly how Jesus' first followers thought of these things.

It bears repeating that the envisaged liberation would not have been simply economic in character but social as well. I have argued above that Jesus' call on his wealthy interlocutor entailed the latter's entering a society which had effectively obliterated social ordering according to an economic scale. This datum is indirectly corroborated by observing from the above passage (Luke 14.12–14) that Jesus commended meals as the venue for associating with the poor. By so doing, Jesus not only embraced the poor as part of his circle, but also seemed to have used meals, including not least the counter-cultural seating arrangement he enjoined in these settings, as part of a broader attempt to destabilize the rigid social hierarchy.[78] In the first-century world the poor, blind, and crippled belonged to the social margins. But in the world of Jesus' making, symbolically created through dining practices and dining stories, it was the likes of the poor, the blind, and the crippled that were singled out as the guests of honor. This is more than a courtesy towards the social underdog at mealtimes. As Jesus was well aware, once the poor were established alongside or in place of the wealthy at the top of the social pecking order (and no social custom reinforced this pecking order more than meals), the pecking order itself would eventually fall into obsolescence. By teaching his followers that they should honor the poor through everyday symbolic gestures, Jesus was in effect instigating a quiet revolution.

Summary

The account of the woman who anointed Jesus at Bethany not only confirms the socially radical nature of the Jesus movement, but sharpens its contours in several respects. First, the event provides excellent evidence that the Jesus movement was a kind of clearing-house that met the needs of the poor and, in this respect, the initial impression drawn from the evidence of Mark 10.17–22 (The Rich Young Man) is simply confirmed. Second, given Jesus' allusion to Deuteronomy 15 in the context, we have solids grounds for identifying this interest in the poor as part of an effort to fulfill the scriptural obligation of canceling debts. This in turn must be seen against a larger backdrop of an eschatological jubilee.

Beyond this, I maintain that Jesus' jubilee program finds its fundamental ground on his self-understanding as the eschatological high priest. Just as the community behind 11Q13 held forth the hope of a Melchizedekian high priest who would redeem the land, deliver Israel, and judge the wicked, so did Jesus. In Jesus' case, however, the hope devolved upon himself. Given Jesus' indications of being the eschatological temple-builder, this comes as little surprise. The messianic rebuilder of the temple would also be the one

---

[78] Luke 14.7–11; Matt. 22.1–14; 23.6a; John 13.1–17.

to officiate over the same. This was no innovation on Jesus' part: in Second-Temple Judaism, messiahship and high priesthood consistently went hand in hand.[79]

Synthesis

Jesus and his immediate followers embraced a lifestyle of poverty and ministered to the impoverished. In adopting this way of life, which was short of absolute destitution, Jesus was no socially isolated ascetic, but kept table fellowship with those who would have been considered 'poor', meaning people who were either economically or socially disenfranchised – in most cases both. Moreover, he and his movement sought to meet the economic needs of the destitute by brokering alms; he also called others to take part in carrying out a voluntary redistribution of goods. Through both his teachings and his actions, Jesus was for, among, and about the poor. This was a defining feature of his movement.

The reasons for this are to be traced back to Jesus' conviction that God was about to do something to remediate Israel's systemic failure. Despite scripture's provisions for ensuring that debt, servitude, and alienation from one's ancestral land would be temporary conditions, eventually to be reversed through the jubilee, there is no evidence that the high priesthood ever implemented these injunctions in the Second-Temple period. Nor, from Jesus' standpoint, was there any evidence that things were going to get better any time soon. As time wore on, more and more landholdings were being transferred from the evicted householders into the hands of a relatively small collection of Jerusalem-based families. While the rich grew richer, the foreclosed-upon – if they were fortunate enough to serve as tenant-farmers – would be consigned to increasing degrees of indignity and deprivation. Unable to get out from under the crushing weight of debt, the poor were often forced into unfavorable and high-risk loan arrangements, invariably resulting in insolvency, the irretrievable loss of inheritance and fundamental capital. All this could of course have been averted through the application of the Levitical laws; the neglect of the same served to aggravate the divide between the rich and poor.

Reneging on their responsibility to reverse the disenfranchisement of the poor, and indeed taking their own measures to perpetuate it, Israel's high-priestly leadership had undermined Israel's basic *raison d'être*. Since Yahweh's proprietorship of the land could only be vouchsafed through the faithful practice of jubilee, the high priest's continued failure to convey the expropriated tracts back to the disinherited was tantamount to saying to God, 'This land is our land; it isn't your land.' This omission implicitly not only

---

[79] See Fletcher-Louis 2006, 2007.

divested the land of its sacral character, but also put on hold Israel's return from exile, the outstanding prerequisite of full restoration. In its stubborn refusal, the leadership had decisively compromised Israel as a people of worship and Israel as the place of worship. As long as this state of affairs persisted, Jesus reasoned, true worship would be impossible. From his point of view, the main thing separating Israel from its destined task of worship was, ironically enough, the priesthood itself.

What was needed, Jesus surmised, was a new priesthood. Such a priesthood would need to demonstrate the core requirement of the priestly office and that which the current priesthood singularly lacked: righteousness – a righteousness made concrete in caring for the poor. Since the failure to observe jubilee frustrated the national calling of worship, such a priesthood would also have to apply itself somehow to the reappropriation of land, as was necessary both for the reintegration of the worshipping community and the restoration of the land. All this would be requisite preparation for the ushering in of the final temple. As for those who opposed this program of restoration, including the wicked priests themselves, Jesus seems to have reasoned in accordance with the prophetic texts that these would one day meet with the wrath of Yahweh. Given the apocalyptic invective preserved in the tradition, it seems that he spoke of this judgment in no uncertain terms.

This new priesthood was of course constituted by Jesus himself, and one of the basic ways in which he worked out this priesthood in daily life was through his identification with and presence among the poor. First, by dedicating himself to 'doing righteousness' (almsgiving), Jesus not only threw into shade the oppressive practices of the high priesthood, but also established himself as a true priest – more exactly, *the* true priest. Jesus' actions were in this respect a public demonstration of his priestly credentials. Second, by modeling himself on certain scriptural figures who stood with the poor, Jesus sought to symbolize his own representative role on their behalf, which involved priestly and therefore redemptive suffering. This fits the picture of this historical Jesus. Given the weight of various testimonies, it is virtually undeniable that Jesus saw suffering as integral to his ministry, reckoned himself to be the focal point of that suffering, and finally expected his disciples to share this suffering in some way as well.[80] As the prelude to the future temple, suffering was necessary because, according to the scriptural logic, it was integral to God's redemptive purposes for the poor. In short, Jesus had to suffer as one of the prophesied 'poor', for he saw himself as the poor *par excellence*. By identifying himself this way and therewith recapitulating the story of remnant Israel in his own life, Jesus enacted a return from exile and the fulfillment of the well-known story of the oppressed

---

[80] Mark 2.20 par.; 8.34–38 par.; 10.38–40.

faithful one being delivered out from under the yoke of his oppressors. It was a theme to which the prophetic texts, a sure source of inspiration for Jesus, gave variation.[81]

The dramatic announcement of return from exile and restitution through a much-delayed release was no pie-in-the-sky matter, for in receiving alms and re-dispensing them to the poor, Jesus was also *doing* jubilee. While the poor certainly needed their daily bread, the greatest need for long-term improvement of their economic lot lay in their ability to acquire surplus. I have suggested that the movement's brokering of alms not only targeted immediately pressing needs, but also over the long haul would have provided a springboard for escaping the vicious cycle of debt. The provision of this money seemed to come through almsgiving, the transfer of wealth to the poor, all prompted by Jesus' announcement that those with surplus should now share their meals. While there is no telling to what extent the local indigent were able to realize the potential of this open commensality, it nevertheless seems the case that Jesus established a counter-society which enabled those with insufficient means to take some initial steps to re-investiture. By breaking down the socio-economic barriers that stood between the stratified classes, and enabling a flow of resources between these classes, the community sought to make the forgiveness of personal debt a real possibility.

In his symbolically conveying the jubilee character of his movement and giving the same principles practical expression, Jesus was seeking to restore land and people for the worship of Yahweh. Jubilee was not an end in itself, just as liberation from Egypt or Assyria was never considered an end in itself. The main point of land redistribution and debt forgiveness was that God's temple might soon pick up where it left off. This time, however, at the tenth jubilee and at the climax of the period of exile, Israel would find that their temple had a whole new look. Through messiah, Israel's God was building a temple whose treasure would neither decay nor go missing. The breathtaking news for Jesus' peers lay in his claim that that temple-building was going on in the present.

Conclusion

At the close of the previous chapter, I raised two questions provoked by the temple cleansing: (1) What hope remained for the dispossessed? and (2) What would become of the priests and the office which they held? At the close of this chapter, I am in a position to answer these and will do so in reverse order.

First, what about the high priests and the high priesthood itself? Given the likelihood that Jesus appropriated the scriptural story of the champion

---

[81] Isa. 25.1–10; 41.17–20; 61.1–6; Ezek. 22.29–31; 46.18; Zech. 7.10–14; 9.8–12; 13.1–9; etc.

of the poor as his own, it is to be inferred that he also assigned his opponents the same part assigned to the wicked within the prophetic texts. They would, in other words, meet their just deserts at the hands of God. As for the high priesthood, this now belonged to Jesus. From his perspective, he now was the exemplar of covenantal righteousness and it fell to him, precisely in his role as high priest, to proclaim the jubilee at last. Jesus does not stipulate a point at which this changing of the guards was to take place: he only intimates that it was taking place and would take place, partially through his agency.

Second, what would be the fate of those who had been oppressed by the high priesthood, the dispossessed? Here Jesus' actions and teachings speak clearly enough. Since return from exile was underway, this meant the prospect of the poor regaining the land that was theirs by a strange, unexpected justice. This was a real hope involving the real restitution of land at some future indeterminate point; this was also in part a present reality, being realized in an anticipatory way through the purposeful sharing of the Jesus movement. The prospective pay-out of future hope was underwritten by the cash down-payment of present practice.

Seeing himself as the divinely commissioned counter to the high priest in Jerusalem, Jesus placed a premium on righteousness, expressed most clearly in almsgiving. Also, having been convinced that eschatological jubilee was underway, he sought to lead his movement in establishing a presence among the poor and effecting reappropriation of expropriated properties. As long as the poor were being systematically removed from their ancestral lands, as long as jubilee legislation was being ignored, land and temple would remain in a state of defilement. In calling his followers to identify socially with the poor and participate in the voluntary redistribution of wealth, Jesus sought to restore the ruined socio-economic foundations of Israel's cultic life. Without these foundations in place, the rebuilding of the temple would be for naught. Even if Yahweh's standard of jubilee could not be observed across Israel as a whole, it was enough to begin within the movement itself. In this sense, Jesus was reconstituting Israel around himself. It was not Jesus' intention to restore temple worship because Israel was continuing through him. Rather it was his intention to witness the continuation of Israel amidst his own ranks because he was restoring Israel's temple.

Yet Jesus' jubilee project does not tell the whole story. A reconstituted socio-economic fabric was a necessary condition for the re-investiture of Israel as the world's priest, but it was not a sufficient condition. Obedience to the socio-economic principles inherent in jubilee legislation might have been a central component in the restoration of culticly pure worship, but it was not enough by itself. Something else was required. If the political philosophies to which the priestly elite had subscribed were out of place, this too had to give way. A new temple demanded a new body politic – and with it a new political vision.

5

'Thy kingdom come!'

Implementing the kingdom among the impure

Introduction

The jubilee release was not strictly or even originally a Jewish idea; it arose in the context of Ancient Near Eastern royal ideology. In antiquity, when a sovereign assumed the throne, it was not uncommon for the new ruler to issue a decree (called a *misharum* or *andurarum*) effectively canceling all debt.[1] Originally born out of political expediency, the practice at least in some cultures became a standing tradition embedded in the ritualistic cycle of life. For example, we might take note of the Mesopotamian *akîtu* festival, a regular celebration which spanned the millennia right down into the time of Jesus. The highlight of this twice-a-year tradition centered on an enacted drama whereby the high priest would oversee, first, the ritual re-entry of the local god into the city, then the cleansing of the god's temple, next a ritual enthronement within the temple, and then acts of justice on behalf of the poor. Finally, the high priest would drag 'the king before the deity where he was made to prostrate himself and give account for his administration of both cultic affairs and social justice'.[2] If nothing else, the ritualized event would serve as a regular reminder that the priestly king was the god's vice-gerent on earth and therefore was obliged to act like it. How the ancient ruler discharged his responsibilities for vertical (cultic) and horizontal (social) realities was no private matter.

The storyline dramatized in the *akîtu* festival is strikingly parallel to the events of Jesus' last week. After entering the city as the representative of Israel's God, Jesus cleanses the temple, and in so doing, he stands in solidarity with the poor and calls the temple rulers out for their maladministration of the cult and negligence of social justice. I raise the comparison not in order to prove that the *akîtu* festival was the inspiration for Jesus' script (it would be impossible to adduce evidence that he was even aware of the Mesopotamian practice), but to suggest that he was appealing to a common grammar of royal-priestly rule, broadly shared in the Ancient Near East. Those who ruled

---

[1] The primary purpose of this was to level the steep differences between the rich and poor, with a view to stabilizing the society and winning the support of the lower classes. See Weinfeld 1985; Bergsma 2007: 19–52.

[2] Bergsma 2007: 31.

the nation (kings in the case of Mesopotamia, high priests in the case of Judea) were seen as holding a fiduciary trust ensuring, on the one side, social justice for the people, and, on the other side, faithful oversight of the god's representative institution. While Jesus consistently found his impetus in the scriptures of Israel, on a more general level his protest was goaded by the conviction that within Israel even pagan standards of justice, to which the royal priests of surrounding nations were beholden, had been violated. It was time for Jesus the rightful high priest to cleanse the temple, call local rulers to account, and actualize social justice, beginning with his own movement.

For the historical Jesus and his followers, who operated according to a more specific storyline laid out in the scriptures, there was even more at stake. Jesus' take on Israel's situation was simple enough: in their idolatrous greed, the temple elite had helped themselves to the temple coffers and expropriated the poor from their inherited lands through foreclosure. The former activity had the effect of profaning the temple; the latter not only wreaked economic havoc on the poor, but also exerted its own desecrating force: the failure to observe jubilee – indeed, systemic expropriation amounting to an anti-jubilee – meant that the land, like the temple, had also become unclean. For many pious Jews of the day, the profaned temple grounds and land had together become the proverbial elephant in Israel's living room – a glaringly huge problem which betrayed no obvious solutions.

Like other dissident sectarians who had gone before, Jesus and his followers were persuaded of such realities, but were also convinced that Israel's God was on the verge of issuing a drastic response. Thus fell to Jesus, for starters, the two-fold task of naming what was wrong with current cultic practices and painting a living, breathing picture of temple life as it was supposed to be. He employed many of the same brushes as the temple dissidents that came under review in Chapter 1; their much-studied model was also his; that is, the eschatological temple. At the same time, Jesus did not paint with all the same colors, for his vision was unique. His distinctiveness as a prophetic voice within Judaism did not consist so much in what he looked for but in how he saw it, and in how he represented this in-breaking temple in his own day. Like others before him, Jesus saw both himself and his community as a new temple. But unlike anything we meet in Second-Temple Judaism, Jesus leaves no firm boundary between his own interim temple-project and the final, eschatological temple. Quite the contrary, according to Jesus' radical understanding: the heavenly temple had already come to earth and was beginning to coalesce within his own community.

Plausible as this reconstruction may be, we are still left with at least two issues unresolved. The first pertains to Jesus' central metaphor: the kingdom of God. As virtually all scholars agree, the historical Jesus made much of the kingdom. If the upstart Galilean's symbolic enactment of debt release raised the specter of an incipient regime change, his doing so in conjunction with preaching on the kingdom clarified his basic expectation (even if the character of that kingdom remained rather mysterious). Add to this Jesus' entering Jerusalem to shouts of 'Hosanna!' and his public intimations of a destroyed temple, then by his eleventh hour it would have been clear to even the dimmest of his contemporaries: Jesus was claiming to usher in the promised kingdom. But if the kingdom of God was *the* recurring theme in Jesus' public communication, then what does all this have to do with the eschatological temple? The relationship between this kingdom and the temple reality I have been describing needs to be addressed.

There is a second problem, not so much an issue in my reconstruction of Jesus, but a hurdle which he would have undoubtedly faced, if my account is accurate. It is the problem of the land and its violated purity. Even if Jesus saw the temple elites as priestly pretenders and his own following as rightful heirs to the cultus, this reassignment of roles does not necessarily explain how the desecrations of the standing priesthood would be reversed. On the assumption that the carpenter saw his native Palestine as having been despoiled, largely on account of its inhabitants' toxic failure to observe jubilee, then one might expect his movement not just to clarify the nature of true righteousness, but also to articulate some mechanism by which the desecrated land could be restored – or at least be shown as restored. The declaration of jubilee and the corresponding symbolic reappropriation of the land were necessary conditions for renewed worship within Israel, but these were by themselves not sufficient conditions. There had to be some tangible assurance that the desecrated land had in effect been exchanged for a newly sanctified space. What would have made this task particularly difficult was the fact that the Judaism of the day did not seem to have any ready-made or agreed-upon expectations as to what such assurance looked like. *That* Yahweh intended to re-consecrate the land was beyond dispute; *how* and *when* he was going to do – or had done – this remained an altogether open question.[3]

In the present chapter, I will suggest that these two issues, the kingdom's relationship to the eschatological temple and the problem of the ritually impure land, can actually be seen as converging and informing each other within two of Jesus' most characteristic activities: first, his healing and exorcising a good number of troubled individuals, and second, his eating with a variety of table companions, including some pretty unsavory ones. To describe these two aspects of Jesus' life, John Dominic Crossan uses the taxonomy

---

[3] Second-Temple Judaism's ambivalence on this point comes to concrete expression, for example, in 1 Maccabees. Uncertain as to what to do with the altar desecrated under the pogrom of Antiochus IV, the Hasmoneans 'thought it best to tear it down . . . and stored the stones in a convenient place on the temple hill until a prophet should come to tell what to do with them' (1 Macc. 4.45–46).

of 'magic and meals'. My own categories will be almost the same, less the alliteration: first, healing and exorcism, and then, second, meals. Working my way from particulars to more general statements regarding Jesus' aims, I seek to show that these two sets of behaviors signal the inauguration of the kingdom and, simultaneously, the creation of renewed sacred space. Proper consideration of healing/exorcism and meals will ultimately lead us to see that the kingdom of God is actually one and the same as the eschatological temple being made present. This co-identification provides a crucial backdrop; by it, we better understand how Jesus brought together his eschatology (vision of the end) and ethics (the good life). Ultimately, my claim that Jesus saw himself as the temple will lastingly commend itself only inasmuch as it provides a convincing explanation of the data and *a posteriori* holds heuristic promise for theological and ethical reflection.

Healing and exorcism

Healing

Whether Jesus did heal or even could heal raises a host of historiographical and philosophical issues which cannot be fully resolved here. I will take up these questions very briefly in my discussion of exorcism (where our modern scientific sensibilities risk more serious affront), but for the present it is enough to assume (1) that Jesus perceived himself to be a healer, and (2) that his public shared in this perception. Neither of these points is very controversial among scholars these days.[4]

In regarding Jesus as a healer, we see a figure who is not alone on the horizon of the first-century world. Others, both within Judaism and outside of it, were known to heal all kinds of illnesses. In many of these cases, the source of the healing was thought to be inherent within the healer himself or herself. By virtue of a certain intrinsic power, often accompanied by certain rituals or incantations, such a person could purportedly bring about real transformation in the bodies of the unwell. We might term healings of this kind as magical.[5]

Alternatively, healings could also be undertaken with reference to a particular deity, and when they were, location was often highly relevant. To be more exact, in cases of non-magical healing in antiquity, the role of

---

[4] See, e.g., Crossan 1991: 320; Blackburn 1994; Davies 1995; Theissen and Merz 1998 [1996]: 281–315; Twelftree 1999; Eve 2002. Meier (1994: 630–1) summarizes the matter well: 'Put dramatically but with not too much exaggeration: if the miracle tradition from Jesus' public ministry were to be rejected *in toto* as unhistorical, so should every other Gospel tradition about him. For if the criteria of historicity do not work in the case of the miracle tradition . . . [t]he question would simply have to be abandoned.'

[5] Crossan (1991: 304–10) originally framed 'magic' in purely socio-political terms, but later on, as Powell (1998: 97) notes, seems to have backed down from this position under criticism.

temple could hardly be overstated. In Judaism, no less than in Greco-Roman paganism, when the sick and diseased found no relief in either physicians or medicine, they would often go to the temple of their healing god. Temple visitation was important not simply in order to show true earnestness on the part of the supplicant, but simply because the ancient world took seriously the concept of sacred space. (The concept of sacred space in turn – much against our westernized judgment – reserves ahead of time the deity's right to work in a special way in a special place.) It made sense to go 'to the source', that is, the god's earthly seat, not least because in the ancient mentality, holy space was *de facto* healing space.[6]

The connection between cultic space and healing is particularly strong in ancient Judaism, for it was understood that the temple was the locus of creative and re-creative power – and what is bodily healing if not a form of re-creation? Having alluded above to the overlap between Jewish notions of temple and creation, amply attested in the secondary literature, I will not belabor the point.[7] Suffice it to say that when the temple was built, it was designed as a microcosm of creation, for in some sense it *was* creation. The wash basins, the altar, the temple veil – the major fixtures of the temple area – were all symbolic components of the universe; they corresponded, respectively, to the sea, earth, and heavens. The ark, hidden mysteriously within the Holy of Holies, was Yahweh's footstool; above the ark, nothing at all, for God is unseen.[8] Yahweh inhabits, sustains, and rules creation from within the inner sanctuary, even as, paradoxically, he takes his throne in the heavenly temple above. In praying to Yahweh as resident in Zion, Jewish supplicants were essentially asking the author of light and life and all that exists to change the creational script.[9] When it came to divine healing (and all healing was ultimately seen as occurring through divine agency), there was no better place to find it than in the temple.[10]

Jesus' acts of healing easily lend themselves to being interpreted within just this cultic context. The evangelists report that Jesus made the blind to see, the lame to walk, the lepers to be whole, the deaf to hear, and the dead to live again (Matt. 11.5//Luke 7.22). Whether some or all these predications are intended in a metaphorical sense, the Gospels nevertheless describe Jesus' healing in realistic terms, effecting real physical transformation. Similar attestation is recorded in other, independent sources as well.[11] Whatever was actually taking place in these healing encounters (and certain scholars have been led by their metaphysical pre-commitments to pre-empt certain options

---

[6] See Hogan 1992; Avalos 1995: 56–72, 192–222, 299–394; Petsalis-Diomidis 2005.
[7] See above, Chapter 4, pp. 139–40. On the fluidity between creational and cultic images in ancient Jewish texts, see Levenson 1984; Hayward 1996; Beale 2004: 31–38; Klawans 2006: 111–44.
[8] 1 Chron. 28.2; Pss. 99.5; 132.7; *4 Ezra* 6.1.
[9] On prayers to Yahweh in his temple, see, e.g., Pss. 5.7; 11.4; 18.6; 20.2; 2 Chron. 6.20.
[10] Also, see Levenson 1986 [1976]: 11–13.
[11] See *Hul.* 2.22–23; *b. Sanh.* 43a; cf. Sanders 1985: 166.

or prescind from the question altogether), it is, as I have said, certainly clear that Jesus claimed to be a healer and that even his fiercest opponents granted the point. That the itinerant Jesus attained his fame primarily through his therapeutic abilities, together with the fact that the temple was the primary venue for healing within Judaism, makes it altogether plausible that Jesus' healing ministry, which he apparently shared with his disciples (Matt. 10.1; Mark 3.15), was meant to mark off the movement as the mobile embodiment of the temple. While it would be difficult to infer Jesus' self-identification with the temple simply on the evidence of his healing actions, this does not preclude us from saying that Jesus, in his role as healer, was giving symbolic reinforcement to his basic claim. For my overall argument, Jesus' acts of healing furnish corroborative (as opposed to probative) evidence.[12]

Exorcism

While Jesus histories of an earlier day had a chronic tendency to demythologize the evangelists' accounts of Jesus' exorcisms, translating what 'befuddled first-century folk' thought of as demon possession into what we as 'enlightened humanity' now know as mental illness or hysteria, times have changed: more recent New Testament scholarship has shown signs of wiggling loose from the straitjacket-like assumptions of such epistemologically unself-conscious rationalism. For some modern-day interpreters, this kind of demythologization might seem necessary on both a theological and historical level in order to make sense of Jesus' actions. But the complications which typically attend this risky procedure far outweigh any derivable hermeneutical benefit. The difficulty we face is this: that in providing a historically critical account of Jesus the exorcist, we as scholars have placed him and his contemporaries on a cultural map which they would have found utterly alien and unrecognizable.

Against such anachronism, and its entailed reductionism, which follows from what Charles Taylor calls our 'exclusive humanism', I propose that if we wish to understand Jesus, then we must take him on his own terms and in his own context.[13] A step in this direction in our analysis of Jesus the exorcist is to acknowledge that whatever theoretical or moral misgivings we might have in regard to things like demons and demonic possession, the ancient

---

[12] As Herzog (2000: 131) puts it more stringently: 'Insofar as God has chosen "a son of man" to declare forgiveness and mediate healing power, God has rejected the temple priesthood and opened an alternative way.' The eschatological context for Jesus' healings can also, I think, be established. The point is certainly relevant to my argument but, standing at several removes from my immediate interest, must await another space.

[13] Taylor (2007: 569) contends 'that the power of materialism today comes not from the scientific "facts", but has rather to be explained in terms of the power of a certain package uniting materialism with a moral outlook, the package we could call "atheist humanist", or exclusive humanism'.

Jew assumed both of these as unquestioned realities. By the writing of Tobit, several centuries before Jesus' time, Judaism had already developed an advanced demonology. And in the first century (CE), most Hellenized Jews and pagan Greeks alike shared a belief in the spiritual world, populated by malignant, personal forces. Thus we find both Greek and Rabbinic historians looking back, quite unflinchingly, on their favorite first-century exorcists: the Rabbi Hanina ben Dosa or the Neo-Pythagorean Apollonius among them.[14] If history records that Jesus cast out demons, he had some company.

Jesus' activities as an exorcist must also be situated within a trajectory that would carry on among his followers long after his death. Canonical and non-canonical texts speak abundantly to the practice of exorcism in the early Church.[15] Quite clearly, the early Church thought of itself as taking on the mantle of Jesus' role as exorcist in a realistic sense. To suppose for some reason that Jesus and his post-Easter followers did not see themselves along similar lines not only removes the most likely explanation for the early Church's characteristic practices but also imposes an arbitrary and historically unwarranted fissure. Just as exorcism was an integral part of the early Church's life and practice, the same obtains for the historical Jesus. The historian who dismisses the Gospel accounts of Jesus' exorcism as fictive mythography *a priori* is therefore also obliged to apply the same scalpel to exorcism as it continued to be practiced through church history. The historian may of course exercise just this option, but in so doing he or she must recognize that this move leaves matters far more unexplained than explained. If the goal of history is ultimately a constructive one, then the blunt instrument of rationalism brings us no closer to our goal.

This is not to commend going back to an anachronistic, pre-critical reading of the Gospels, but rather to refuse our own western dogmatism unlimited license to foreclose upon the text. It is not the role of the fair-minded historian to pronounce the evangelists' accounts of Jesus' exorcisms dead on arrival, for this almost inevitably presumes, quite mistakenly, that the ancient writers had great difficulty distinguishing observable phenomena from mythography. At bottom, such presumption is nothing more than a re-iteration of the tired Enlightenment myth, namely, that what sets us moderns apart from those pre-moderns we study is our unique ability to separate out scientific observation from tribal interpretation. (The myth is of course self-legitimizing: once you dispense with it, the foundations of the Enlightenment project as a whole, including its distinctive approaches to history, begin to erode.) I would suggest that people of the first-century world, no less than us, knew that they lived in a world of facts and were indeed ultimately constrained by those same facts in their efforts to explain reality.

---

[14] For the former, see *y. Ber.* 1.9d; *y. Maʿas Š.* 5.56; *b. Ber.* 34b; *Eccl. Rab.* 1; for the latter, see Philostratus, *Life of Apollonius of Tyana*. See Twelftree 1993: 23–6.

[15] Twelftree 2007.

We as twenty-first-century historians should reserve the right to disagree with first-century interpretation of its own sensory perceptions or to offer specific hypotheses as to how the ancient thought-world may have distorted those same perceptions as they came to be preserved, but it is only epistemological hubris which permits us to take metaphysically untidy facts and sweep them under the rug. Many New Testament scholars are now finally putting away the old prejudice relating to the reported facts, and it is high time.

The story of the Gergesene demoniac as history

To one set of reported facts we now turn: in this case, an episode recorded in Mark 5.1–20, a passage which recounts Jesus' meeting a demon-possessed man who (or whose demons) went by the name of 'Legion'.[16] The text reads as follows:

> They came to the other side of the sea, to the country of the Gerasenes. And when he had stepped out of the boat, immediately a man out of the tombs with an unclean spirit met him. He lived among the tombs; and no one could restrain him any more, even with a chain; for he had often been restrained with shackles and chains, but the chains he wrenched apart, and the shackles he broke in pieces; and no one had the strength to subdue him. Night and day among the tombs and on the mountains he was always howling and bruising himself with stones. When he saw Jesus from a distance, he ran and bowed down before him; and he shouted at the top of his voice, 'What have you to do with me, Jesus, Son of the Most High God? I adjure you by God, do not torment me.' For he had said to him, 'Come out of the man, you unclean spirit!' Then Jesus asked him, 'What is your name?' He replied, 'My name is Legion; for we are many.' He begged him earnestly not to send them out of the country. Now there on the hillside a great herd of swine was feeding; and the unclean spirits begged him, 'Send us into the swine; let us enter them.' So he gave them permission. And the unclean spirits came out and entered the swine; and the herd, numbering about two thousand, rushed down the steep bank into the sea, and were drowned in the sea. The swineherds ran off and told it in the city and in the country. Then people came to see what it was that had happened. They came to Jesus and saw the demoniac sitting there, clothed and in his right mind, the very man who had had the legion; and they were afraid. Those who had seen what had happened to the demoniac and to the swine reported it. Then they began to beg Jesus to leave their neighborhood. As he was getting into the boat, the man who had been possessed by demons begged him that he might be with him. But Jesus refused, and said to him, 'Go home to your friends, and tell them how much the Lord has done for you, and what mercy he has shown you.' And he went away and began to proclaim in the Decapolis how much Jesus had done for him; and everyone was amazed.[17]

---

[16] The parallels in Matt. 8.28–34 and Luke 8.26–39 are shorter and presumed to be later.
[17] Mark 5.1–20.

While the historicity of this astounding episode is variously granted, questions still arise regarding certain portions of the narrative and their historical worth.[18] First of all, there have been difficulties in identifying the precise location of the event. On consideration of the three best text-critical alternatives, commentators generally take Mark as having originally noted that all this occurred in the 'country of the Gerasenes' (5.1), which puts us somewhere in the neighborhood of modern-day Jerash (Gerasa). While this is theoretically possible, we are still left to wonder how a town some thirty miles southeast of the Sea of Galilee could possibly provide the setting for a scene which ends with two thousand pigs plunging into the same sea. Pounding hooves over rocky hill and dale, even the fittest of the pigs would die of exhaustion before making it anywhere near the shore! Second, Mark's description of a shackle-ripping man and self-drowning pigs seems to beggar belief. The account is said to be more the stuff of superhero comic-strips than anything resembling human experience. For some, these details are best explained not as factual report but as the effort of the early Church to underscore the fantastic effectiveness of the exorcism. Third, the denouement of the story (vv. 16–20), which has Jesus sending the former demoniac back home into the Decapolis in order that he might 'tell them how much the Lord has done for you, and what mercy he has shown you' (5.19), has the smell of early Christian missiology, potentially calling itself if not the whole pericope into historical question. For one or more of these reasons, a number of scholars have come to see the passage as patchwork of fact and fancy – or as fancy altogether.

While the list of objections to Mark 5.1–20 as a unified historical account appears at first sight to be rather daunting, I believe that our accepting the text as reasonably accurate reportage requires no special pleading, but only a willingness to hold some of our well-entrenched prejudgments more lightly. As for the location of the miracle, this is difficult to pin down simply because the conflicting manuscript evidence for Mark 5.1 leaves us with no decisively best reading. True, the reading of 'Gergesenes' commends itself by virtue of being the more difficult (and therefore in theory the less likely to be inserted later) reading. But here I suggest that the better part of wisdom is to chalk up this particular more difficult reading, which in this case leaves us with a monstrously large stage for the miracle, to the hand of a geographically challenged scribe. On the widely held assumption that the cycle of miracles to which Mark 5.1–20 belongs was pre-Markan and therefore probably stemmed from a mind with a decent knowledge of Palestinian geography, we should assume rather as a matter of course that the earliest traditionalists knew enough to know which town was which.[19] For this reason,

---

[18] On the methodological difficulties inherent in these assessments, see Craffert 2008: 3–76.

[19] On Mark 5.1–20 as part of a larger, contiguous pre-Markan tradition, see Achtemeier 2008: 67–8.

either of the two alternatives at 5.1, 'Gadara' or 'Gergesa', is to be preferred. The former option (attested in manuscripts A and C) would put us in the modern-day Um Qeis, bringing us twenty-five miles closer to the water. But since this reading may have easily entered the manuscript tradition through the influence of Matthew 8.28, we are left with 'Gergesa', a reading which, though not commanding the weightiest manuscripts, does show the broadest distribution among the three possibilities. Both Origen and Eusebius lend support by locating the miracle near this town; its first-century existence is confirmed by rabbinic and archaeological evidence.[20] This site (identifiable with modern-day Kursi on the northeast coast of the Sea of Galilee) not only boasts a steep cliff plunging into the waters below, but also sits alongside one of Herod's important citadels at Hippos (a point to which I will return momentarily).[21]

As for the bizarre actions of the demoniac and the pigs, we should be on guard against a rash skepticism. Quite apart from the reality or non-reality of demonic forces, it may be observed that in the field of mental health, incidents which involve super-human displays of strength are not unheard-of. And, true, while it may be unusual for pigs to stampede *en masse* and drown (skeptics remind us that swine are both independent thinkers *and* adept swimmers!), we should not lose sight of the fact that Mark is self-consciously depicting all this as a miraculous event and would have heartily agreed that the animals' behavior was unusual to say the least. Still, 'unusual' is not the same thing as impossible. It doesn't convince to insist that such behavior is absolutely beneath an agitated swineherd when most of us have taken in reports of human beings stampeding, even to a drowning death.[22] Along these lines, it is equally a misreading of the scene to think that the sub-plot of the drowning pigs was the early Church's inventive and belated way of proving Jesus' effectiveness as an exorcist.[23] It must be recalled that for the ancient exorcist, getting the spirits out was usually only half the job. The next step often involved transferring the demonic spirits or illness to another carrier, be it water or a stone or dogs or pigs.[24] Just because Jesus is not described as executing this transference in other exorcism accounts, this does not mean that he never did or that his decision to do so here would have been out of place.

Finally, as for the event being dramatically reworked in order to stir the Church to its mission to the Gentiles, this argument too has only limited force. While it is probable that the Gergesene demoniac was a Gentile and

---

[20] See brief but fine discussion, along with bibliography, in Edwards 2002: 153–4.
[21] For further discussion of the text-critical question, see Annen 1976: 201–6.
[22] As has sadly and recently happened in Varanasi (India) just several months before my writing this.
[23] Notably, Annen (1976: 192) sees the pigs' stampeding response as overly spectacular and thus a deal-breaker so far as historicity is concerned.
[24] See Twelftree 1993: 75–6; Collins 2007: 270.

that this is a matter of significance for Mark, there are few signs that the evangelist is *mainly* interested in highlighting this point in the story, as seems to be the case, say, with the Syro-Phoenecian woman (Mark 7.24–30). And, true, while it is often observed that the episode occurs in 'Gentile territory', the point should not be over-pressed. The territory on the east side of the Sea of Galilee was in fact originally Jewish before the incursion of the Romans under Pompey, and continued – so archaeology tell us – to witness a ponderous Jewish presence down into Jesus' own day.[25] Moreover, the former demoniac's response of telling his story 'in the Decapolis' would have involved his going not only to distinctively 'Gentile areas', but 'Jewish areas' as well.[26] The story may have lent itself reasonably well to the early Christians as they sought to motivate one another in their missionary endeavors, but there is little explicit indication in the text that suggests it was invented for this purpose.

Objections to the basic integrity of this passage as a historical window on Jesus fall short.[27] Their force typically derives from not only speculative source-critical hypotheses, involving multiple layers of tradition rooted in unsubstantiated settings,[28] but also a strange determination to distance Jesus, who was obviously regarded as remarkable in his own time, from remarkable actions. As an organic unity, Mark's account in its major components coheres well with the details of Palestinian geography and fits the broader tradition that ascribes exorcistic abilities to Jesus. Its usefulness as a datum in historical Jesus studies remains intact.

Jesus and the 'unclean spirit'

This being the case, an initial point of interest lies in the fact that the demoniac is described as having an 'unclean spirit' (5.2, 8). While first-century Judaism was already fully cognizant of a connection between the demonic and the impure, the phrase is unusual not only on account of its relative infrequency as a way of referring to demons, but also, and all the more so, on account of its frequency in the synoptic tradition.[29] The distribution of the phrase in the Gospels forbids us to think of it as peculiar to Mark; instead, it makes most sense to attribute the expression to a fairly stable, pre-Markan

---

25 Meyers 1997: 62; Collins 2007: 267.

26 One of the most important cities in the Decapolis was Scythopolis, which sat along the trade route on the western side of the Jordan. See Parker 1975: 437–41.

27 Although his incomplete grasp of history of religions backgrounds (in particular, ancient exorcistic techniques) prevented him from admitting a historical core, Bultmann (1968 [1921]: 210) affirmed that 'clearly this story is essentially intact in its original form'.

28 So Collins 2007: 266; *pace* Pesch 1972; Meier 1991: 650.

29 While the notional connection between 'unclean' and a demonic spirit occurs, e.g., in 1QapGen 20.16–28; the phrase 'unclean spirit', apparently deriving from Zech. 13.2, occurs with limited range and frequency: 1QS 4.22; 4Q444; 11Q5; *T. Ben.* 5.1–2 (see discussion in Wahlen 2004: 24–68). Its usage in the synoptic tradition is stunning by comparison: outside Mark 5.1–20, see Matt. 12.43; Mark 1.23, 26; 3.30; 7.25; 9.25 (2×); Luke 4.33; 9.42; 11.24.

tradition which broadly impacted the synoptic texts.[30] As to who popularized this term as a designation of the demonic, we could hardly do better than locate its origins within the earliest community, perhaps even with Jesus himself.

The latter possibility becomes increasingly likely on several considerations. First, as the past fifteen or so years of scholarship has now recognized, it was pre-eminently Jesus (and not the early Church) who framed so much of his ministry in terms of cultic purity: clean and unclean.[31] Obviously, within the first-century Palestinian Jewish context, cultic purity was an issue of immense importance for observant Jews, and Jesus – despite certain appearances to the contrary – does not seem to have been an exception to the rule. Moreover, discussions revolving around issues of clean and unclean became progressively moot within the early Church (Mark 7.19; Acts 11.9), and in the New Testament literature outside of Palestine, such terminology is fairly rare except in a transposed ethical sense. In short, if we are forced to choose between the setting of Jesus and that of the early Church in stipulating the origins of the phrase 'unclean spirit', we would on these grounds be more inclined to the former.

Whether it was Jesus or the early Church who introduced the phrase 'unclean spirit' also depends on some consideration of its meaning within the scriptural context. Its only occurrence is found in Zechariah 13:

> On that day, says the LORD of hosts, I will cut off the names of the idols from the land, so that they shall be remembered no more; and also I will remove from the land the prophets and the *unclean spirit*.[32]

But before attending to the meaning of this verse within its co-text, we must first inquire into the likelihood that Jesus concerned himself with the passage at all. I believe that he did and that this can be shown, in the first place, on a brief overview of Zechariah's oracle and its dramatization in Jesus' actions. The verse Zechariah 13.2 is itself contained within a larger section of scripture (Zechariah 9—14). Following a word of judgment assuring that Israel's enemies will be cleared from the land to make way for the faithful (Zech. 9.1–7), the oracle continues:

> Then I will encamp at my house as a guard, so that no one shall march to and fro; no oppressor (*yiggoś*) shall again overrun them, for now I have seen with my own eyes. Rejoice greatly, O daughter Zion! Shout aloud, O daughter Jerusalem! Lo, your king comes to you; triumphant and victorious is he, humble (*'änî*) and riding on a donkey, on a colt, the foal of a donkey.[33]

---

[30] So, too, Klutz 1999: 161; Wahlen 2004: 88.
[31] Chilton 1996; Kazen 2002; Klawans 2006.
[32] Zech. 13.2.
[33] Zech. 9.8–9.

Within Zechariah these verses form part of a larger chapter focusing on a royal figure who is paradoxically triumphant and humble or, better, poor (*'ānî*). As one of the *'ānî*, the same royal figure belongs to a category of people who suffer at the hands of the powerful (7.10) and count themselves among the flock slated for slaughter (11.7). In Zechariah 9.8–9, the appearance of the poor shepherd-king is associated with Yahweh defending his temple against marauders; that is, those who 'oppress'.[34] Interestingly, the verbal root (*ngś*) behind our translation 'oppressor' in Zechariah 9.8, used sparingly in the Hebrew scriptures, invokes both the Exodus story and certain Deuteronomic legislation involving debt remittance. In these texts the agents of oppression are, respectively, Pharaoh's taskmasters (Exod. 3.7; 5.6, 10, 13–14) and those who refused to cancel the debt of a fellow Israelite (Deut. 15.2–3). While the modern exegete would do well to avoid inferring too much semantic payload from such wide-spanning links, we are less interested in what the historical Zechariah meant than in how he would have been understood by a Jew like Jesus. And for the first-century Jewish reader, scripture always interpreted scripture: the 'oppressor' in Zechariah 9.8 would have been quite naturally – perhaps even necessarily – regarded as an instantiation of the Egyptian taskmaster and the greedy Israelite creditor. Such meaning could not have been far from the prophet's mind, in any case, especially since the shepherd-king is the one who on Yahweh's behalf would reverse the unjust conditions afflicting the disenfranchised poor (Zech. 7.8–9), pay back their enemies (9.10–15; 10.1–3; etc.), and perhaps even witness the destruction of the temple with its despoiled shepherds (11.1–3). Once the righteous poor were delivered along with the shepherd through the tribulation (13.7–9), true worship could resume (14.6–21). Out of the kaleidoscopic array of prophetic imagery, a compelling messianic storyline begins to emerge: the shepherd-king will come to suffer with a view to releasing the poor from exile and the thrall of pagan creditors, and the final goal of restoring proper worship in an idealized temple.[35]

And, significantly enough, Zechariah's shepherd-king comes down from the Mount of Olives (Zech. 14.4), towards Jerusalem on a donkey (9.9), and all on account of the 'blood of the covenant' (11.11). He comes, in other words, much in the same way that the historical Jesus came to Jerusalem. This does not begin to touch on the likely relevance of the broader Zecharian plot, where Yahweh's poor are pitted against their 'oppressors', to Jesus' socio-economic reform and critique of official leadership. Jesus did not correlate his own actions with that of the shepherd-king in an atomistic way. Rather, it was the broader prophetic narrative which prompted him to re-enact the scriptural storyline in his own temple movement. This is in keeping with other like-minded revolutionary figures of his day. As Craig Evans states:

---

[34] On the messianic import of this figure, see Schmidt 1997.
[35] A similar story plays out in Ezekiel 40—48.

[G]iven the observation that other Jewish figures in the late second Temple period acted out scriptural patterns and oracles, we should resist the 'critical' impulse to assign scriptural correlations in the Gospel narratives to the theological and literary creativity of the evangelists (or tradents before them). In my judgment it is probable that Jesus' behavior while in Jerusalem was guided by elements and themes in Zechariah.[36]

Not only 'while in Jerusalem', but throughout his career, Jesus drew deeply and self-consciously on the post-exilic prophet.

From here one can hardly resist supposing that Jesus interpreted his own conflict with the temple against the backdrop of – among other texts – Zechariah 13. Here is a passage which tells of the clash between the true, Davidic 'shepherd' of Yahweh (v. 7), on the one side, and the 'false prophets' (vv. 2–6) who abuse their charge as they are carried along by the 'unclean spirit' (v. 2), on the other. Jesus' conflict with the temple dignitaries of course comes to a head at his arrest, a moment which, according to Mark 14.27// Matthew 26.31, he seems to have anticipated and interpreted in light of Zechariah 13.7. The ascription of this Zecharian verse to Jesus himself is well accepted by many scholars today, in large part because 13.7–9 coheres splendidly with Jesus' assumed role as the tribulation-bearing shepherd.[37] The narrative of Zechariah 13 is not only plausible as background for Jesus' self-understanding, it is patently likely.

Given Jesus' recurring self-emplotment within Zechariah, including not least the thirteenth chapter, I conclude that it was the master himself who pulled the phrase 'unclean spirit' from Zechariah 13.2 and pushed it to the forefront of the community's consciousness. Not only is there no better explanation for the univocal application of the term in the earliest tradition, it also fits hand-in-glove with Jesus' self-perception as I have reconstructed it. Comparing his own conflict with the temple to that which takes place between Zechariah's shepherd-king and the false prophets, he applied the phrase 'unclean spirit' not only to fill out the scriptural interpretive grid which he commended, but to give distinctive significance to his own exorcistic powers.

At the risk of 'over-reading' Jesus' dependence on Zechariah 13 (and 13.2 in particular), it is possible to draw from this template certain implications which shed light on his ministry of exorcism. True as it may be that Jesus' first biographers tended to emphasize his power over the demonic as evidence of his messianic authority (*exousia*), the *primary* interests of the historical Jesus seem to have lain more directly elsewhere. For one who dispensed forgiveness to the individual Israelite as a parabolic token of Yahweh's forgiveness of the nation as a whole, his exorcisms seem to have served an analogous double

---

[36] Evans 1999: 388; so too Kim 1987: 138–40; Wright 1996: 586; McKnight 2005: 177–205.
[37] Meyer 2002 [1979]: 216; Wright 1996: 599–600; Theissen and Merz 1998 [1996]: 107–8; Dunn 2003: 89; Pitre 2005: 466–78.

duty: they were not intended simply for the sake of the individuals, but were public emblems of an impending upheaval, just the kind of redemptive-historical shift envisaged in Zechariah 13. While most contemporary readers of the Gospels are conditioned to think of the afflictions of an 'unclean spirit' as occurring strictly on an individualized level, we are probably on firmer ground in thinking of this ministry of exorcism as indicating something far deeper and broader – the eschatological removal of a spirit that bedevils the land as a whole.[38]

This insight in turn sharpens our understanding of Jesus' ministry as a whole and the temple cleansing in particular. On reconsideration, it seems that the final target of Jesus' temple action was not the idolatrous 'false prophets' who occupied the high-priestly office: the real enemy consisted of the invisible forces of darkness which inspired them. This much at any rate can be inferred from Zechariah 13.2: 'I will cut off the names of [1] the idols from the land ... I will remove from the land [2] the prophets and [3] the unclean spirit'. Zechariah's terrible troika is hardly unique to this text but is simply a restatement of what Judaism assumed as a matter of course: wherever you find false leaders in Israel, an unclean spirit and ensnaring idols are not far below the surface.[39] Along these lines, Israel's moral failure at the highest religio-political levels, spotlighted so dramatically in Jesus' temple cleansing, was symptomatic of a nation-wide apostasy. But beneath, behind, in, and through it all lingered the influence of malignant spiritual forces. Because demons and idols were thought to enjoy a symbiotic existence, Jesus knew that any attempt to restore the purity of the land must include a purging of the 'unclean spirit' *and* its venerated haunts. This suggests that Jesus intended to prosecute his holy campaign not only within some invisible sphere of reality beyond ordinary human perception, but also on the plain of observable phenomena, among the visible symbols and public practices – the very idols – to which the unclean spirit gave rise.

The meaning of exorcism

In situating Jesus' exorcistic activity within the context of Zechariah 13, that is, as a symbolic expression of Yahweh's imminent intention to purify the land of idolatry and dark spiritual forces, we recognize its inextricable political charge within the first-century context. Clearly, it would have been impossible for Jesus or anyone in his community to dissociate the problem of the invisible 'unclean spirit' from the very visible Roman presence in the land. The Roman Gentiles threatened the purity of the Jewish theocracy not

---

[38] This sense is preserved in the synoptic tradition, including here, where paradoxically the unclean spirit dwells in the demoniac (Mark 5.8), but more principally the demoniac literally dwells 'in an unclean spirit' (v. 2), so as to suggest the spirit being something closer to a totalizing, cosmic force than a contagion.

[39] Ps. 106.34–39; Ezekiel 13—14.

so much on account of who they were, but on account of what they did; the basic problem was not one of ethnicity, but of false worship.[40] Like murder and certain forms of sexual transgression, idolatry was seen to be intrinsically defiling.[41] Throughout the post-exilic era, what made close relations (be it intermarriage or table fellowship) with Gentiles unthinkable was the assumption that they through their idolatry lived in a protracted state of defilement. Such association would have been potentially problematic not only in terms of the individual Jew's freedom to enter temple grounds, but also in terms of Israel's long-term freedom to remain in the land (Lev. 18.24–25). Like the spate of intermarriages which so vexed the post-exilic community (Ezra 9—10), idolatry was less a personal problem (although it was a personal problem indeed) than a social issue with social consequences.[42] As pious first-century Jews saw it, linking hands with the Romans was the steep slippery slope to the incursion of idolatry, demonic spirits, and ultimately the desecration of the land, which had been one of the central precipitating causes of the exile.

But it was not simply the Romans in their capacity as idol-worshipping Gentiles that raised red flags for Israel, but the Romans in their capacity, well, as Romans. By Jesus' day, the great empire had established quite a long and bloodied track record for itself: by all accounts, it was determined to use whatever force necessary to extend and secure its imperial interests. Along these lines, it is with as much realism as rhetoric that the tribal British chieftain Calgacus rallies his forces, when he says that the Romans are the

> robbers of the earth, for after depleting the land by altogether ravaging it, they ransack the sea. If the enemy is rich, they are greedy; if poor, they are ruthless. Neither the East nor the West has satisfied them. Unique among all people they lust for domination over those in poverty and opulence, and do so with equal desire. Robbery, massacre, seizure – these they call by the false name of empire; they make a wasteland and call it peace.[43]

Undoubtedly, almost any Jew of Jesus' day would have wholeheartedly agreed with Calgacus' summary, including, I think, Jesus himself. True, while Israel had in some sense brought its political problems on itself through covenantal disobedience, it was also quite clear in the Jewish mind that the nation (along perhaps with many others) would one day be avenged by a still higher power and that the Romans would have to answer for their relentless voracity. It was a voracity that on the level of everyday experience was most acutely felt (in economic terms) through taxation and (in military terms) through the

---

[40] To be sure, while at least certain Jews of Jesus' day regarded the Gentiles as inherently unclean, this was only in an indirect sense; cf. Alon 1977: 146–89; Kazen 2002: 8.

[41] See Lev. 19.31; 20.1–3. Klawans (1998) convincingly argues that the defilement from these sins was not merely metaphorical, but actual.

[42] See Hayes 1999.

[43] Tacitus, *Agr.* 30. The translation is my own.

presence of the nearest imperial outpost. Meanwhile, on an ideological level, the imperium's heavy handedness was consistently underwritten by a certain religio-political script, one which attempted to highlight the practical advantages of Roman rule as well as its (alleged) inherent appropriateness. By appealing to the benefits of security and peace, the central propaganda machine routinely sought to legitimize an otherwise amoral pursuit of economic and military dominance. But on a much deeper level, the imperial city and its supporters continued to find warrant for Roman exploits by construing the rest of the known world as satellites of 'the City', and all of history as a lead-up to the climactic establishment of the glorious Principate. Meanwhile, the ethnic superiority of the Roman race was presumed all along. The unlimited pursuit of dominance and wealth were justified on a particularly 'imperium-centric' mapping of time, space, and humanity, all of which then became fully integrated into the religious identity of the *cives* (citizens). It is only in modern times that worship and ideology can be separated: in the first-century world this was not possible. Jesus and his fellow Palestinian Jews would have recognized without question that the Romans' state religion and their quest for domination, both equally inspired by demons, were but two sides of the same coin. Oppressive military self-assertion was merely the outworking of demonic activity – and vice versa.

In this connection, it is worth returning to my earlier point that the exorcism recorded in Mark 5.1–20 was carried out on the northeast shore of the Sea of Galilee, just on the north side of Herod's magnificent fortress in Hippos. The location of this miracle is significant in the first place, since it would have not been a natural stopping-point for either Jesus or, for that matter, anyone of his sensibilities. According to the passage, when he and the disciples land, they arrive close to a gravesite and a space reserved for a large herd of swine. On either count, Jesus the Jew would have considered such an environment an unwelcome one, having the potential to inflict both himself and his disciples with impurity associated with the dead or unclean animals – or both.[44] It is patently unlikely that Jesus sought out this distant stretch of Palestine as a place of respite; the surroundings of Kursi would have not struck any first-century Jew as either a get-away spot or 'the place to be'. From this, I think, we can surmise a certain degree of intentionality in Jesus' visit to the eastern shore. In other words, he arrived at Gergesa with a particular purpose, one might even say a mission. Couple this with the probability that the demoniac, given his extreme condition, seems to have been something of a notorious phenomenon in his own region and beyond, and it soon becomes clear that Jesus sailed where he did because he knew who and what he was going to find there. In this case, too, he likely had a pretty good idea as to what he intended to do.

---

[44] The dead and their resting-places were deemed especially egregious sources of uncleanness; cf. *m. Kelim* 1.1–4.

So then, what were Jesus' aims in approaching the demoniac? One clue presents itself in the possessed man's words to Jesus: 'What have you to do with me, Jesus, Son of the *Most High God*?' (v. 7). As is regularly noted, the phrase 'Most High God' is a peculiarly Gentile way of referring to divinity, and in this context acknowledges both the superiority of Yahweh and Jesus as Yahweh's duly appointed agent.[45] So far as Mark sets it up, then, the components of the pericope combine to depict a titanic clash between, on the one side, Jesus, representative of the 'Most High God', and, on the other side, the gods of the 'unclean spirit'. It is of course a contest which, as the narrative makes clear, Jesus/Yahweh wins decisively. Whereas the attempt to cast Jesus' meeting on the eastern shore as a divine face-off may in theory have been an innovation on the evangelist's part, in my mind it is very hard to accept the intentionality behind the historical Jesus' journey without also admitting his determination to frame the encounter as a demonstration of divine power over the demonic. In other words, Mark's preserved dialogue between Jesus and the demoniac, ultimately initiated by the traveling exorcist, seems to attest to a dynamic that was inherent in the situation itself: by the power of Yahweh, Jesus saw himself as serving public notice to the 'unclean spirit'.

It bears noting here that the name of the demon (or demons) occupying the demoniac was 'Legion'. Pertaining to more than the extremity of the demoniac's condition, the word 'Legion' would have drawn especial attention to the correspondence between the demonic world and the Roman military, which was implicitly understood in any case.[46] That the tradition bothered to preserve the demon's name, together with the fact that the Romans maintained a detachment of the Tenth Legion (*Fretensis*) right next door in Hippos, sways me to think that the inclusion was not politically innocent. As to whether the occurrence of 'Legion' here reflects Mark's hand, the actual word of the demon, or something lying in between, is a slightly more difficult question. While it is true that the Tenth Legion took its place alongside others in combating the First Jewish Revolt, a fact which may prompt us to see the demon's name as redactional, it is also true that the same legion – and only this legion – was at a much earlier point responsible for ruthlessly putting down the Jewish uprising following Archelaus' deposition (6 CE). The Archelaan uprising and its subsequent violent suppression occurred when Jesus was a boy and must therefore have had a lingering impact on his generation's collective memory. The perlocutionary effects of the word 'Legion' against either of these contexts demands a political reading of Mark 5.1–20; as to whether the politics are those of Jesus or Mark is another question.

---

[45] Lane 1974: 183 n. 14; Collins 2007: 268.

[46] The connection between 'Legion' and Rome at Mark 5.9 is developed by, among others, Winter 1961: 129; Hollenbach 1981; Theissen 1983: 255; Wengst 1987: 65–8; Crossan 1991: 313; Myers 2008 [1988]: 190–3.

For several reasons, I submit that Jesus stands behind it. First of all, if, as I have argued, this encounter with the demoniac is a prophetic speech act, in effect declaring that the 'unclean spirit' of pagan Rome was due to be dislodged, then its orchestration makes much more sense as having been the brainchild of Jesus' creativity rather than the fancy of Mark or pre-Markan tradition. I have argued above that the detail of the herd's demise is historically founded. Jesus' exorcism then would have not only effected a substantial loss of animal property, but also, given that the Roman soldiers garrisoned at nearby Hippos would have likely depended on the swine as a food source, served to deprive the legionnaires of a staple delicacy. In this respect, Jesus' measures amounted, albeit in an indirect way, to an act of political sabotage. The symbolic irony could hardly have been lost on those present: the destruction of the pigs would have been a subtle but nonetheless telling indication that Rome was perhaps more vulnerable than it would have otherwise liked to believe, and on a level of which it was largely unaware. It is, however, all these likely details – the nearby presence of the Roman fort, their enjoyment of the swine, the deleterious effects of the swine's destruction on the garrison's diet – that do not so much as receive a hint in Mark's account. Historical reconstruction of Jesus' setting leaves us with a far more incisive anti-Roman polemic than either Mark or his prior tradition was willing to exploit.

My second reason for ascribing the episode's original political freight to Jesus also has to do with the herd of swine. As the Galilean exorcist himself would have been aware, the wild boar was as much symbolic of Torah-based impurity as it was of Roman power. In the first place, the wild boar was the mascot of the Tenth Legion, which occupied Palestine and therefore also Hippos.[47] In the second place, the wild boar was symbolic of both Rome and Roman power, as can be confirmed by the numismatic evidence showing the same animal on Caesar Augustus' coinage. You don't have to be a sports expert to realize that when an over-zealous fan throws a snowball at the opposing team's mascot, it is not really the mascot he is attacking but what the mascot represents. By driving two thousand living Roman mascots into the sea, Jesus was, as it were, throwing his own snowball. He was also of course capitalizing on one very well known dramatic moment to portray another. Mindful of the narratives of creation and Exodus, both containing stories of God's overcoming his opposition in the sea in order to establish sacred space, Jesus saw circumstances on the far shore as an opportunity – and planned accordingly. It was a perfect convergence of factors which Jesus manipulates in order to dramatize a cosmic-level storm, a storm which was now ready to burst in his own time and through his own movement. And at the end of the driving rains, Jesus seemed to reason, a renewed and purified

---

[47] The boar's mascot status may be deduced from its image being affixed to the standards of the legion, as it was to that of the First Legion (*Italica*) and Twentieth Legion (*Victrix*).

space would emerge. In ridding the promised land of the unclean spirit and the quintessential symbol of its human minions, Jesus is clearing sacred space and in effect purifying the land.

Jesus the exorcistic high priest

The establishment of sacred space was of course the remit of the high priest. In the previous chapter, I argued that Jesus, no less than the Qumran community, looked to a final Melchizedek to introduce the last jubilee. However, in the case of the former's convictions, the high-priestly figure turned out to be Jesus himself. The implementation of jubilee was not the only responsibility of the anticipated high priest: the eschatological figure would also deal with Yahweh's enemies and the spirit thereof. Likewise, Jesus is playing not only the role ascribed to the Zecharian shepherd-king, but also the role ascribed to the Melchizedekian high priest. In 11Q13 we read:

> Concerning what scripture says, 'How long will you judge unjustly and show partiality to the wicked? Selah' (Ps. 82.2) the interpretation applies to Belial and the spirits predestined to him, because all of them have rebelled, turning from God's precepts and so becoming utterly wicked. Therefore Melchizedek will thoroughly prosecute the vengeance required by God's statutes. In that day he will deliver them from the power of Belial, and from the power of all the spirits predestined to him ... 'Your divine being' is Melchizedek, who will deliver them from the power of Belial.[48]

The eschatological high priest will restore Israel by delivering the remnant from the demonic power and sitting in judgment on the Gentiles (that is, Yahweh's enemies). Both of these elements of the Melchizedek narrative in turn find their source in Psalm 110, which speaks not only to the high priest's vanquishing of Israel's enemies (vv. 1–2, 5–6), be they human or demonic, but also, and presumably most importantly, to the restoration of proper worship (v. 3). In the psalm the preparation of sacred space is in fact the high priest's climactic task, as it was for the eschatological Melchizedek. On reflection, the ancient Jews' decision to assign an exorcistic role to the one who would bring the eschatological jubilee seems to have its own compelling logic. The socio-economic goal of reappropriating the land to its rightful heirs through jubilee release would be empty without a corresponding removal of the demons and their ideologies which simultaneously oppressed and seduced Israel. The land needed to be not only re-deeded, but also re-purified, for only on a purified land would it be possible to enjoy pure worship. For Jesus no less than the Qumran covenanters, both tasks – crucial for the future salvation of Israel – would fall to the eschatological high priest, Melchizedek.

In discerning the source of Jesus' purifying power, one might linger on two interesting bits of data: Jesus' peculiar style of invocation (or lack thereof)

---

[48] 11Q13 2.11b–13, 24b–25.

and his apparent indifference to surrounding impurity. First, a few comments are in order regarding the way in which Jesus conducted his exorcism. While almost as a rule, ancient exorcistic practices required invocations, chants, charms, and the like, we find in the Jesus tradition a salient absence of any such rituals or props. What we have is merely Jesus' word itself. Drawing on Habermehl, Christian Strecker comments on this observation as follows:

> As already noted, the exorcistic practice of Jesus of Nazareth was similarly lacking in techniques. According to the Jesus tradition, his exorcistic action was confined essentially to the appeal to the demon to leave, the so-called *apopomē* (*exelthe ex*: 'come out of' Mark 1.25; 5.8; 9.25). Apart from that, only a request for a name (Mark 5.9), an *epipomē* (the departure of demons and their entry into swine, according to Mark 5.13), and a prohibition to reenter (Mark 9.25) are mentioned. Corresponding to exorcists who function as mediums, Jesus' effectiveness, to all appearances, was due to his presence, which obviously was regarded as the *presence of some high power manifest in him*. In other words, when casting out demons, Jesus of Nazareth appeared as a *medium of divine power*.[49]

This is no insignificant point. Jesus was confident of his abilities to deal with the possessed, ultimately because he was also confident that the divine power rested not only in his movement but also, in some inscrutable way, within himself in particular.

This may have something to do with the fact that Jesus, though clearly violating the purity codes of his day and clearly, too, incurring in this event what for any other Jew would have been defiling contact in that gravesite, remains unscathed. The question as to how Jesus, as is he presented in this and other pericopae, sat towards purity remains a vibrant one in current scholarly debate, and one which has attracted a handful of various suggestions.[50] Given my argument so far, one plausible explanation for both Jesus' seeming cultic indifference and spare exorcistic technique begins to come to surface. In Judaism, defilement was generally thought to have moved centrifugally, that is, the flow of uncleanness was understood to move outward so as to infect any clean objects that connected with it. The singular exception to this was thought to be the altar, for it was the altar, as the presence of God, which would transform that which was unclean into a purified state. Perhaps Jesus' remarkable lack of concern for his unclean environment in Mark 5.1–20, rather than being evidence of his flouting purity laws, speaks to his conviction that the laws have been redefined according to the eschatological moment. If Jesus was convinced that he himself was the temple, perhaps he reasoned – in a way that other counter-temple groups of

---

[49] Strecker 2002: 126; emphasis added. Likewise, Klutz 1999: 159–60, 164–5.
[50] Sanders (1985: 209–10) doubts that Jesus' handling of purity was controversial within his Judaism at all; similarly, Fredriksen 2000: 197–207; Levine 2006: 21–33. Borg (1984) and Riches (1990), on the other hand, see Jesus as having relaxed purity standards altogether.

his era did not – that he himself was not just the medium of divine power but its very locus on earth. What if, in other words, the location and methods of Jesus' exorcistic practices could be attributed to a radical self-identity as the embodied eschatological temple? For the present, I hold this as a tentative hypothesis, subject to corroboration.[51]

Meals

Among miraculous events ascribed to Jesus in the gospel tradition, few have attracted more speculation than the two-fold event which Mark describes in the Feeding of the Five Thousand (6.30–44) and the Feeding of the Four Thousand (8.1–10). While a few readers stoutly refuse to believe anything like the stories which the evangelist records happened, a sizable bulk of Jesus interpretation happily accepts that the core of these accounts have a secure footing in history, either as one event or two. The feeding event has multiple attestation in spades: with common agreements of the Matthean (Matt. 14.13–21, 15.29–39) and Lukan (Luke 9.10–17) accounts against Mark, and what is likely a separate tradition in John (John 6.1–15), it is possible to discern three lines of tradition (Mark, Q, and John) going back very early, almost certainly originating from the time of Jesus.[52] Whether Jesus actually did multiply the loaves and fishes, as the Gospel writers report, is certainly no inconsequential matter.[53] For my purposes, adjudicating the point would take us too far afield. It will be sufficient to affirm, along with a good deal of historical-critical scholarship, that Jesus did indeed on one or more occasions find himself in a far-off place in the company of a large crowd, which he proceeded to feed in a such way that was publicly deemed as miraculous.[54]

It may be possible to go further and say a few things about the social makeup of these same crowds. First, according to the words of Jesus in the Fourth Gospel, the throngs followed in order to be fed (John 6.25–27). Although the surrounding passage is highly stylized, the remark accords with what we would otherwise assume to be the case. No one minds a free meal and free – not to mention miraculously delivered – food would have been compelling incentive especially for those who could not count on regular mealtimes. Moreover, the crowd's willingness to travel substantial distances

---

[51] This is very close to the view of Kazen (2002: 338–9), who explains Jesus' indifference to impurity in this scene as reflective of the overriding priority of the kingdom.

[52] As rightly stressed by Bammel (1984: 211); Meier 1994: 951–6.

[53] Some take up the standard rationalist reading of the pericope and see the miracle not in the actual multiplication of the loaves and fishes, but in the fact that everyone shared. I admit to being at more than a few family meals where generous-minded self-restraint would have been something of a small miracle. All the same, as Strauss stringently asserts, this way of interpreting the passage is completely at odds with what the four evangelists intend.

[54] Meier (1994: 959–67) provides an excellent defense, which Dunn (2003: 687) commends. See now Blomberg 2009: 238–9.

into remote areas with families in tow suggests that not many among the multitude were anchored in routine employment; many, if not the overwhelming majority, could be supposed to belong to a transient, landless class. In the previous chapter, I offered some reasons as to why Jesus attracted the 'poor and needy'; here we have some indication as to what he did with them: on at least one or two occasions, he led them out into the desert and fed them. The main beneficiaries of these large-scale feedings seem to have been the wandering poor.

A few things may also be inferred about the cultic status of those whom Jesus fed; that is, whether or not they were *kashrut* (ritually clean). If the crowd did indeed consist largely of peasants, then for various reasons it may be assumed almost as a matter of course that some of them were in an uninterrupted state of ritual impurity. The historical record also stresses the size of these crowds, numbering in the thousands. The social status of these desert stragglers together with their sheer number would have made it impossible for Jesus or the disciples to have expected the group meal to have conformed to standards of ritual purity as they were construed in the day. This is significant inasmuch as first-century Judaism maintained strict prescriptions for the Jew *and* his or her table fellows. In the normal course of things, to eat with one who was ritually impure was to incur impurity. But unless the Gospel traditions have deliberately and independently distorted the record, purity concerns do not seem to have entered into the thinking of Jesus and his disciples as they administered these mass feedings.

If the poor and impure attended these gatherings, we also have evidence that at least one meal was attended by Gentiles. In his account of the Feeding of the Four Thousand (Mark 8.1–21), the evangelist takes pains to make this clear. His Jesus remarks, 'Some have come *from a great distance (makrothen)*' (8.3). The adverb appears redactional, undoubtedly serving as a circumlocution for 'Gentiles'.[55] The second feeding, clearly Mark's attempt to present a 'plus-Gentile version' of the earlier Jewish feeding (6.30–44), also seems of a narrative piece with the account of the Syro-Phoenecian Woman (7.24–30), which takes place in the far north (Gentile territory) of Tyre (7.24). The storyline subsequently has Jesus heading towards the sea but by way of the Decapolis (7.31), which of course provided the setting for the episode of the Gergesene Demoniac (5.1–20). Finally, if we tentatively assume that the presence of Pharisees in Dalmanutha (8.10–11) points to a location on the western shore, then Jesus' arrival there by boat (v. 10), rather than walking along the coast, may suggest an origination point on the opposite, eastern (and largely Gentile) shore.[56] The indicators are consistent: Mark wishes his

---

55 On similar usages, see Mark 5.6; 11.13; 14.54; 15.40. On its reference to Gentiles, see Josh. 9.6 (LXX); Isa. 60.4 (LXX); Acts 2.39; 22.21; Eph. 2.11–12.

56 But in this case one must also assume along with the Caesarean recension of Mark 8.10 that the otherwise unknown Dalmanutha is actually Magadala (near present-day Tiberias).

readers to think of the second feeding as occurring in Gentile territory with a good number of Gentile interlopers in attendance.

Without a doubt, there is no light theological freight contained within the fact that the Feeding of the Four Thousand was a 'Gentile miracle', one within a string of several (7.24–8.21), and this payload is underscored by the evangelist's decision to leave subtle geographical clues along the narrative way. But it would be unwarranted to infer from the evangelist's obvious narrative interest in Jesus' activity in non-Jewish surroundings that this setting had little connection to the historical facts. The opposite conclusion seems more likely. In the first place, whatever the chronological relationship between the historical feeding(s) and the historical encounter with the demoniac (5.1–20), the latter's almost certain occurrence on the eastern shore (whether Gadara, Gergesa or Gergesenes) lays a pattern of Jesus' interest in the same parts. If the historical Jesus made his way to the further side of the Jordan on one occasion, why not on several, including the event described in Mark 8.1–21? Second, if Jesus did carry out one public mass feeding prior to the event known as the Feeding of the Four Thousand, and did so in Jewish territory (which seems to be the case if the event was indeed separate), then one might have expected him for the sake of self-preservation to settle on a venue right along the lines of Mark's description. Mindful of John the Baptizer's execution and the brooding presence of Herod's informants (Luke 13.31), Jesus would have surely found any encore feedings performances – politically dangerous enough at the debut – better suited for a stage well outside of his chief critic's jurisdiction. Third, the former disciple of John the Baptizer would have found the desert regions beyond the Jordan to be a familiar stomping ground. John himself, partially to minimize the political effrontery of his movement, stayed within the desert and apparently received Gentile listeners there (Luke 3.10–14). On the assumption that Jesus learned at least a few good tricks from his erstwhile master and as the heir apparent to John's movement who had an interest in continuing at least some aspects of his program, we might well have expected Jesus to have visited the trans-Jordan, much as Mark leads us to believe. The Gentile character of certainly one feeding appears beyond serious question.

This much seems clear: the Jesus tradition represents its hero as having conducted mass meals involving people who (1) matched the socio-economic profile of those Jesus sought to attract, that is, the 'poor'; and who, as such, (2) failed to maintain the level of ritual purity which would have been normally presupposed in a *kashrut* meal; and who (3) included among their numbers, at least on one occasion (even if it was the only occasion), a sizeable contingency of Gentiles. This reconstruction of the constituency of the crowds receives excellent corroboration on our considering what most scholars take to be indisputable, namely, that over more private dinner-tables Jesus consorted shamelessly with 'sinners', including the poor and the ritually unclean. Although there is no evidence that Jesus privately ate with Gentiles, the purity status of some of his dinner companions would have put them only a small remove from the category of 'Gentiles' at any rate. Apparently, Jesus' private meals with such socially poor were only small-scale anticipations or recapitulations of the mass feedings. The striking feature of Jesus' dining habits – and one of the main criticisms which his opponents lay at his feet – was the company he kept. His trespass was that he consorted with the poor, the ritually unclean, and on at least one occasion Gentiles as well. Most shockingly, he did all this with seemingly complete indifference to issues of purity and impurity.

Between the recent and welcome scholarly insistence on Jesus' essential Jewish character, on the one side, and his apparent nonchalance in regard to purity issues, on the other, there is an obvious tension. It is a tension which Jesus scholars have sought to resolve in different ways. In my view, the most promising explanation must be one which not only describes what Jesus (uniquely) believed about purity, but also explains the reasons for his belief. Historical explanations, even explanations within the history of religious ideas, prefer to identify a cause, a precipitating spark.

The most promising 'spark' in my view begins to appear on the observation of two data: the timing of the feedings and the topographical location. In Mark's narrative, the Feeding of the Five Thousand (6.30–44) follows on the heels of Herod's execution of John the Baptizer (6.14–29); the later Feeding of the Four Thousand (8.1–10) is likewise tied to Jesus' remarks regarding the corrupting 'yeast of the Pharisees and that of Herod' (8.15). The tradition which Matthew lays hold of also connects the feeding miracles to John's death: 'Now when Jesus heard this, he *withdrew* (*anechōrēsen*) from there in a boat to a *deserted place* (*erēmon topon*) by himself. But when the crowds heard it, they followed him on foot from the towns . . .'[57] Matthew's word choice to denote Jesus' withdrawal (*anachōreō*) consistently appears in contexts where one is seeking refuge from oppressive political forces; the same pattern obtains, among other places, in the remaining Gospel tradition.[58] Meanwhile Luke connects the Feeding of the Five Thousand (Luke 9.10–17) with Herod's perplexity following his execution of the Baptizer (9.7–9). John alone omits any explicit connection between Herod's actions against John and the feedings, but the note that the feeding took place in Passover season (John 6.4), corroborated by other intimations of Passover in the synoptic Gospels (Mark 8.14–19 par.), would suggest that John also is reporting an event which took place not just close to Passover, but also not long after the Baptizer's death. While it is theoretically possible that the connecting link between John's death and the feeding miracles was forged on the anvil of post-Easter tradition, it makes far more sense to take the pairing of the events as true to historical fact. Any contemporary with an ounce of common sense would have supposed that if Herod was willing to get rid of John, popular

---

[57] Matt. 14.14.
[58] Matt. 2.14, 22; 4.12; 14.13; 15.21; 27.5; Mark 3.7; John 6.15.

as he was with the people, there would be nothing stopping him from making Jesus his next victim: there would also have been no better time for Jesus and his followers to beat a retreat into the wilderness, just as the synoptic tradition recounts. The question it seems is not whether the evangelists' depiction of Jesus' withdrawal after John's death has a footing in history; the question is whether, given the fact of the Baptizer's death, it is plausible for the historical Jesus to have done any differently. There is excellent warrant for supposing that the desert feedings took place soon after word of John's death got out.

Before unpacking the possible significance of this point, it is worthwhile registering a second observation bearing on the locale of Jesus' feedings. Matthew stipulates the topographical setting of the Feeding of the Four Thousand; John does the same for the Feeding of the Five Thousand:

> After Jesus had left that place, he passed along the Sea of Galilee, and he went up *the mountain (to oros)*, where he sat down.[59]

> When Jesus realized that they were about to come and take him by force to make him king, he withdrew again to *the mountain (to oros)* by himself.[60]

The decision of John's Jesus to withdraw to the mountain 'again' implies that the miracle occurred at the same mountain, just as it did for the Feeding of the Four Thousand, according to Matthew. The term *oros* need not signify a 'mountain' in the sense of 'mountain peak'; it is quite possible that for both evangelists something like a high plateau was in view. Thus one need not assume any discrepancy between these witnesses and the designation of the feeding venues elsewhere as a 'deserted place'.[61] While Matthew's special interest in mountains may initially prompt us to see this as a redactional move, and while it is possible that John for his part conformed his narrative to the mountain motif of Ezekiel 34 (vv. 6, 13, 14, 26), the fact that both traditions independently remark on the mountainous setting of the feedings suggests that the detail originates not in any coincidentally shared theological imagination but in historic reality. This is no hard teaching, for as anyone familiar with the geography east of the Sea of Galilee can attest, mountains (such as can fairly be called *oros*) are in no short supply. Moreover, it is *a priori* unlikely that the mountain detail originated as a bit of theological flourish *despite* the facts: given the vast numbers present, the precise location of the feedings must have quickly become a matter of enduring and widespread public knowledge, even to the time of the evangelists. Historically reliable tradition tells us that for whatever reason, Jesus held these gatherings on a mountain. In sum, having argued above that Jesus and the disciples hosted a massive meal with the poor, the unclean, and even the Gentiles in attendance,

---

[59] Matt. 15.29.
[60] John 6.15.
[61] Mark 6.31, 32, 35; Luke 9.12.

I wish to add that Jesus did so shortly after Herod's execution of John and on a mountain-top.

The facts are in, but the facts do not on the surface seem to speak to any obvious intention. So when we ask ourselves what to do with this odd assortment of jigsaw puzzle pieces, perhaps the best first move is to look for a corresponding jigsaw puzzle box-top – some underlying image or rubric – that might make sense of the stray data. The most promising box-top, the most probable underlying rubric, I suggest, is to be found in the prophet Isaiah, in his seminal depiction of the great eschatological meal:

> On that day the LORD will punish the host of heaven in heaven, and on earth the kings of the earth. They will be gathered together like prisoners in a pit; they will be shut up in a prison, and after many days they will be punished. Then the moon will be abashed, and the sun ashamed; for the LORD of hosts will reign on Mount Zion and in Jerusalem, and before his elders he will manifest his glory. O LORD, you are my God; I will exalt you, I will praise your name; for you have done wonderful things, plans formed of old, faithful and sure. For you have made the city a heap, the fortified city a ruin; the palace of aliens is a city no more, it will never be rebuilt. Therefore strong peoples will glorify you; cities of ruthless nations will fear you. For you have been a refuge to the poor, a refuge to the needy in their distress, a shelter from the rainstorm and a shade from the heat. When the blast of the ruthless was like a winter rainstorm, the noise of aliens like heat in a dry place, you subdued the heat with the shade of clouds; the song of the ruthless was stilled. On this mountain the LORD of hosts will make for all peoples a *feast of rich food (mištēh šemānîm)*, a feast of well-aged wines, of rich food filled with marrow, of well-aged wines strained clear. And he will destroy on this mountain the shroud that is cast over all peoples, the sheet that is spread over all nations; he will swallow up death forever. Then the Lord GOD will wipe away the tears from all faces, and the disgrace of his people he will take away from all the earth, for the LORD has spoken. It will be said on that day, Lo, this is our God; we have waited for him, so that he might save us. This is the LORD for whom we have waited; let us be glad and rejoice in his salvation. For the hand of the LORD will rest on this mountain.[62]

A few observations on the text are in order. First, the eschatological meal (25.6) is prompted by a word of judgment against the kings of the earth (Isa. 24.21). Over and against the earthly kings, the Lord himself will reveal his glory before watching elders, and exercise his kingship (24.23); according to Isaiah, when the kingdom of God comes, it will come as a direct response to wayward actions of wicked earthly rulers. The kingdom of Yahweh is also an inaugurated kingdom, and so the scholarly suggestion that Isaiah's eschatological meal is in fact modeled on the Ancient Near Eastern coronation

---

[62] Isa. 24.21—25.10a.

celebration cannot be set aside.[63] Second, the focal point of Yahweh's judgment and hosted celebration is Zion (24.23), also called 'this mountain' (25.6, 7, 10). No doubt drawing on Yahweh's self-revelation on Mount Sinai (Exod. 24.9–11), Israel's first temple after the Exodus, Isaiah looks forward to another divine visitation on a future temple mount.[64] Third, the Isaianic text focuses on the final banquet as part and parcel of Yahweh's concern for the poor (vv. 4–5), who suffer disgrace (v. 7). Lifted from out of their humiliation, the poor will take their seat at Yahweh's feast. Among their number will also be Gentiles: it will be a feast 'for *all* peoples' (v. 6).[65] Their shared meal, consisting of 'rich food, a feast of well-aged wines, of rich food filled with marrow, of well-aged wines strained clear' (v. 6), is specifically cultic fare.[66] In partaking of this temple-mount meal, they are – so Isaiah seems to intimate – constituting themselves as priests in their own right. While more remains to be said in regard to this fascinating passage, not to mention its reception within later Judaism, for now it is sufficient to focus on these points: Isaiah's vision portrays a time when in direct response to the wickedness of earthly kings, Yahweh will install his kingdom, an event that will be celebrated by bringing together the poor and the Gentiles at a common banquet table on the eschatological temple mount. To put it conversely, for any discerning first-century reader of Isaiah, whenever the poor, the unclean, and the Gentiles are found reclining together on a mountain, sharing a solemnly blessed meal (Mark 6.41; 8.6 par.), all on the heels of Yahweh's famed prophet being martyred at the hands of a wicked king, this would be certain evidence of an eschatological meal before its time. This would be intimation that the poor, the unclean and the Gentiles have been made clean by virtue of their participation in a priestly meal and thereby have become both a temple and priests. This would be a sign too that the kingdom of God has come.

If the counter-temple community at Qumran speculated on its own participation in the future messianic banquet, we should not be too surprised to see something similar within Jesus' band, precisely in its capacity as the bridge to the eschatological temple.[67] One might even expect as much, given that the very motifs flagged up in Isaiah 25 were already being – or about to be – worked out within the context of Jesus' community, as I have already touched on. When Jesus cites Isaiah 56.7 in the midst of cleansing the

---

[63] Childs 2001: 184; Oswalt 1986: 463, with bibliography.

[64] On the echoes of the covenant-making meal in Exodus 24, see Clements 1980: 208. On the temple mount in Isaiah, see Isa. 2.2; 4.5; 11.9; 65.25.

[65] The in-gathering of the Gentiles is thematic in Isaiah (14.1–2; 19.18–25; 45.20–25; etc.), and is closely associated with the eschatological temple mount as well (2.2–3; 60.1–22).

[66] The fat portions were typically reserved for Yahweh's altar (Lev. 3.3–17; 4.8–10; Deut. 32.37–38; 2 Chron. 7.7; 29.35; 1 Esd. 1.14) as well as the priests in the promised eschatological future (Jer. 31.14).

[67] See 1QSa 2.11–22; CD 13.7–8.

temple, he is implying that his new temple ministry would carry with it the fulfillment of one of the premier eschatological promises: the in-gathering of the Gentiles to Zion. When Jesus publicly devotes himself to the redistribution of capital among the poor, his intentions for reinstating the 'poor' within Israel could not be any clearer. The conversion of the Gentiles and justice for the poor, the *sine qua non* of Yahweh establishing his temple-based kingdom – such eschatological realities were front and center in Jesus' consciousness. Since the same constellation of bright points also occurs within the context of a temple meal in Isaiah 25, and since this text becomes the singular point of departure for later elaborations much closer to the time of Jesus, it is hardly unreasonable to suppose that Jesus' mountain-top meal, involving both the 'poor' and Gentiles, was inspired by Isaiah 25 as well.[68] Jesus must have concluded that John's death was proof positive that the tribulation was well underway and that therefore the kingdom was also on its way.

That it was the historical Jesus and not post-Easter tradition that understood his meals as proleptic eschatological meals is sustained by several external supports. The first, and perhaps most obvious, lies in the event of the Last Supper (Mark 14.22–23 par.). While the complexities surrounding this very pivotal moment exceed the limits of my discussion here, a few bare observations are in order. First of all, if we grant the Last Supper as a historical reality (as almost all scholars do), then it may be – and repeatedly has been – argued that whatever Jesus intended at that mysterious meal, at least part of what he wished to accomplish was a kind of sacrifice.[69] Moreover, it was a sacrifice in which he invited his disciples to partake. Their having done so equally implies their own conscious participation in a priestly ritual. It was, after all, only priests who were allowed to feed themselves on the sacrificial meal.

The second kind of confirmation for Jesus' self-conscious appropriation of the messianic banquet motif lies with two sayings, both of which may be traced back to the historical Jesus. The first is found in Jesus' mouth as he remarks on the Gentile centurion's faith:

> I tell you, many will come from east and west and will eat with Abraham and Isaac and Jacob in the kingdom of heaven, while the heirs of the kingdom will be thrown into the outer darkness, where there will be weeping and gnashing of teeth.[70]

> There will be weeping and gnashing of teeth when you see Abraham and Isaac and Jacob and all the prophets in the kingdom of God, and you yourselves

---

[68] On Isaiah 25 as a unique witness to the eschatological banquet within the Hebrew scriptures, see Wildberger 1978: 960. Later developments of the messianic meal can be found in *4 Ezra* 6.52; *2 Bar.* 29.4–8; *1 En.* 10.18–19; 25.4–6; 60.24; 62.13–16; *b. Bat.* 74b; *Num. Rab.* 13.2; cf. Priest 1992.

[69] As most recently argued and argued well by McKnight 2005.

[70] Matt. 8.11–12.

thrown out. Then people will come from east and west, from north and south, and will eat in the kingdom of God.[71]

Quite clearly, Matthew understands the banquet to include Gentiles much like the centurion he commends (it would make little sense otherwise). For Luke, even if the Gentiles are not explicitly in view, the saying fits well within his thematic of reversal; it suits to illustrate how the 'last will be first and the first will be last'.[72] In the eyes of the third evangelist, the 'last' would probably include the category of Gentiles. At the same time, there is no indication in either Gospel that such kingdom celebrants would be exclusively Gentile: the kingdom and those who entered therein would entail a good measure of Jews as well. The double tradition affirms the banquet guests' participation by virtue not of their ethnic identities, but of their disposition to respond to the call. The same principle obtains for Q's treatment of the invited banquet guests. Those who are invited to the messianic supper are those who have oriented their lives around Jesus.

In the Markan tradition we have what appears to be a reference to the messianic banquet in a text where Jesus is taken to task for his disciples' failure to fast. Jesus responds to his interlocutors:

> Jesus said to them, 'The wedding guests cannot fast while the bridegroom is with them, can they? As long as they have the bridegroom with them, they cannot fast. The days will come when the bridegroom is taken away from them, and then they will fast on that day.'[73]

The implication is that as long as the 'bridegroom', that is, the host of the banquet, is present, it would be unthinkable to fast. Who that bridegroom may be, Mark leaves his readers to decide (the unspoken answer of course is Jesus himself). If Mark equated 'disciples' with 'those who followed him' (2.15), then the tax collectors and sinners who ate with him would also be included in that category (2.16–17). They are the wedding guests, and the meals which Jesus enjoys with them Mark deems to be proleptic anticipations of the messianic banquet. For Mark, as for the so-called Q tradition, participation in the messianic banquet is not ethnically but ethically determined. Throughout the synoptic tradition, one's reservation at the future repast is secured through one's present relationship to Jesus.

The dominical sayings relating to the messianic banquet have a stand-alone quality which speaks to their authenticity. On the one side, we find no indication on the level of either form or substance of a retrojected Eucharistic theology (as, say, appears to be the case in John 6). Nor do we recognize any attempt on the redactor's part to shape these references to the eschatological

---

[71] Luke 13.28–29.

[72] Luke 13.30. This hardly supports the view of Smith (1991, 2003) that Jesus' meals were Greco-Roman style symposia, a thesis I think ably refuted by Blomberg 2009.

[73] Mark 2.19–20.

meal as narrative harbingers of the Last Supper. On the other side, what sets Jesus' words apart from other attestations to the messianic banquet within the Jewish milieu is that which I have just noted: namely, the absence of any implicit ethnic criterion in determining who will be and who will not be in attendance on that feast day. Much along the lines of how Jesus challenges the wealthy ruler of Mark 10, the fundamental soteriological question revolves around one's position in respect to Jesus. This alone of course is quite un-Jewish and therefore cannot be a stock form which the Palestinian church carelessly inserted into their master's mouth. For good reason, both of these sayings enjoy wide support as reflecting the voice of Jesus.

In this case, it appears that just as Jesus saw the in-gathering of the Gentiles (Isaiah 56) and the redemption of the poor (Zechariah 9—14) as now taking place through his own ministry, he also saw the messianic banquet (Isaiah 25) as something occurring in the present. I believe that it is precisely this latter conviction that undergirds his eating with the marginalized and his hosting large crowds in the desert. These were sincere acts, born out of a genuine concern for his followers' welfare, but they were also deeply and self-consciously symbolic. Just as through his exorcism, Jesus wished to signal that the 'unclean spirit' of Israel was on its way out, now through the meals which pointed proleptically to the last meal, he sought to express what was on the way in.

And what was on the way in but the very banquet hall of the eschatological meal: the temple. It was Jesus' conviction that the eschatological temple was breaking in and through his own ministry, and it was this conviction which in turn emboldened him to do that for which he was so bitterly criticized: eating with the poor and the impure, and keeping company with the Gentiles. Just as from the era of the tabernacle the temple priests confirmed and fortified their priestly status by consuming the showbread, so too would the eschatological community of Isaiah 25 come to define themselves as priests by partaking of the eschatological supper. Jesus' community, as the embodiment of that eschatological community, saw themselves in these terms. Jesus was never indifferent to purity codes. But in his own ministry he redefined those same codes so that purity now revolved around him and his community. Where he was – there was the temple, and so also his sanctified temple community.

Synthesis and conclusion

Jesus of Nazareth's most distinctive activities, healings/exorcisms, and meals were public signs that he had reconstituted time, space, and a people around himself, the new convergence of heaven and earth, the new temple. What Second-Temple Judaism had customarily conceived as being in the future, Jesus symbolically through his actions brought into the immediate present. The kingdom of God had come, which was another way of saying that the kingdoms of the world, under sway of the dark ruler of this world, were coming to an end (Mark 3.20–30 par.). In short, the future was now. And the future was unfolding in the space occupied by Jesus. If Jesus' interaction with the demoniac at Gergesa raised the possibility that Jesus saw in himself the locus of God's presence and purity, his meals for the masses – properly understood against the background of Isaiah 25 – have now all but settled the question. As the embodied realization of the eschatological temple, Jesus and his community were the newfound source of cultic power and purity. To meet up with Jesus was to have within one's grasp the prospect of deliverance; to eat with Jesus was to partake in a new holiness and to acquire a new priest–like status. The exorcisms and public meals were thus socially constitutive. This is borne out by the evangelists' report. Following his encounter with Jesus, the restored demoniac knew that he could now be reintegrated into society; he hoped that that society was the one which centered around his deliverer (Mark 5.18). Meanwhile, the crowds who followed along in the desert also formed an alliance by virtue of their eating together, one which found its focal point in the one who offered the priestly blessing and provided the food. Through his exorcisms and healings, Jesus was in effect saying, 'The time is now, the sacred space is here, centered around me, and the people of God are those who have made the radical choice of reorienting their daily lives as if both these affirmations were unquestionably true.'

Because Jesus' exorcisms and feedings had symbolically reframed reality in a way that stood opposed to competing worldview scripts, for example, that of the reigning imperium, which held that all temporal, spatial, and ethnic roads led to Rome, such actions were inexorably political. Jesus had no intention of establishing a temple that stood aloof from the political issues of the day. Indeed, just as the Cleansing of the Temple flagged up a national pathology on both socio-economic and political levels, Jesus' turning over the tables was only the climactic gesture of what he had been doing all along. In funneling resources from the haves to the have-nots, the movement was adding practice to symbol: Jubilee was on its way, even as jubilee must be enacted in the here and now. Such was the heart of Jesus' socio-economic program. But there was also a political program of sorts. First of all, in healing and exorcising demons, Jesus was effectively purging the 'unclean spirit' from the land, but he was also declaring that those things that went with it, idols and false ideology, were also on borrowed time. However daunting the Roman way of life may have been as a cultural force, Jesus' exorcism of the 'Legion' of demons exposed the soft underbelly of the empire and all that it stood for, its alleged glory and values. The power of the itinerant temple was greater than the icon of the worshipped Roman standard. The accompanying ideology of Rome, based as it was on *faux* power and violence, also could not stand before that array of ethical values that the eschatological temple held as unquestioned. Jesus' temple ethics, encompassing all of life, were grounded in the eschatological come-uppance that was drawing nearer day by day. The very same could be said of Jesus' mass feedings. A public meal on a deserted mountain, involving the poor, the unclean, and Gentiles together – all this was a way of saying that a new society was being formed. It was a society not of rapacious greed and violence, but one of sharing and receiving. It was, in the terms of Isaiah 25, a society which could look past death to the resurrected state (Isa. 25.6–7). It was a society for whom resurrection was in some sense a present reality. The fencing between heaven and earth was beginning to show gaping holes, and the kingdom of heaven was perceptibly becoming visible amidst the rough and tumble of first-century life.

Through healing, exorcising, and dining, the Jesus movement was driving its own political stake in the ground. Most fundamentally, it was challenging the powerful few who shaped the culture and for all intents and purposes defined the controlling narrative of day-to-day life and ethics. Yes, the center of the cosmos could indeed be located, but not in Rome or Zion. The Creator God's new fresh point of departure was the movement of Jesus. More precisely, the new temple was beginning to take shape amidst the community even as God's presence remained, for the time being anyway, within the temple in Jerusalem. Once again, Jesus' actions said as much.

We are now in a position to return to our two questions posed at the beginning of this chapter. First, if Jesus did indeed see his movement primarily in 'temple terms', what does all this have to do with his central motif: the kingdom of God? The short answer, I believe, is 'Everything'. At one level, this should be completely obvious, for what else is the temple of God but the palace of Yahweh, the location from which he, as one enthroned between the cherubim, rules and dwells. For example, when in Daniel 7 we read about the enthronement of the Son of Man before the Ancient of Days, it is highly likely – as has been well argued – that the entire scene, reflecting the shift of power from the doomed kingdoms to the kingdom of God, is one which takes place in the heavenly temple.[74] The throne room of the Son of Man and the Ancient of Days is invisible to the human eye, yet nonetheless intersects with and impinges upon the realities of the time–space continuum in absolute terms. Where the now-present eschatological temple is, there one finds the kingdom of God – and vice versa. While, like the kingdom, this temple is already dynamically present, it is not yet fully present. It is here in a sense, but not yet completely so.

If my portrayal of Jesus is accurate, then through healings and exorcisms, as well as through meals, the one who claimed to bring in the kingdom was basically claiming to establish a reality that was simultaneously political and – to borrow two awkward terms – 'religious' or 'spiritual'. The establishment of the true temple of Yahweh brooked no rivals and would certainly give no quarter to the worship of gods other than Yahweh. Because Jesus knew full

---

[74] The argument of Lacocque (1993) along these lines is convincing.

well that the worship of idols unavoidably carried with it an implicit (or explicit) allegiance to a competing narrative of an unavoidably political nature, he also knew that any attempt to establish the true temple would have to be accompanied by a clarification of political ideals. Jesus found no better shorthand way of describing the complex of ideals he espoused than the highly freighted phrase 'kingdom of God'. Against the military power of Rome, quintessentially summed up in the icon of the wild boar, Jesus asserted the power of Yahweh. Against the conniving violence of John's executioner, the ruler Herod, Jesus asserted a new kind of rule and celebrated this reality with a feast that effectively demolished all pre-existing social caste systems. The net effect was the creation of a new people. No longer beholden to any supposed master race, even less under the influence of the controlling narrative of the same dominant culture, this new community joined together, perhaps even not fully aware as they were doing so, in rewriting 'the script'. A properly functioning temple, where people gave themselves fully to the one true God, could countenance no less. The eschatological temple arrived on earth was one and the same as the kingdom of God, almost by necessity.

The same eschatological temple or kingdom was also the source of purifying power. And here we come to the heart of the second question raised at the chapter's beginning, namely: if the land had been profaned through the idolatrous greed of the high priests, how did Jesus expect restoration to occur? Perhaps we are not as yet in a position to answer that question in a comprehensive way. But I do think we can say this: that precisely in his status as the temple of God, Jesus believed that his presence and activity, through which the divine was mediated to the earthly, served to impart purity. A new temple meant a new way of configuring purity: from now on, those who sought to worship Yahweh properly would have to align themselves with the cause and movement of Jesus. As a result, those who up to that point had been considered pure had no guarantee; those who had been considered impure, but who nonetheless threw in their lot with Jesus, were now suddenly and inexplicably counted as pure. This proved as true for the Gergesene demoniac as it did for the countless people who ate their fill of bread that day on the mountaintop. For Jesus as for any Jew, purity mattered deeply. The main difference lay in how, in light of the redemptive-historical shift that was underway, one planned to attain such purity. Even as purity was never an end in itself but was only defined by one's standing vis-à-vis the temple, from now on the only path to right temple standing was right through the center of the Jesus movement. After all, as had become clear not only through the climactic temple-cleansing, but also through actions for the poor, healings and exorcism, and finally, meals, Jesus was the temple. Others before him had also claimed to lay the foundations of the eschatological temple, but Jesus' project was a temple of a different kind. It was a temple society that the world had never quite seen the likes of before and one which has never been successfully imitated since.

Conclusion

Issuing some new tables and tabling some new issues

Born into the world of first-century Palestine, the historical Jesus comes to us as an exotic figure. We western readers especially should be little surprised if the ancient Galilean and his drama of many acts strike us as unfamiliar. In fact, if Jesus is not strange to us in some sense, it almost certainly means that we have distorted matters, domesticated the one they came to call 'Lord', and finally, in an effort to overcome the alienation, conformed him into our own cultural and theological likeness. I do not rule out the possibility that in writing this book I have fallen into the same trap. Sometimes overturning one comfortably established table only gives rise to another equally tendentious; sometimes the way we (on a deeply unconscious level) want the story to unfold hampers our ability to get the story straight. So I freely admit that the historical reconstruction presented in these pages may be wide of the mark – on this score, future scholars and other thoughtful readers will have to decide for themselves. If I am mistaken, if the historical Jesus did *not* consider himself the temple in the way I have suggested, then there would presumably be more compelling explanations for the presenting data. I trust that time and considered judgment will tell. If, on the other hand, Jesus did see himself as spearheading a counter-temple movement in a way analogous to what we find at Qumran, or behind the *Psalms of Solomon* or within the Baptizer's sect, more than that, if he saw himself as the temple, then this raises a number of important implications.

I began the book by making a plea for leaving open the possibility that Jesus and Paul (as a major representative of early Christianity) situated themselves along the same notional trajectory. The trajectory in this case was also – so I argued in Chapter 1 – shared by John the Baptizer and characterized by certain basic features. The Baptizer, Jesus, and the early Church were convinced that the temple had become irretrievably corrupt, and in this light also concluded that the appointed hour of tribulation was at hand. Since Judaism was inconceivable apart from a temple or apart from at least some apparatus that served the temple's role, these three movements took it upon themselves to take stop-gap measures. Of course there were profound differences between the Baptist's movement, Jesus' association, and the early Church. Notwithstanding these differences, members of all these groupings agreed that the God of Israel was mysteriously on the move and that this same God would use the suffering of his faithful priests to expedite the in-breaking of his saving reign. In fulfillment of the scriptures, Yahweh was now poised to take the throne; the kingdom of God, the sacred temple space in which God reigned, would imminently take recognizable earthly form. Though the arrival of the temple itself was regarded as a cataclysmic event, rumblings of its arrival came as no utter surprise to the first-century world: countless first-century Jews were desperately looking for the full return from exile, the restoration of the tribes, and – the point of it all – the establishment of proper worship. From Israel's perspective, the *telos* of human history, the anticipated climax of the scriptural narrative, was to be set on the stage of the final temple. This was the only appropriate venue in which Israel could lay hold of its destiny: the worship of the Creator God. Against this backdrop, Jesus of Galilee entered the stage of history. Against this backdrop, too, Jesus was dramatizing his unprecedented claim that the kingdom temple was *now* materializing through him and his followers.

While a fuller discussion of the kingdom as a cultic reality must remain for another day, there are nevertheless a few things worth saying now. To begin with, it bears stating what the kingdom was *not*. First of all, the kingdom which Jesus preached was not fundamentally an individualized entity. It could be neither reduced to an interior experience nor co-identified with an egocentric reality or process. Today, on an academic and popular level, the concept of the subjectivized kingdom regularly underwrites statements to the effect that while first-century Jews sought a political kingdom, the more heavenly minded Jesus came to install a 'spiritual kingdom'. The implication here is that the theocracy set up under Moses was merely the outward, carnal husk to the inward, spiritual kernel, the point to which all of biblical revelation was tending: the establishment of the kingdom of God in the human heart, the only earthly purpose of which was to prepare the individual for heaven. Such an understanding is viable only on what I think is a misunderstanding of Jesus' actions.

It is not hard to see why this somewhat Gnostic vision of a 'spiritual kingdom' took hold within the history of interpretation. Invoking religious legitimacy for their own agenda, emerging European nation-states often failed to distinguish the interests of local Christendom, which were at bottom national interests, from the interests of the kingdom. But ultimately the recurring fusion of the kingdoms could be leveraged only on a particular way of reading Jesus. Only by relegating the thrust of Jesus' teachings to the sphere of personal ethics could the post-Constantinian state and its sponsored institutions carry on with business-as-usual with its corporate conscience no worse for the wear. Caught up in the nationalistic spirit, Bible scholars and theologians writing towards the end of the early modern European period – all those who functioned as chaplains to the nation-states – were generally all too eager to lend their support. The legacy of this portrait lives on, as does its baneful influence. Once Jesus is debarred from speaking to the realms of socio-economics and politics, the question as to how society ought to live is then referred to its cultural powerbrokers and their best self-interested guesses. If Jesus doesn't speak to such matters, then somebody has to, for nature abhors a vacuum.

All the same, those who seek to confine the kingdom of Jesus within the boundaries of the human soul have failed to do justice to the facts. Wittingly or unwittingly, such have become co-conspirators in distorting the voice of the historical Jesus. When Jesus came to cleanse the temple and thereby threw himself on the wheel of history, it was not his intention to speak only to a privatized piety. Nor was his turning over the tables on that day an indication that he had some minor suggestions on the day-to-day running of the temple. No, he was shouting into Israel's central public square, the realm of socio-economic, political, and religious exchange. He was announcing that time had expired on the regnant wicked priests, that the kingdom had come through him, and that as a result Israel could never go home again. To imagine that Jesus was interested merely in bringing a 'spiritual kingdom', in the sense that the West has come to define the phrase, is to run aground on the shoals of history. The modern sundering of personal piety and socio-political action would have been quite foreign to Jesus the first-century Jew. Piety, if it was true piety at all, would have to translate into acts of social and political justice.

There are also theological reasons why the kingdom as temple has been largely ignored. If Luther offered 'gospel' as God's answer to 'law', Protestant theology (whose shaping influence on the modern study of Jesus can hardly be overestimated) has generally failed to take into account the cultic frame-work within which both law and gospel are to be found. My critique is not so much of Luther but of Platonizing and anti-priestly tendencies, inherent in post-Lutheran historiography, which have failed properly to appreciate the Jewish cult on its own terms, as well as, so I suggest, the cultic tenor of the Jesus movement.[1] As is clear enough on even a brisk reading of the Pentateuch, law and cult presuppose each other. Even so, the temple remains the more fundamental reality. To interpret the law was in essence to discern the way of life appropriate to the temple; to obey the law was to maintain right standing in relation to the cultus. As Lohmeyer aptly puts it: 'one takes part in the cult not because it is commanded in the Torah; rather one fulfills the Torah in order to be pure enough to be able to take part in the cult', that is, 'the cult is ... the basis of life, the Law is the imperative derived from it'.[2] Thus it will not do, as so much of New Testament theology has done, to frame Jesus' objections against the law as an absolute abrogation of what had gone before. Just as Adam had his garden temple, Moses had his tabernacle, Solomon had his house, and Zerubbabel had his (somewhat less glorious) house too, the historical Jesus was convinced that he too had his own house. The temple of Jesus was seen as the continuation and climax of the same trajectory. Even though Jesus had redefined temple in radical ways (which had the effect of reconstituting the law), and this redefinition would not

---

[1] On the former point, see above all Klawans 2006.
[2] Lohmeyer 1961: 14, 10. Similarly, Klinzing 1971: 154.

begin to settle out until after the resurrection, the change in modality did not alter the basic continuity. Neither would Paul and his fellow early Christians see themselves as being disconnected from what Jesus had begun. Their temple was Jesus' temple, a sacred space that had secured a foothold during his earthly existence and which after his death, resurrection, and ascension was beginning to expand. The temple of the early Christians was in fact the body of Jesus – and in some sense their bodies as well. While the historical Jesus would have undoubtedly thought about these matters in a slightly different way, on a certain level they would not have agreed more. Differences between Jesus and his contemporaries on the proper interpretation of law, if they are to be properly assessed at all, must be situated within the context of a basic shared assumption: the God of Israel willed to dwell with his people through a divinely appointed space where heaven and earth met. Modern New Testament study's preoccupation with the law, together with Luther's dichotomizing of law and gospel, has obscured the historical fact that Jesus had far more in common with the likes of the Baptizer and Paul than he had difference. Properly appreciated in his historical context, Jesus' message cannot be said – as Bultmann famously wrote – to be the 'presupposition' of New Testament theology.[3] He stands in substantial continuity; his message is part of that theology itself.

My thesis also challenges the widely received impression that Jesus addressed himself to humanity as an undifferentiated mass. In my view, this is a grave misunderstanding. Jesus' introduction of the new temple would seem to suggest that his ethical teachings were not primarily meant as a 'raising of the bar' so far as humanity or even Judaism was concerned, but were an attempt to give content and norms to the unique society he was establishing. As an apocalyptic preacher, he was not so interested in introducing a universal ethic, as in giving contour and color to the kingdom he was proclaiming. While the summons to the kingdom went out to all those who had 'ears to hear', Jesus primarily directed his teachings to those who aspired to be his fellow priests. We suspect that his message was simple, that he spoke to the possibility of true worship and, correspondingly, an undreamt-for possibility of escaping idolatry. The two-sided call, to eschew idols and to worship the God of Israel with all one's heart, cannot be divorced from the eschatological moment. Now more than ever, Jesus proclaimed, was the time to turn. It was time to turn because the kingdom was at hand, for the current temple would be destroyed, and a new one would be built in its place; the purity of the land would be restored through jubilee and the poor of Israel would finally take their due inheritance; finally, the pagan powers – including their demonic idols and sustaining scripts – would succumb to Yahweh's righteous unfolding judgment and give way to a new priestly

---

[3] Bultmann 1951: 3.

society. We have every reason to believe that Jesus' ethics radically depended on this basic eschatological frame.

What was needed in this hour, Jesus reasoned, was a new society. It was to be a strange society, where 'the first will be last and the last will be first' (Mark 9.35; 10.41). Here in the company of Jesus and his comrades, adherents could be safe from the destructive pecking order imposed by the god of mammon, for in this community human worth was no longer measured against the scale of wealth or social position. As a kingdom of priests, the temple community would have to be free of all idolatry, which was profaning, and hence free from all greed. Here individuals within the community worked together to empower those who were socio-economically disempowered. If the poor could be integrated into the community, they could be made to flourish and eventually they too would become agents of human flourishing for others. This vision was no will-o'-the-wisp but seems to have been a very practical set of ideals for Jesus.

What was needed in this hour, Jesus reasoned, was a new body politic. Here within this community centering around the rightful high priest, the forces of paganism, the dark spiritual powers and the equally dark narratives which gave them warrant, would no longer hold sway. That which the dominant Roman culture worshipped and valued, Jesus seems to have said, was no competition for the life enjoined by the God of Israel and would eventually be rendered null and void. The sign of paganism's obsolescence lay not only in Jesus' powers over the demonic but in the emerging reality of a diverse rabble that found its shared sustenance and point of orientation in Jesus himself. In orchestrating exorcisms and mass feedings as he did, Jesus had publicly demonstrated that the promised eschatological temple was now taking palpable form in his body and in the midst of those who followed him. Jesus' healings, exorcisms, and meals were simultaneously a sign of an impending reality *and* a means by which such reality would be realized. Against the Roman *imperium* which had culturally overpowered the world by its own narratives, narratives involving time, space, and true humanity, Jesus had effectively laid out his own counter-script. For him the *telos* of human history was not Roman supremacy or any manifest destiny, but the establishing of the temple. If there was an *axis mundi* at all, it was not found in 'the City' or any metropolis or empire, but in the humble gathering of Jesus' followers. Humanity at its best was not modeled on Caesar Augustus or his imposing statues, but on the person of Jesus himself.

Perhaps the most significant difference between Caesar and Jesus on this last point, that is, in their respective visions of true humanity, lies in their respective construals of power and suffering. For the Romans, the acquisition of power together with wealth and self-glory was a kind of norming norm; to orient one's life to such things was a noble ideal. For Jesus, on the other hand, true humanity emerged, at least in the present eschatological crisis, through the crucible of suffering. For Jesus and his followers, suffering was no random happenstance but the very means by which God's people, his chosen priests, would help usher in the kingdom of God. I decline to be much more specific than this, for I confess, as to precisely how suffering helps advance the divine purpose remains something of a partially veiled mystery to me. While there may be a number of plausible explanations which may begin to get at Jesus' thinking on this matter, I believe that one could hardly find a better summary than one which comes from the pen of Thomas F. Torrance:

> The fact that Israel was called to be the people 'entrusted with the oracles of God', which it could not be without embodying these oracles in its way of life, brought upon Israel intense suffering, physical and mental, in its relations with other peoples. But Israel had to suffer above all from God, precisely as the chosen medium of his self-revelation to mankind, for divine revelation was a fire in the mind and soul and memory of Israel burning away all that was in conflict with God's holiness, mercy and truth. By its very nature that revelation could not be faithfully appropriated and articulated apart from conflict with deeply ingrained habits of human thought and understanding and without the development of new patterns of thought and understanding and speech as worthy vehicles of its communication.[4]

Suffering was as necessary for the remnant constituted by Jesus as it was for Israel itself. Since the message of Yahweh's salvation is bound only by the messengers who proclaim it, the followers of Jesus eventually followed their master in so many ways and accepted the importance of being enlarged through tribulation. Tribulation shapes the messenger; it also grants the message a certain clarity and weightiness that it would not otherwise have. Thus through their afflictions, Jesus' priests would help force an existential crisis among the wavering. The final temple may have been a unilateral act of God, but this would not occur without a good measure of human suffering along the way.

Having emphasized that Jesus' ethics remain firmly rooted in his historic moment, a moment in which his followers even today arguably share, it must also be acknowledged that the Galilean also seems to have modeled and enjoined a certain transcendent, theocentric ideal. How Jesus could simultaneously be both wild-eyed eschatological prophet and sagacious pronouncer of ethical abstractions is a very good question. The relationship between his apparently timeless truths and his warnings of imminent judgment has been a source of long-standing scholarly puzzlement. At this point I would venture that perhaps the best resolution of such puzzlement comes to light in the portrait I have been advancing. I have argued that Jesus announced the immediate presence of the eschatological temple and yet also, paradoxically, its imminent arrival. If this account is accurate, then one might expect as a matter of course that Jesus, as forward-looking eschatological

---

[4] Torrance 1992 [1983]: 8.

priest, would enjoin a particular ethic as appropriate to the hour of crisis. One might also expect that this same Jesus, in his role as reigning high priest, made it his business and the business of his followers to image in the present moment the character of Yahweh, 'merciful and gracious, slow to anger, abounding in steadfast love and faithfulness' (Exod. 34.6). Poised between two ages, Jesus commended an ethic that was both particular to the hour of tribulation and universally reflective of the unchanging character of God. The 'already' and the 'not yet', Jesus the prophet and Jesus the sage, converge within and easily subsume themselves under the category of Jesus the temple.

As far as Jesus himself is concerned, one might dare to go further. I have been maintaining that Jesus had come to establish a new temple and a correspondingly new priesthood. Over that temple and priesthood stood Jesus himself as the new high priest. This gives us pause to ponder, for the high priest was not only required to be like God, but he was also called *in some sense* to be God – at least God to the people. With reference to the high-priestly office, Fletcher-Louis explains:

> Wider considerations of the function of high priestly clothing in Exod. 28—29 and in later interpretation . . . indicate that the high priest wears the divine Name *precisely because he is the visible and ritual embodiment of Israel's god*. In his gold and jewel-studded garments he *is* (ritually and dramatically) Yahweh. His garments have a designer label, with the designer's (the creator's) name emblazoned on his headgear because in his official duties he plays the role of the creator and savior.[5]

Although Fletcher-Louis's argument has yet to command a consensus regarding the historical origins of the worship of Jesus, it is provocative and, in light of the present study, inviting. In reference to the scholarly question as to how a first-century carpenter could be promoted to the office of messiah, and then from messiah to the divine Son of God, the argument I have laid out in these pages has the prospect of laying hold of a fresh thread. It is a thread that leads back to the swaddling clothes, the workaday cloak, and the bloodied last-worn robe of the historical Jesus; it is also a thread that goes beyond him to the priestly ephod which the early Church would eventually place on its Risen Lord. As *soi-disant* builder of the eschatological temple, Jesus claimed for himself the title of messiah. As claimant to the final high-priestly office, he may well have been staking an even more radical claim. More work needs to be done on what Jesus taught about God, God's relationship to the kingdom and God's relationship to Jesus himself; more work also needs to be done on how Jesus' final actions and death, all taking place after the temple cleansing, related to his temple work and role as divine representative.

---

[5] Fletcher-Louis 2004: 88.

In the meantime, we return to where we began, namely with Paul and his mention of Jesus Christ the 'cornerstone'. And as we do, we now conclude that the phrase is no arbitrarily deployed comparison. Rather the apostle's temple imagery incorporates a whole world of meaning unto itself. It was a world which not only had its origins long before the time of Jesus and Paul, but also would climax at some indeterminate point after both had come and gone. The early Christian language about Jesus the temple was a way of speaking that drew together all that Israel hoped and longed for, all that God's people – so went the firm belief – would one day see. It is also a world that stands to be explored today. When the historical Jesus overturned the tables, he effectively announced that the kingdom had come and, as a result, worship, the very point of human existence, was now about to be possible in a whole new way. Just what this whole new way means we have yet to understand or experience fully.

References

Abegg, M. G., M. O. Wise and E. M. Cook (2005 [1996]), *The Dead Sea Scrolls: A New Translation* (San Francisco: HarperSanFrancisco).

Aberbach, M. (1951), 'The Historical Allusions of Chapters IV, XI, and XIII of the *Psalms of Solomon*', *JQR* 41: 379–91.

Achtemeier, P. J. (2008), *Jesus and the Miracle Tradition* (Eugene, Or.: Wipf & Stock).

Ådna, J. (1999), 'The Encounter of Jesus with the Gerasene Demoniac', in B. Chilton and C. A. Evans (eds), *Authenticating the Activities of Jesus* (NTTS 28/2; Leiden/Boston: Brill): 279–301.

Ådna, J. (2000), *Jesu Stellung zum Tempel: Die Tempelaktion und das Tempelwort als Ausdruck seiner messianischen Sendung* (WUNT 2/119; Tübingen: Mohr Siebeck).

Albertz, R. (1983), 'Die "Antrittspredigt" Jesu im Lukasevangelium auf ihrem alttestamentlichen Hintergrund', *ZNW* 74: 182–206.

Allison, D. C. (1985), *The End of the Ages Has Come: An Early Interpretation of the Passion and Resurrection of Jesus* (Philadelphia: Fortress).

Allison, D. C. (1998), *Jesus of Nazareth: Millenarian Prophet* (Minneapolis: Fortress).

Alon, G. (1977), *Jews, Judaism, and the Classical World: Studies in Jewish History in the Times of the Second Temple and Talmud* (Jerusalem: Magnes).

Anderson, G. A. (2007), 'Redeem Your Sins by the Giving of Alms: Sin, Debt, and the "Treasury of Merit" in Early Jewish and Christian Tradition', *LtSp* 3: 37–67.

Annen, F. (1976), *Heil für die Heiden: Zur Bedeutung und Geschichte der Tradition vom besessenen Gerasener (Mk 5, 1–20 parr.)*, (FTS 20; Frankfurt: Knecht).

Applebaum, S. (1989), 'Josephus and the Economic Causes of the Jewish War', in L. H. Feldman and G. Hata (eds), *Josephus, the Bible, and History* (Detroit: Wayne State University Press): 237–64.

Arnal, W. E. (2001), *Jesus and the Village Scribes: Galilean Conflicts and the Setting of Q* (Minneapolis: Fortress).

Atkinson, K. (1998), 'Toward a Redating of the *Psalms of Solomon*: Implications for Understanding the *Sitz im Leben* of an Unknown Jewish Sect', *JSP* 17: 95–112.

Atkinson, K. (2001), *An Intertextual Study of the* Psalms of Solomon: *Pseudepigrapha* (SBEC 49; Lewiston, NY: Mellen Press).

Atkinson, K. (2004), *I Cried to the Lord: A Study of the* Psalms of Solomon's *Historical Background and Social Setting* (JSJSup 84; Leiden/Boston: Brill).

Aune, D. E. (1998), *Revelation 6–16* (WBC 52b; Dallas: Word).

Avalos, H. (1995), *Illness and Health Care in the Ancient Near East: The Role of the Temple in Greece, Mesopotamia, and Israel* (HSM 54; Atlanta: Scholars Press).

Avemarie, F. (1999), 'Ist die Johannestaufe ein Ausdruck von Tempelkritik? Skizze eines methodischen Problems', in B. Ego and A. Lange (eds), *Gemeinde ohne Tempel: Zur Substituierung und Transformation des Jerusalemer Tempels und seines Kults im Alten Testment, antiken Judentum und frühen Christentum* (WUNT 118; Tübingen: Mohr Siebeck): 395–410.

Bachmann, M. (1994), 'Himmlisch: der "Tempel Gottes" von Apk 11:1', *NTS* 40: 474–80.

Baldensperger, W. (1898), *Der Prolog des vierten Evangeliums: Sein polemisch-apologetischer Zweck* (Freiburg: Mohr Siebeck).

Bammel, E. (1968), 'Πτωχός', in G. Kittel (ed.), *Theological Dictionary of the New Testament: Vol. 6: Πε–Ρ* (Grand Rapids: Eerdmans): 885–915.

Bammel, E. (1984), 'The Feeding of the Multitude', in idem and C. F. D. Moule (eds), *Jesus and the Politics of His Day* (Cambridge: Cambridge University Press): 211–40.

Barker, M. (2002), 'Wisdom: The Queen of Heaven', *SJT* 55: 141–59.

Barrett, C. K. (1953), 'Paul and the "Pillar" Apostles', in J. N. Sevenster and W. C. van Unnik (eds), *Studia Paulina in honorem Johannis de Zwaan, Septuagenarii* (Haarlem: Bohn): 1–19.

Barrett, C. K. (1975), 'The House of Prayer and the Den of Thieves', in E. E. Ellis and E. Grässer (eds), *Jesus und Paulus: Festschrift für Werner Georg Kümmel zum 70sten Geburtstag* (Göttingen: Vandenhoeck & Ruprecht): 13–20.

Bauckham, R. (1988), 'Jesus' Demonstration in the Temple', in B. Lindars (ed.), *Law and Religion: Essays on the Place of the Law in Israel and Early Christianity* (Cambridge: Clarke): 72–89.

Bauckham, R. (1995), 'James and the Jerusalem Church', in idem (ed.), *The Book of Acts in its Palestinian Setting* (Grand Rapids: Eerdmans; Carlisle: Paternoster): 415–80.

Bauckham, R. (2006), *Jesus and the Eyewitnesses: The Gospels as Eyewitness Testimony* (Grand Rapids: Eerdmans).

Bayer, H. F. (1986), *Jesus' Predictions of Vindication and Resurrection: The Provenance, Meaning, and Correlation of the Synoptic Predictions* (WUNT 2/20; Tübingen: Mohr Siebeck).

Beale, G. K. (1999), *The Book of Revelation: A Commentary on the Greek Text* (NIGTC; Grand Rapids: Eerdmans; Carlisle: Paternoster).

Beale, G. K. (2004), *The Temple and the Church's Mission: A Biblical Theology of the Dwelling Place of God* (NSBT 17; Leicester: Apollos; Downers Grove: InterVarsity).

Beale, G. K. (2005), 'Eden, the Temple, and the Church's Mission in the New Creation', *JETS* 48: 5–31.

Beare, F. W. (1970), *The First Epistle of Peter* (3rd edn; Oxford: Blackwell).

Beavis, M. A. (2006), *Jesus and Utopia: Looking for the Kingdom of God in the Roman World* (Minneapolis: Fortress).

Becker, J. (1972), *Johannes der Täufer und Jesus von Nazareth* (BibS[N] 63; Neukirchen-Vluyn: Neukirchener Verlag).

Becker, J. (1998), *Jesus of Nazareth* (New York: de Gruyter).

Beckwith, R. T. (1981), 'Daniel 9 and the Date of Messiah's Coming in Essene, Hellenistic, Pharisaic, Zealot and Early Christian Computation', *RevQ* 10: 521–42.

Beckwith, R. T. (1996), *Calendar and Chronology, Jewish and Christian: Biblical, Intertestamental and Patristic Studies* (AGJU 33; Leiden: Brill).

Berger, K. (2006), *Von der Schönheit der Ethik* (Frankfurt am Main: Insel).

Berges, U. and R. Hoppe (2009), *Arm und Reich* (NEchtB 10; Würzburg: Echter).

Bergsma, J. S. (2007), *The Jubilee from Leviticus to Qumran: A History of Interpretation* (VTSup 115; Leiden: Brill).

Betz, H. D. (1994), 'Jesus and the Cynics: Survey and Analysis of a Hypothesis', *JR* 74: 453–75.

Betz, H. D. (1997), 'Jesus and the Purity of the Temple (Mark 11:15–18): A Comparative Approach', *JBL* 116: 455–72.

Bietenhard, H. (1951). *Die himmlische Welt im Urchristentum and Spätjudentum* (WUNT 2; Tübingen: Mohr Siebeck).

Binder, D. D. (1999), *Into the Temple Courts: The Place of Synagogues in the Second Temple Period* (SBLDS 169; Atlanta: Society of Biblical Literature).

Blackburn, B. (1994), 'The Miracles of Jesus', in B. D. Chilton and C. A. Evans (eds), *Studying the Historical Jesus: Evaluations of the State of Current Research* (NTTS 19; Leiden: Brill): 353–94.

Blank, J. (1968), *Paulus und Jesus: Eine theologische Grundlegung* (SANT 18; Munich: Kösel-Verlag).

Blenkinsopp, J. (2001), 'Did the Second Jerusalemite Temple Possess Land?' *Transeu* 21: 61–8.

Blomberg, C. L. (2009), 'The Authenticity and Significance of Jesus' Table Fellowship with Sinners', in D. L. Bock and R. L. Webb (eds), *Key Events in the Life of the Historical Jesus: A Collaborative Exploration of Context and Coherence* (WUNT 247; Tübingen: Mohr Siebeck): 215–50.

Bock, D. L. and R. L. Webb (eds), (2009), *Key Events in the Life of the Historical Jesus: A Collaborative Exploration of Context and Coherence* (WUNT 247; Tübingen: Mohr Siebeck).

Bockmuehl, M. N. A. (1996 [1994]), *This Jesus: Martyr, Lord, Messiah* (Downers Grove: InterVarsity).

Bockmuehl, M. N. A. (2006), *Seeing the Word: Refocusing New Testament Study* (Grand Rapids: Baker).

Bockmuehl, M. N. A. (2007), 'Peter between Jesus and Paul: The "Third Quest" and the "New Perspective" on the First Disciple', in T. D. Still (ed.), *Jesus and Paul Reconnected: Fresh Pathways into an Old Debate* (Grand Rapids: Eerdmans): 67–102.

Borg, M. J. (1984), *Conflict, Holiness & Politics in the Teachings of Jesus* (SBEC 5; New York: Mellen Press).

Borg, M. J. (1995), *Meeting Jesus Again for the First Time: The Historical Jesus and the Heart of Contemporary Faith* (San Francisco: HarperSanFrancisco).

Borg, M. J. (2006), *Jesus: Uncovering the Life, Teachings, and Relevance of a Religious Revolutionary* (San Francisco: HarperSanFrancisco).

Boring, M. E. (1989), *Revelation* (IBC; Louisville: Westminster/John Knox).

Bornkamm, G. (1977 [1969]), *Paulus* (Stuttgart: Kohlhammer).

Brandon, S. G. F. (1967), *Jesus and the Zealots: A Study of the Political Factor in Primitive Christianity* (New York: Scribner).

Briggs, R. A. (1999), *Jewish Temple Imagery in the Book of Revelation* (StudBL 10; New York: Peter Lang).

Brooke, G. J. (1999), 'Miqdash Adam, Eden and the Qumran Community', in B. Ego and A. Lange (eds), *Gemeinde ohne Tempel: Zur Substituierung und Transformation des Jerusalemer Tempels und seines Kults im Alten Testment, antiken Judentum und frühen Christentum* (WUNT 118; Tübingen: Mohr Siebeck): 285–301.

Brown, R. E. (1968 [1961]), 'The Pater Noster as an Eschatological Prayer', in R. E. Brown, *New Testament Essays* (Garden City, NY: Doubleday): 275–320.

Brown, R. E. (1970 [1966]), *The Gospel according to John* (2 vols.; AB 29; New York: Doubleday).

Bryan, S. M. (2002), *Jesus and Israel's Traditions of Judgement and Restoration* (SNTSMS 117; Cambridge: Cambridge University Press).

Buchanan, G. W. (1959), 'Mark 11:15–19: Brigands in the Temple', *HUCA* 30: 169–77.

Buchanan, G. W. (1964), 'Jesus and the Upper Class', *NovT* 7: 195–209.

Buchanan, G. W. (1991), 'Symbolic Money-Changers in the Temple', *NTS* 37: 280–90.

Büchler, A. (1968), *Types of Jewish-Palestinian Piety from 70 B.C.E. to 70 C.E.: The Ancient Pious Men* (New York: KTAV).

Bultmann, R. K. (1934 [1926]), *Jesus and the Word* (New York: Scribner).

Bultmann, R. K. (1951), *Theology of the New Testament*, vol. 1 (New York: Scribner).

Bultmann, R. K. (1968 [1921]), *The History of the Synoptic Tradition* (rev. edn; Oxford: Blackwell).

Bultmann, R. K. (1969 [1933]), *Faith and Understanding* (New York: Harper & Row).

Burkett, D. (1999), *The Son of Man Debate: A History and Evaluation* (Cambridge/ New York: Cambridge University Press).

Buth, R. and B. Kvasnica (2006), 'Temple Authorities and Tithe Evasion: The Linguistic Background and Impact of the Parable of the Vineyard, the Tenants and the Son', in R. S. Notley, M. Turnage and B. Becker (eds), *Jesus' Last Week* (JCP 11; Leiden/ Boston: Brill): 53–80.

Capper, B. J. (1995), 'The Palestinian Cultural Context of Earliest Christian Community of Goods', in R. Bauckham (ed.), *The Book of Acts in its Palestinian Setting* (Grand Rapids: Eerdmans; Carlisle: Paternoster): 323–56.

Capper, B. J. (2006), 'Essene Community Houses and Jesus' Early Community', in J. H. Charlesworth (ed.), *Jesus and Archaeology* (Grand Rapids: Eerdmans): 472–502.

Cardellini, I. (1981), *Die biblischen 'Sklaven' – Gesetze im Lichte des heilschriftlichen Sklavenrechts: Ein Beitrag zur Tradition, Überlieferung und Redaktion der alttestamentlichen Rechtstexte* (BBB 55; Bonn/Königstein: Hanstein).

Carson, D. A. (1981), *Divine Sovereignty and Human Responsibility: Biblical Perspectives in Tension* (NFTL; Atlanta: John Knox).

Casey, M. (1997), 'Culture and Historicity: The Cleansing of the Temple', *CBQ* 59: 306–32.

Catchpole, D. R. (1984), 'The "Triumphal" Entry', in E. Bammel and C. F. D. Moule (eds), *Jesus and the Politics of His Day* (Cambridge: Cambridge University Press): 319–34.

Chae, Y. S. (2006), *Jesus as the Eschatological Davidic Shepherd: Studies in the Old Testament, Second Temple Judaism, and in the Gospel of Matthew* (WUNT 2/216; Tübingen: Mohr Siebeck).

Chance, J. B. (1988), *Jerusalem, the Temple, and the New Age in Luke–Acts* (Macon, Ga.: Mercer University Press).

Charette, B. (1992), *The Theme of Recompense in Matthew's Gospel* (JSNTSup 79; Sheffield: JSOT Press).

Charlesworth, J. H. (1992), 'From Messianology to Christology: Problems and Prospects', in J. H. Charlesworth (ed.), *The Messiah: Developments in Earliest Judaism and Christianity: The First Princeton Symposium on Judaism and Christian Origins* (Minneapolis: Fortress): 3–35.

Childs, B. S. (2001), *Isaiah: A Commentary* (OTL; Louisville: Westminster John Knox).

Chilton, B. (1992), *The Temple of Jesus: His Sacrificial Program within a Cultural History of Sacrifice* (University Park, Pa.: Pennsylvania State University Press).

Chilton, B. (1996), *Pure Kingdom: Jesus' Vision of God* (SHJ; Grand Rapids: Eerdmans; London: SPCK).

Chilton, B. and C. A. Evans (1997), *Jesus in Context: Temple, Purity, and Restoration* (AGJU 39; Leiden/New York: Brill).

Chilton, B. and C. A. Evans (eds) (1999), *Authenticating the Activities of Jesus* (NTTS 28/2; Leiden/Boston: Brill).

Chirichigno, G. (1993), *Debt-Slavery in Israel and the Ancient Near East* (JSOTSup 141; Sheffield: JSOT Press).

Christiansen, E. J. (1995), *The Covenant in Judaism and Paul: A Study of Ritual Boundaries as Identity Markers* (AGJU 27; Leiden/New York: Brill).

Clements, R. E. (1965), *God and Temple: The Idea of the Divine Presence in Ancient Israel* (Oxford: Blackwell).

Clements, R. E. (1980), *Isaiah 1—39* (NCBC; Grand Rapids: Eerdmans).

Collins, A. Y. (2007), *Mark: A Commentary* (Hermeneia; Minneapolis: Fortress).

Collins, R. F. (1999), *First Corinthians* (SP 7; Collegeville, Minn.: Liturgical Press).

Coloe, M. L. (2001), *God Dwells with Us: Temple Symbolism in the Fourth Gospel* (Collegeville, Minn.: Liturgical Press).

Craffert, P. F. (2008), *The Life of a Galilean Shaman: Jesus of Nazareth in Anthropological-Historical Perspective* (MBMC 3; Eugene, Or.: Cascade Books).

Cranfield, C. E. B. (1951), 'Riches and the Kingdom of God: St. Mark 10:17–31', *SJT* 4: 302–13.

Cranfield, C. E. B. (1975), *A Critical and Exegetical Commentary on the Epistle to the Romans*, vol. 1: *Chapters 1–8* (ICC; Edinburgh: T. & T. Clark).

Crossan, J. D. (1991), *The Historical Jesus: The Life of a Mediterranean Jewish Peasant* (San Francisco: HarperSanFrancisco).

Crossan, J. D. (1994), *Jesus: A Revolutionary Biography* (San Francisco: HarperSanFrancisco).

Dahl, N. A. (1976), *Jesus in the Memory of the Early Church: Essays* (Minneapolis: Augsburg).

Davies, G. I. (1991), 'The Presence of God in the Second Temple and Rabbinic Doctrine', in W. Horbury (ed.), *Templum Amicitiae: Essays on the Second Temple Presented to Ernst Bammel* (Sheffield: JSOT Press): 32–6.

Davies, S. L. (1995), *Jesus the Healer: Possession, Trance, and the Origins of Christianity* (London: SCM Press; New York: Continuum).

Davies, W. D. (1974), *Gospel and the Land: Early Christianity and Jewish Territorial Doctrine* (Berkeley: University of California Press).

Davies, W. D. and D. C. Allison (1988–97), *A Critical and Exegetical Commentary on the Gospel According to Saint Matthew* (3 vols.; ICC; Edinburgh: T. & T. Clark).

Derrett, J. D. M. (1972), '"Eating Up the Houses of Widows": Jesus' Comment on Lawyers?', *NovT* 14: 1–9.

Desmond, W. (2006), *The Greek Praise of Poverty: Origins of Ancient Cynicism* (Notre Dame: University of Notre Dame Press).

Dietrich, W. (1985), '"... Den Armen das Evangelium zu verkünden" vom Befreienden in biblischer Gesetze', *TZ* 41: 31–43.

Dimant, D. (1981), 'A Cultic Term in the Psalms of Solomon in the Light of the Septuagint', *Textus* 9: 28–42.

Dimant, D. (1986), '4QFlorilegium and the Idea of the Community as Temple', in A. Caquot, M. Hadas-Lebel and J. Riaud (eds), *Hellenica et Judaica: Hommage à Valentin Nikiprowetzky* (REJ 3; Leuven: Peeters): 165–89.

Dodd, C. H. (1953), *The Interpretation of the Fourth Gospel* (New York: Cambridge University Press).

Donahue, J. R. (1989), 'Two Decades of Research on the Rich and the Poor in Luke–Acts', in W. J. Harrelson, D. A. Knight and P. J. Paris (eds), *Justice and the Holy: Essays in Honor of Walter Harrelson* (Atlanta: Scholars Press): 129–44.

Donner, H. (1964), *Israel unter den Völkern: Die Stellung der klassischen Propheten des 8. Jahrhunderts v. Chr. zur Aussenpolitik der Könige von Israel und Juda* (VTSup 11; Leiden: Brill).

Dubis, M. (2002), *Messianic Woes in First Peter: Suffering and Eschatology in 1 Peter 4:12–19* (StudBL 33; New York: Peter Lang).

Dumbrell, W. J. (1984), *Covenant and Creation: An Old Testament Covenantal Theology* (Exeter: Paternoster).

Dunn, J. D. G. (1991), *The Partings of the Ways: Between Christianity and Judaism and their Significance for the Character of Christianity* (London: SCM Press; Philadelphia: Trinity Press International).

Dunn, J. D. G. (1993), *The Epistle to the Galatians* (BNTC; London: Black; Peabody, Mass.: Hendrickson).

Dunn, J. D. G. (2003), *Christianity in the Making*, vol. 1: *Jesus Remembered* (Grand Rapids: Eerdmans).

Edwards, J. R. (2002), *The Gospel according to Mark* (PNTC; Grand Rapids: Eerdmans).

Ego, B. and A. Lange (1999), *Gemeinde ohne Tempel: Zur Substituierung und Transformation des Jerusalemer Tempels und seines Kults im Alten Testment, antiken Judentum und frühen Christentum* (WUNT 118; Tübingen: Mohr Siebeck).

Ehrman, B. D. (1999), *Jesus: Apocalyptic Prophet of the New Millennium* (Oxford/New York: Oxford University Press).

Eichrodt, W. (1970), 'Prophet and Covenant: Observations on the Exegesis of Isaiah', in J. I. Durham and J. R. Porter (eds), *Proclamation and Presence: Old Testament Essays in Honour of Gwynne Henton Davies* (Richmond: John Knox Press): 167–88.

Elliott, M. A. (2000), *The Survivors of Israel: A Reconsideration of the Theology of Pre-Christian Judaism* (Grand Rapids: Eerdmans).

Eppstein, V. (1964), 'Historicity of the Gospel Account of the Cleansing of the Temple', *ZNW* 55: 42–58.

Esler, P. F. (1987), *Community and Gospel in Luke–Acts: The Social and Political Motivations of Lucan Theology* (SNTSMS 57; Cambridge/New York: Cambridge University Press).

Evans, C. A. (1989), 'Jesus' Action in the Temple: Cleansing or Portent of Destruction?', *CBQ* 51: 237–70.

Evans, C. A. (1992), 'Opposition to the Temple: Jesus and the Dead Sea Scrolls', in J. H. Charlesworth (ed.), *Jesus and the Dead Sea Scrolls* (ABRL; New York: Doubleday): 235–53.

Evans, C. A. (1995), *Jesus and his Contemporaries: Comparative Studies* (AGJU 25; Leiden/New York: Brill).

Evans, C. A. (1995 [1989]), 'Jesus' Action in the Temple and Evidence of Corruption in the First-Century Temple', in C. A. Evans, *Jesus and His Contemporaries: Comparative Studies* (AGJU 25; Leiden/New York: Brill): 319–44.

Evans, C. A. (1995 [1993]), 'Jesus and the "Cave of Robbers": Toward a Jewish Context for the Temple Action', in C. A. Evans, *Jesus and His Contemporaries: Comparative Studies* (AGJU 25; Leiden/New York: Brill): 345–65.

Evans, C. A. (1999), 'Jesus and Zechariah's Messianic Hope', in B. Chilton and C. A. Evans (eds), *Authenticating the Activities of Jesus* (NTTS 28/2; Leiden/Boston: Brill): 373–88.

Eve, E. (2002), *The Jewish Context of Jesus' Miracles* (JSNTSup 231; London: Sheffield Academic Press).

Ewald, H. (1868 [1841]), *Die Propheten des alten Bundes: Band 3: Die jüngsten Propheten des alten Bundes mit dem Büchern Barukh und Daniel* (Göttingen: Vandenhoeck & Ruprecht).

Fiensy, D. A. (1999), 'Leaders of Mass Movements and the Leader of the Jesus Movement', *JSNT* 74: 3–27.

Fitzmyer, J. A. (1998), *The Acts of the Apostles: A New Translation with Introduction and Commentary* (AB 31; New York: Doubleday).

Fitzmyer, J. A. (2007), *The One Who is to Come* (Grand Rapids: Eerdmans).

Fitzmyer, J. A. (2008), *First Corinthians: A New Translation with Introduction and Commentary* (AB 32; New Haven: Yale University Press).

Fletcher-Louis, C. H. T. (2002), *All the Glory of Adam: Liturgical Anthropology in the Dead Sea Scrolls* (STDJ 42; Leiden: Brill).

Fletcher-Louis, C. H. T. (2004), 'Alexander the Great's Worship of the High Priest', in L. T. Stuckenbruck and W. E. S. North (eds), *Early Jewish and Christian Monotheism* (JSNTSup 263; London/New York: T. & T. Clark): 71–102.

Fletcher-Louis, C. H. T. (2006), 'Jesus and the High Priestly Messiah, Part 1', *JSHJ* 4: 155–75.

Fletcher-Louis, C. H. T. (2007), 'Jesus and the High Priestly Messiah, Part 2', *JSHJ* 5: 57–79.

Fredriksen, P. (1990), 'Jesus and the Temple, Mark and the War', in D. J. Lull (ed.), *Society of Biblical Literature 1990 Seminar Papers* (SBLSP 29; Atlanta: Scholars Press): 293–310.

Fredriksen, P. (1999), *Jesus of Nazareth, King of the Jews: A Jewish Life and the Emergence of Christianity* (1st edn; New York: Knopf).

Fredriksen, P. (2000), *Jesus of Nazareth, King of the Jews: A Jewish Life and the Emergence of Christianity* (New York: Knopf).

Fredriksen, P. (2007), 'The Historical Jesus, the Scene in the Temple, and the Gospel of John', in P. N. Anderson, F. Just, and T. Thatcher (eds), *John, Jesus, and History*, vol. 1: *Critical Appraisals of Critical Views* (SBLSymS 44; Atlanta: Society of Biblical Literature): 249–76.

Freedman, D. N. (1981), 'Temple without Hands', in D. N. Freedman (ed.), *Temples and High Places in Biblical Times* (Jerusalem: Hebrew Union College–Jewish Institute of Religion): 21–9.

Freyne, S. (1988), *Galilee, Jesus, and the Gospels: Literary Approaches and Historical Investigations* (Philadelphia: Fortress).

Freyne, S. (1992), 'Urban–Rural Relations in First-Century Galilee: Some Suggestions from the Literary Sources', in L. I. Levine (ed.), *Galilee in Late Antiquity* (New York: Jewish Theological Seminary of America): 75–91.

Fuglseth, K. (2005), *Johannine Sectarianism in Perspective: A Sociological, Historical, and Comparative Analysis of Temple and Social Relationships in the Gospel of John, Philo, and Qumran* (NovTSup 119; Leiden/Boston: Brill).

Funk, R. W. (1998), *The Acts of Jesus: The Search for the Authentic Deeds of Jesus* (San Francisco: HarperSanFrancisco).

Gäbel, G. (2006), *Die Kulttheologie des Hebräerbriefes: Eine exegetisch-religionsgeschichtliche Studie* (WUNT 2/212; Tübingen: Mohr Siebeck).

Gärtner, B. E. (1965), *The Temple and the Community in Qumran and the New Testament: A Comparative Study in the Temple Symbolism of the Qumran Texts and the New Testament* (SNTSMS 1; Cambridge: Cambridge University Press).

Gaston, L. (1970), *No Stone on Another: Studies in the Significance of the Fall of Jerusalem in the Synoptic Gospels* (NovTSup 23; Leiden: Brill).

Gaventa, B. R. (1990), 'The Maternity of Paul: An Exegetical Study of Galatians 4:19', in R. T. Fortna and B. R. Gaventa (eds), *The Conversation Continues: Studies in Paul and John in Honor of J. Louis Martyn* (Nashville: Abingdon): 189–201.

George, T. (1994), *Galatians* (NAC 30; Nashville: Broadman & Holman).

Goeij, M. de (1980), *De Pseudepigrafen: Psalmen van Salomo, IV Ezra, Martyrium van Jesaja* (Kampen: Kok).

Goodacre, M. S. and N. Perrin (2004), *Questioning Q: A Multidimensional Critique* (London: SPCK; Downers Grove: InterVarsity).

Goodman, M. (1982), 'The First Jewish Revolt: Social Conflict and the Problem of Debt', *JJS* 33: 417–27.

Goodman, M. (1987), *The Ruling Class of Judaea: The Origins of the Jewish Revolt Against Rome, A.D. 66–70* (Cambridge/New York: Cambridge University Press).

Gray, T. C. (2009), *The Temple in the Gospel of Mark: A Study in its Narrative Role* (WUNT 2/168; Tübingen: Mohr Siebeck).

Green, J. B. (1994), 'Good News to Whom? Jesus and the "Poor" in the Gospel of Luke', in J. B. Green and M. Turner (eds), *Jesus of Nazareth: Lord and Christ: Essays on the Historical Jesus and New Testament Christology* (Grand Rapids: Eerdmans; Carlisle: Paternoster): 59–74.

Green, J. B. (1997), *The Gospel of Luke* (NICNT; Grand Rapids: Eerdmans).

Gundry, R. H. (1982), *Matthew: A Commentary on his Literary and Theological Art* (Grand Rapids: Eerdmans).

Haenchen, E. (1971), *The Acts of the Apostles: A Commentary* (Philadelphia: Westminster).

Hägerland, T. (2006), 'Jesus and the Rites of Repentance', *NTS* 52: 166–87.

Hamilton, N. Q. (1964), 'Temple Cleansing and Temple Bank', *JBL* 83: 365–72.

Hamm, D. (1990), 'Faith in the Epistle to the Hebrews: The Jesus Factor', *CBQ* 52: 270–91.

Han, K. S. (2002), *Jerusalem and the Early Jesus Movement: The Q Community's Attitude toward the Temple* (JSNTSup 207; London/New York: Sheffield Academic Press).

Hands, A. R. (1968), *Charities and Social Aid in Greece and Rome* (AGRL; Ithaca, NY: Cornell University Press).

Harland, P. A. (2002), 'The Economy of First-Century Palestine: State of the Scholarly Discussion', in A. J. Blasi, P.-A. Turcotte and J. Duhaime (eds), *Handbook of Early Christianity: Social Science Approaches* (Walnut Creek, Calif.: AltaMira Press): 511–27.

Harvey, A. E. (1982), *Jesus and the Constraints of History* (Philadelphia: Westminster).

Hauck, F. (1965), 'Θησαυρός', in G. Kittel (ed.), *Theological Dictionary of the New Testament*, vol. 3: *Θ–Κ* (Grand Rapids: Eerdmans): 136–8.

Hayes, Christine (1999), 'Intermarriage and Impurity in Ancient Jewish Sources', *HTR* 92: 3–36.

Hays, C. M. (2009), 'By Almsgiving and Faith Sins are Purged? The Theological Underpinnings of Early Christian Care for the Poor', in B. W. Longenecker and K. D. Liebengood (eds), *Engaging Economics: New Testament Scenarios and Early Christian Reception* (Grand Rapids: Eerdmans): 260–80.

Hayward, C. T. R. (1996), *The Jewish Temple* (London/New York: Routledge).

Hayward, R. (1987), *The Targum of Jeremiah: Translated, with a Critical Introduction, Apparatus, and Notes* (ArBib 12; Wilmington, Del.: Glazier).

Headlam, A. C. (1923), *The Life and Teaching of Jesus the Christ* (New York/London: Oxford University Press).

Heil, J. P. (1997), 'The Narrative Strategy and Pragmatics of the Temple Theme in Mark', *CBQ* 59: 76–100.

Hengel, M. (1968), 'Das Gleichnis von den Weingärtnern Mc 12:1–12 im Lichte der Zenonpapyri und der rabbinischen Gleichnisse', *ZNW* 59: 1–39.

Hengel, M. (1971), *Was Jesus a Revolutionist?* (Philadelphia: Fortress).

Hengel, M. (1974), *Property and Riches in the Early Church: Aspects of a Social History of Early Christianity* (London: SCM Press; Philadelphia: Fortress).

Herrmann, J. (1965), '*nḥlh* and *nḥl* in the OT', in G. Kittel (ed.), *Theological Dictionary of the New Testament*, vol. 3: *Θ–Κ* (Grand Rapids: Eerdmans): 769–76.

Herzog, W. R. (2000), *Jesus, Justice, and the Reign of God: A Ministry of Liberation* (Louisville: Westminster John Knox).

Hoffmann, P. (1994), *Studien zur Frühgeschichte der Jesus-Bewegung* (SBAB 17; Stuttgart: Katholisches Bibelwerk).

Hogan, L. P. (1992), *Healing in the Second Temple Period* (NTOA 21; Göttingen: Vandenhoeck & Ruprecht).

Hollenbach, P. W. (1981), 'Jesus, Demoniacs and Public Authorities: A Socio-Historical Study', *JAAR* 99: 567–88.

Hooker, M. D. (1988), 'Traditions about the Temple in the Sayings of Jesus', *BJRL* 70: 7–19.

Horbury, W. (1984), 'The Temple Tax', in E. Bammel and C. F. D. Moule (eds), *Jesus and the Politics of His Day* (Cambridge: Cambridge University Press): 265–86.

Horbury, W. (1991a), 'Herod's Temple and "Herod's Days"', in W. Horbury (ed.), *Templum Amicitiae: Essays on the Second Temple Presented to Ernst Bammel* (Sheffield: JSOT Press): 103–49.

Horbury, W. (ed.) (1991b), *Templum Amicitiae: Essays on the Second Temple Presented to Ernst Bammel* (Sheffield: JSOT Press).

Horbury, W. (1996), 'Land, Sanctuary and Worship', in M. D. Hooker, J. M. G. Barclay and J. P. M. Sweet (eds), *Early Christian Thought in its Jewish Context* (Cambridge/New York: Cambridge University Press): 207–24.

Horsley, R. A. (1986), 'High Priests and the Politics of Roman Palestine: A Contextual Analysis of the Evidence in Josephus', *JSJ* 17: 23–55.

Horsley, R. A. (1987), *Jesus and the Spiral of Violence: Popular Jewish Resistance in Roman Palestine* (San Francisco: Harper & Row).

Horsley, R. A. (1995), *Galilee: History, Politics, People* (Valley Forge, Pa.: Trinity Press International).

Horsley, R. A. (2003), *Jesus and Empire: The Kingdom of God and the New World Disorder* (Minneapolis: Fortress).

Horsley, R. A. (2008), *Jesus in Context; Power, People, and Performance* (Minneapolis: Fortress).

Horsley, R. A. and J. S. Hanson (1985), *Bandits, Prophets, and Messiahs: Popular Movements at the Time of Jesus* (NVBS; Minneapolis: Winston Press).

Hoskyns, E. C. (1940), *The Fourth Gospel* (London: Faber & Faber).

Hughes, G. (2003), *Transcendence and History: The Search for Ultimacy from Ancient Societies to Postmodernity* (EVIPP; Columbia, Mo.: University of Missouri Press).

Jeremias, J. (1958), *Jesus' Promise to the Nations* (SBT 24; London: SCM Press; Naperville, Ill.: Allenson).

Jeremias, J. (1969), *Jerusalem in the Time of Jesus: An Investigation into Economic and Social Conditions during the New Testament Period* (Philadelphia: Fortress; London: SCM Press).

Jeremias, J. (1971a), 'Die Drei-Tage-Worte der Evangelien', in J. Jeremias, H.-W. Kuhn and H. Stegemann (eds), *Tradition und Glaube: Das frühe Christentum in seiner Umwelt. Festgabe für Karl Georg Kuhn zum 65. Geburtstag* (Göttingen: Vandenhoeck & Ruprecht): 221–9.

Jeremias, J. (1971b), *New Testament Theology: The Proclamation of Jesus* (New York: Scribner).

Johnson, S. R. (2007), *Q 12:33–34: Storing Up Treasures in Heaven* (DQ 8; Leuven: Peeters).

Johnstone, W. (2000), 'Hope of Jubilee: The Last Word in the Hebrew Bible', *EvQ* 72: 307–14.

Jones, L. P. (1997), *The Symbol of Water in the Gospel of John* (JSNTSup 145; Sheffield: Sheffield Academic Press).

Juel, D. H. (1977), *Messiah and Temple: The Trial of Jesus in the Gospel of Mark* (SBLDS 31; Missoula, Mont.: Scholars Press).

Karris, R. J. (1978), 'Poor and Rich: The Lukan *Sitz im Leben*', in C. H. Talbert (ed.), *Perspectives on Luke–Acts* (PRS 5; Danville, Va.: Association of Baptist Professors of Religion): 112–25.

Kautsky, J. H. (1982), *The Politics of Aristocratic Empires* (Chapel Hill: University of North Carolina Press).

Kazen, T. (2002), *Jesus and Purity Halakhah: Was Jesus Indifferent to Impurity?* (ConBNT 38; Stockholm: Almquist & Wiksell).

Keener, C. S. (2003), *The Gospel of John: A Commentary* (2 vols.; Peabody, Mass.: Hendrickson).

Kelhoffer, J. A. (2005), *The Diet of John the Baptist: 'Locusts and Wild Honey' in Synoptic and Patristic Interpretation* (WUNT 176; Tübingen: Mohr Siebeck).

Kerr, A. R. (2002), *The Temple of Jesus' Body: The Temple Theme in the Gospel of John* (JSNTSup 220; London: Sheffield Academic Press).

Kim, S. (1987), 'Jesus—The Son of God, the Stone, the Son of Man, and the Servant: The Role of Zechariah in the Self-Identification of Jesus', in G. F. Hawthorne and O. Betz (eds), *Tradition and Interpretation in the New Testament: Essays in Honor of E. Earle Ellis for his 60th Birthday* (Grand Rapids: Eerdmans; Tübingen: Mohr Siebeck): 134–48.

Kinzer, M. (1998), 'Temple Christology in the Gospel of John', in *Society of Biblical Literature 1998 Seminar Papers* (SBLSP 37; Atlanta: Scholars Press): 447–64.

Klausner, J. (1925), *Jesus of Nazareth, Times, Life and Teaching* (New York: Macmillan).

Klawans, J. (1998), 'Idolatry, Incest, and Impurity: Moral Defilement in Judaism', *JSJ* 29: 391–415.

Klawans, J. (2006), *Purity, Sacrifice, and the Temple: Symbolism and Supersessionism in the Study of Ancient Judaism* (Oxford/New York: Oxford University Press).

Kleinknecht, K. T. (1984), *Der leidende Gerechtfertigte: Die alttestamentlich-jüdische Tradition vom 'leidenden Gerechten' und ihre Rezeption bei Paulus* (WUNT 2/13; Tübingen: Mohr Siebeck).

Klinzing, G. (1971), *Die Umdeutung des Kultus in der Qumrangemeinde und im Neuen Testament* (SUNT 7; Göttingen: Vandenhoeck & Ruprecht).

Klutz, T. E. (1999), 'The Grammar of Exorcism in the Ancient Mediterranean World: Some Cosmological, Semantic, and Pragmatic Reflections on How Exorcistic Prowess Contributed to the Worship of Jesus', in C. C. Newman, J. R. Davila and G. S. Lewis (eds), *Jewish Roots of Christological Monotheism: Papers from the St. Andrew's Conference on the Historical Origins of the Worship of Jesus* (JSJSup 63; Leiden/Boston: Brill): 156–65.

Krodel, G. A. (1989), *Revelation* (ACNT; Minneapolis: Augsburg).

Kümmel, W. G. (1963–4), 'Jesus und Paulus', *NTS* 10: 163–81.

Kvalbein, H. (1987), 'Jesus and the Poor: Two Texts and a Tentative Conclusion', *Themelios* 12: 80–7.

Laato, A. (1988), *Who is Immanuel? The Rise and Foundering of Isaiah's Messianic Expectations* (Åbo: Åbo Akademy Press).

Laato, A. (1997), *A Star is Rising: The Historical Development of the Old Testament Royal Ideology and the Rise of the Jewish Messianic Expectations* (ISFCJ 5; Atlanta: Scholars Press).

Lacocque, A. (1993), 'The Socio-Spiritual Formative Milieu of the Daniel Apocalypse', in A. S. van der Woude (ed.), *The Book of Daniel in the Light of New Findings* (BETL 106; Leuven: Leuven University): 315–43.

Lane, W. L. (1974), *The Gospel According to Mark: The English Text with Introduction, Exposition, and Notes* (Grand Rapids: Eerdmans).

Larsson, E. (1993), 'Temple-Criticism and the Jewish Heritage: Some Reflexions on Acts 6—7', *NTS* 39: 379–95.

Leaney, A. R. C. (1963), 'Eschatological Significance of Human Suffering in the Old Testament and the Dead Sea Scrolls', *SJT* 16: 286–96.

Lee, P. (2001), *The New Jerusalem in the Book of Revelation: A Study of Revelation 21—22 in the Light of its Background in Jewish Tradition* (WUNT 2/129; Tübingen: Mohr Siebeck).

Leske, A. M. (1994), 'The Influence of Isaiah 40—66 on Christology in Matthew and Luke: A Comparison', in E. H. Lovering, Jr. (ed.), *Society of Biblical Literature 1994 Seminar Papers* (SBLSP 33; Atlanta: Scholars Press): 897–916.

Levenson, J. D. (1984), 'The Temple and the World', *JR* 64: 275–98.

Levenson, J. D. (1985), *Sinai and Zion: An Entry into the Jewish Bible* (NVBS; Minneapolis: Winston).

Levenson, J. D. (1986 [1976]), *Theology of the Program of Restoration: Ezekiel 40—48* (HSM 10; Atlanta: Scholars Press).

Levine, A.-J. (2005), 'The Earth Moved: Jesus, Sex, and Eschatology', in J. S. Kloppenborg and J. W. Marshall (eds), *Apocalypticism, Anti-Semitism and the Historical Jesus: Subtexts in Context* (JSNTSup 275; London/New York: T. & T. Clark).

Levine, A.-J. (2006), *The Misunderstood Jew: The Church and the Scandal of the Jewish Jesus* (New York: HarperCollins).

Lindemann, A. (2001), 'Hilfe für die Armen: Zur ethischen Argumentation des Paulus in den Kollektenbriefen II Kor 8 und II Kor 9', in C. Maier, K.-P. Jörns and R. Liwak (eds), *Exegese vor Ort: Festschrift für Peter Welten zum 65. Geburtstag* (Leipzig: Evangelische Verlagsanstalt): 199–216.

Lohmeyer, E. (1961), *Lord of the Temple: A Study of the Relation between Cult and Gospel* (Edinburgh/London: Oliver & Boyd).

Lohse, E. (1981), 'Das Evangelium für die Armen', *ZNW* 72: 51–64.

Longenecker, B. W. (2007), 'Good News to the Poor: Jesus, Paul, and Jerusalem', in T. D. Still (ed.), *Jesus and Paul Reconnected: Fresh Pathways into an Old Debate* (Grand Rapids: Eerdmans): 37–65.

Longenecker, B. W. (2009), 'The Poor of Galatians 2:10: The Interpretive Paradigm of the First Four Centuries', in B. W. Longenecker and K. D. Liebengood (eds), *Engaging Economics: New Testament Scenarios and Early Christian Reception* (Grand Rapids: Eerdmans): 205–21.

Longenecker, B. W. and K. D. Liebengood (eds) (2009), *Engaging Economics: New Testament Scenarios and Early Christian Reception* (Grand Rapids: Eerdmans).

Lüdemann, G. (1987), *Das frühe Christentum nach den Traditionen der Apostelgeschichte: Ein Kommentar* (Göttingen: Vandenhoeck & Ruprecht).

McCaffrey, J. (1988), *The House with Many Rooms: The Temple Theme of Jn. 14, 2–3* (AnBib 114; Rome: Pontificio Istituto Biblico).

McKelvey, R. J. (1969), *The New Temple: The Church in the New Testament* (OxTM; London: Oxford University Press).

McKnight, S. (1999), *A New Vision for Israel: The Teachings of Jesus in National Context* (Grand Rapids: Eerdmans).

McKnight, S. (2005), *Jesus and his Death: Historiography, the Historical Jesus, and Atonement Theory* (Waco: Baylor University Press).

Magness, J. (2002), *The Archaeology of Qumran and the Dead Sea Scrolls* (Grand Rapids: Eerdmans).

Maier, J. (2008), 'Bausymbolik, Heiligtum und Gemeinde in den Qumrantexten', in A. Vonach and R. Meßner (eds), *Volk Gottes als Tempel* (SynK 1; Vienna/Berlin: Münster Lit): 49–106.

Manson, W. (1943), *Jesus the Messiah* (CL 36; London: Hodder & Stoughton).

Martyn, J. L. (1997), *Galatians: A New Translation with Introduction and Commentary* (AB 33A; New York: Doubleday).

Matera, F. J. (1992), *Galatians* (SP 9; Collegeville, Minn.: Liturgical Press).

Meier, J. P. (1991), *A Marginal Jew: Rethinking the Historical Jesus*, vol. 1: *Origins of the Problem and the Person* (New York: Doubleday).

Meier, J. P. (1994), *A Marginal Jew: Rethinking the Historical Jesus*, vol. 2: *Mentor, Message, and Miracles* (New York: Doubleday).

Merklein, H. (1989), *Jesu Botschaft von der Gottesherrschaft: Eine Skizze* (SBS 111; Stuttgart: Katholisches Bibelwerk).

Metzdorf, C. (2003), *Die Tempelaktion Jesu: Patristische und historisch-kritische Exegese im Vergleich* (WUNT 2/168; Tübingen: Mohr Siebeck).

Meyer, B. F. (1992), *Christus Faber: The Master Builder and the House of God* (PrTMS 29; Allison Park, Pa.: Pickwick).

Meyer, B. F. (2002 [1979]), *The Aims of Jesus* (London: SCM Press).

Meyers, E. M. (1997), 'Jesus and His Galilean Context', in D. R. Edwards and C. T. McCollough (eds), *Archaeology and the Galilee: Texts and Contexts in the Graeco-Roman and Byzantine Periods* (SFSHJ 143; Atlanta: Scholars Press): 57–66.

Michaels, J. R. (1988), *First Peter* (WBC 49; Waco: Word).

Milavec, A. (2003), *The Didache: Faith, Hope, and Life of the Earliest Christian Communities, 50–70 C.E.* (New York: Newman Press).

Milgrom, J. (1976), 'The Concept of *Ma'al* in the Bible and the Ancient Near East', *JAOS* 96: 236–47.

Miller, R. J. (1991), 'The (A)historicity of Jesus' Temple Demonstration: A Test Case in Methodology', in E. H. Lovering, Jr. (ed.), *Society of Biblical Literature 1991 Seminar Papers* (SBLSP 30; Atlanta: Scholars Press): 235–52.

Morray-Jones, C. (1998), 'The Temple Within: The Embodied Divine Image and its Worship in the Dead Sea Scrolls and Other Early Jewish and Christian Sources', in *Society of Biblical Literature 1998 Seminar Papers* (SBLSP 37; Atlanta: Scholars Press): 400–31.

Moxnes, H. (1988), *The Economy of the Kingdom: Social Conflict and Economic Relations in Luke's Gospel* (OBT 23; Philadelphia: Fortress).

Murphy, C. M. (2002), *Wealth in the Dead Sea Scrolls and in the Qumran Community* (STDJ 40; Leiden/Boston: Brill).

Murphy, C. M. (2003), *John the Baptist: Prophet of Purity for a New Age* (Collegeville, Minn.: Liturgical Press).

Murphy-O'Connor, J. (2000), 'Jesus and the Money Changers (Mark 11:15–17; John 2:13–17)', *RB* 107: 42–55.

Myers, C. (2008 [1988]), *Binding the Strong Man: A Political Reading of Mark's Story of Jesus* (20th anniv. ed.; Maryknoll, NY: Orbis Books).

Neusner, J. (1989), 'Money-Changers in the Temple: The Mishnah's Explanation', *NTS* 35: 287–90.

Nickelsburg, G. W. E. (1981), *Jewish Literature between the Bible and the Mishnah: A Historical and Literary Introduction* (Philadelphia: Fortress).

Nitzan, B. (1994), *Qumran Prayer and Religious Poetry* (STDJ 12; Leiden: Brill).

Oakman, D. E. (1986), *Jesus and the Economic Questions of his Day* (SBEC 8; Lewiston, NY: Mellen Press).

Oakman, D. E. (2008), *Jesus and the Peasants* (MBMC 4; Eugene, Or.: Wipf & Stock).

Oden T. C. and C. A. Hall (1998), *Ancient Christian Commentary on Scripture: Mark* (Downers Grove, Ill.: Intervarsity Press).

Orr, W. F. and J. A. Walther (1976), *1 Corinthians: A New Translation* (AB 32; Garden City, NY: Doubleday).

Oswalt, J. N. (1986), *The Book of Isaiah, Chapters 1—39* (NICOT; Grand Rapids: Eerdmans; Exeter: Paternoster).

Parker, T. S. (1975), 'The Decapolis Reviewed', *JBL* 94: 437–41.

Pastor, J. (1997), *Land and Economy in Ancient Palestine* (London/New York: Routledge).

Pate, C. M. and D. W. Kennard (2003), *Deliverance Now and Not Yet: The New Testament and the Great Tribulation* (StudBL 54; New York: Peter Lang).

Patsch, H. (1972), *Abendmahl und historischer Jesus* (CalTM A/1; Stuttgart: Calwer).

Patterson, S. J. (2009), review of R. Bauckham, *Jesus and the Eyewitnesses: The Gospels as Eyewitness Testimony*, *RBL* 06/2009; no pages; online: http://www.bookreviews.org/pdf/5650_5966.pdf.

Perrin, N. (2007), *Thomas, the Other Gospel* (Louisville: Westminster John Knox; London: SPCK).

Perrin, N. (2008), 'Eschatological Aspects of the Sinai Experience in Patristic Interpretation', in K. E. Pomykala (ed.), *Israel in the Wilderness: Interpretations of the Biblical Narratives in Jewish and Christian Traditions* (Themes in Biblical Narrative 10; Leiden: Brill): 173–82.

Perrin, N. (2010), 'From One Stone to the Next: Messiahship and Temple in N. T. Wright's *Jesus and the Victory of God*', in R. L. Webb and M. A. Powell (eds), *Jesus as Israel's Messiah: Engaging the Work of N. T. Wright* (forthcoming; Library of the Historical Jesus Studies; London/New York: T. & T. Clark).

Pesch, R. (1972), *Der Besessene von Gerasa: Entstehung und Überlieferung einer Wundergeschichte* (SBS 56; Stuttgart: KBW Verlag).

Peterson, D. (2003), *Christ and his People in the Book of Isaiah* (Leicester: Inter-Varsity).

Petracca, V. (2003), *Gott oder das Geld: Die Besitzethik des Lukas* (TANZ 39; Tübingen/ Basel: Francke).

Petsalis-Diomidis, A. (2005), 'The Body in Space: Visual Dynamics in Graeco-Roman Healing Pilgrimage', in J. Elsner and I. Rutherford (eds), *Pilgrimage in Graeco-Roman and Early Christian Antiquity: Seeing the Gods* (Oxford: Oxford University Press): 183–218.

Pfann, S. J. (2006), 'A Table Prepared in the Wilderness: Pantries and Tables, Pure Food and Sacred Space at Qumran', in K. Galor, J.-B. Humbert and J. Zangenberg (eds), *Qumran, the Site of the Dead Sea Scrolls: Archaeological Interpretations and Debates* (STDJ 57; Leiden: Brill): 159–78.

Phillips, T. E. (2003), 'Reading Recent Readings of Issues of Wealth and Poverty in Luke and Acts', *CBR* 1: 231–69.

Pitre, B. (2005), *Jesus, the Tribulation, and the End of the Exile: Restoration Eschatology and the Origin of the Atonement* (WUNT 2/204; Tübingen: Mohr Siebeck; Grand Rapids: Baker Academic).

Pitre, B. (2008), 'Jesus, the New Temple and the New Priesthood', *LtSp* 4: 47–83.

Pomykala, K. (1995), *The Davidic Dynasty Tradition in Early Judaism: Its History and Significance for Messianism* (EJL 7; Atlanta: Scholars Press).

Posner, R. (2007 [1970–1]), 'Charity', in F. Solnik and M. Berenbaum (eds), *Encylopaedia Judaica*, vol. 4: *Blu–Cof* (Detroit: Gale; Jerusalem: Keter): 569–71.

Powell, M. A. (1998), *Jesus as a Figure in History: How Modern Historians View the Man from Galilee* (Louisville: Westminster John Knox).

Priest, J. (1992), 'A Note on the Messianic Banquet', in J. H. Charlesworth (ed.), *Messiah* (Minneapolis: Fortress): 222–38.

Reicke, B. I. (1951), *Diakonie, Festfreude und Zelos in Verbindung mit der altchristlichen Agapenfeier* (UUA 5; Uppsala: Lundequistska).

Reynolds, B. E. (2008), *The Apocalyptic Son of Man in the Gospel of John* (WUNT 2/249; Tübingen: Mohr Siebeck).

Richardson, P. (1992), 'Why Turn the Tables? Jesus' Protest in the Temple Precincts', in E. H. Lovering (ed.), *Society of Biblical Literature 1992 Seminar Papers* (SBLSP 31; Atlanta: Scholars Press): 507–23.

Riches, J. K. (1990), *The World of Jesus: First-Century Judaism in Crisis* (Cambridge: Cambridge University Press).

Rosner, B. S. (2007), *Greed as Idolatry: The Origin and Meaning of a Pauline Metaphor* (Grand Rapids: Eerdmans).

Rost, L. (1955), 'Gruppenbildungen im Alten Testament', *TLZ* 80: 1–8.

Rothschild, C. K. (2005), *Baptist Traditions and Q* (WUNT 190; Tübingen: Mohr Siebeck).

Ruppert, L. (1972), *Der leidende Gerechte: Eine motivgeschichtliche Untersuchung zum Alten Testament und zwischentestamentlichen Judentum* (FB 5; Würzburg: Echter).

Sabourin, L. (1981), '"Evangelize the Poor" (Lk 4:18)', *RSB* 1: 101–9.

Saldarini, A. J. (1992), 'Sanhedrin', in D. N. Freedman (ed.), *Anchor Bible Dictionary*, vol. 5: *O –Sh* (New York: Doubleday): 975–80.

Sanders, E. P. (1985), *Jesus and Judaism* (Philadelphia: Fortress).

Sanders, E. P. (1993), *The Historical Figure of Jesus* (London: Allen Lane/Penguin).

Schaper, J. (1997), 'The Temple Treasury Committee in the Times of Nehemiah and Ezra', *VT* 47: 200–6.

Schenk, W. (1974), *Der Passionsbericht nach Markus: Untersuchungen zur Überlieferungsgeschichte derPassionstraditionen* (Gütersloh: Gütersloher Verlagshaus Mohn).

Schiffman, L. H. (1999), 'Community without Temple: The Qumran Community's Withdrawal from the Jerusalem Temple', in B. Ego and A. Lange (eds), *Gemeinde ohne Tempel: Zur Substituierung und Transformation des Jerusalemer Tempels und seines Kults im Alten Testment, antiken Judentum und frühen Christentum* (WUNT 118; Tübingen: Mohr Siebeck): 267–84.

Schmidt, F. (2001), *How the Temple Thinks: Identity and Social Cohesion in Ancient Judaism* (BS 78; Sheffield: Sheffield Academic Press).

Schmidt, W. H. (1997), 'Hoffnung auf einen armen König: Sach 9,9f als letzte messianische Weissagung des Alten Testaments', in C. Landmesser, H.-J. Eckstein and H. Lichtenberger (eds), *Jesus Christus als die Mitte der Schrift: Studien zur Hermeneutik des Evangeliums* (BZNW 86; Berlin/New York: de Gruyter): 689–709.

Schmithals, W. (1962), 'Paulus und der historische Jesus', *ZNW* 53: 145–60.

Schnackenburg, R. (1971), *Das Johannesevangelium: Teil 2. Kommentar zu Kap. 5–12* (HTKNT 4; Freiburg: Herder).

Scholer, J. M. (1991), *Proleptic Priests: Priesthood in the Epistle to the Hebrews* (JSNTSup 49; Sheffield: JSOT Press).

Schottroff, L. and W. Stegemann (2009 [1986]), *Jesus and the Hope of the Poor* (Eugene, Or.: Wipf & Stock).

Schröter, J. (2008), 'The Gospels of Eyewitness Testimony? A Critical Examination of Richard Bauckham's *Jesus and the Eyewitnesses*', *JSNT* 31: 195–209.

Schüpphaus, J. (1977), *Die Psalmen Salomos: Ein Zeugnis Jerusalemer Theologie und Frömmigkeit in der Mitte des vorchristlichen Jahrhunderts* (ALGHJ 7; Leiden: Brill).

Schüssler Fiorenza, E. (1984), *In Memory of Her: A Feminist Theological Reconstruction of Christian Origins* (New York: Crossroad).

Schwartz, D. R. (1979), 'The Three Temples of 4 Q Florilegium', *RevQ* 10: 83–91.

Schweitzer, A. (2001 [1906]), *The Quest of the Historical Jesus* (Minneapolis: Fortress).

Scott, E. F. (1924), *The Ethical Teaching of Jesus* (New York: Macmillan).

Seccombe, D. (1978), 'Was there Organized Charity in Jerusalem before the Christians?', *JTS* 29: 140–3.

Seeley, D. (1993), 'Jesus' Temple Act', *CBQ* 55: 263–83.

Senior, D. and D. J. Harrington (2008), *1 Peter, Jude and 2 Peter* (SP; Collegeville: Liturgical Press).

Smith, D. E. (1991), 'The Messianic Banquet Reconsidered', in B. A. Pearson, A. T. Kraabel, G. W. E. Nickelsburg and N. R. Petersen (eds), *Future of Early Christianity: Essays in Honor of Helmut Koester* (Minneapolis: Fortress): 64–73.

Smith, D. E. (2003), *From Symposium to Eucharist: The Banquet in the Early Christian World* (Minneapolis: Fortress).

Snodgrass, K. (2009), 'The Temple Incident', in D. L. Bock and R. L. Webb (eds), *Key Events in the Life of the Historical Jesus: A Collaborative Exploration of Context and Coherence* (WUNT 247; Tübingen: Mohr Siebeck): 429–80.

Söding, T. (1992), 'Die Tempelaktion Jesus: Redaktionskritik – Überlieferungsgeschichte – historiche Rückfrage (Mk 11, 15–19 . . .)', *TTZ* 101: 36–64.

Steck, O. H. (1967), *Israel und das gewaltsame Geschick der Propheten: Untersuchungen zur Überlieferung des deuteronomistischen Geschichtsbildes im Alten Testament, Spätjudentum und Urchristentum* (WMANT 23; Neukirchen-Vluyn: Neukirchener Verlag).

Ste Croix, G. E. M. de (1981), *The Class Struggle in the Ancient Greek World* (Ithaca, NY: Cornell University Press; London: Duckworth).

Stevens, M. E. (2006), *Temples, Tithes, and Taxes: The Temple and the Economic Life of Ancient Israel* (Peabody, Mass.: Hendrickson).

Still, T. D. (2007), 'Christos as *Pistos*: The Faith(fulness) of Jesus in the Epistle to the Hebrews', *CBQ* 69: 746–55.

Strecker, C. (2002), 'Jesus and the Demoniacs', in W. Stegemann, B. J. Malina and G. Theissen (eds), *The Social Setting of Jesus and the Gospels* (Minneapolis: Fortress): 117–33.

Strecker, G. (1979), *Eschaton und Historie: Aufsätze* (Göttingen: Vandenhoeck & Ruprecht).

Strobel, A. (1961), *Untersuchungen zum eschatologischen Verzögerungsproblem; auf Grund der spätjüdisch-urchristlichen Geschichte von Habakuk 2,2ff* (NovTSup 2; Leiden: Brill).

Swarup, P. (2006), *The Self-Understanding of the Dead Sea Scrolls Community: An Eternal Planting, a House of Holiness* (LSTS 59; London/New York: T. & T. Clark).

Tan, K. H. (1997), *The Zion Traditions and the Aims of Jesus* (SNTSMS 91; Cambridge/ New York: Cambridge University Press).

Taylor, C. (2007), *A Secular Age* (Cambridge, Mass.: Belknap Press of Harvard University Press).

Taylor, J. E. (1997), *The Immerser: John the Baptist within Second Temple Judaism* (SHJ; Grand Rapids: Eerdmans).

Theissen, G. (1978), *Sociology of Early Palestinian Christianity* (Philadelphia: Fortress).

Theissen, G. (1983), *The Miracle Stories of the Early Christian Tradition* (Philadelphia: Fortress).

Theissen, G. (2004), *Die Jesusbewegung: Sozialgeschichte einer Revolution der Werte* (Gütersloh: Gütersloher Verlagshaus).

Theissen, G. and A. Merz (1998 [1996]), *The Historical Jesus: A Comprehensive Guide* (Minneapolis: Fortress).

Theissen, G. and D. Winter (2002 [1997]), *The Quest for the Plausible Jesus: The Question of Criteria* (Louisville: Westminster John Knox).

Torrance, T. F. (1992 [1983]), *The Mediation of Christ* (Colorado Springs: Helmers & Howard).

Trautmann, M. (1980), *Zeichenhafte Handlungen Jesu: Ein Beitrag zur Frage nach dem geschichtlichen Jesus* (FB 37; Wurzburg: Echter).

Twelftree, G. H. (1993), *Jesus the Exorcist: A Contribution to the Study of the Historical Jesus* (WUNT 2/54; Tübingen: Mohr Siebeck; Peabody, Mass.: Hendrickson).

Twelftree, G. H. (1999), *Jesus the Miracle Worker: A Historical and Theological Study* (Downers Grove: InterVarsity).

Twelftree, G. H. (2007), *In the Name of Jesus: Exorcism among Early Christians* (Grand Rapids: Baker Academic).

Vahrenhorst, M. (2008), *Kultische Sprache in den Paulusbriefen* (WUNT 230; Tübingen: Mohr Siebeck).

Vanderkam, J. C. and P. Flint (2002), *The Meaning of the Dead Sea Scrolls* (San Francisco: HarperSanFrancisco).

Vanhoye, A. (1967), 'Jesus "fidelis ei qui fecit eum" (Heb. 3,2)', *VD* 45: 291–305.

Vonach, A. (2008), 'Der Mensch als "Heiligtum Gottes": Eine alttestamentlich Spurensuche', in A. Vonach and R. Meßner, *Volk Gottes als Tempel* (SynK 1; Vienna/ Berlin: Münster Lit): 9–20.

Vonach, A. and R. Meßner (2008), *Volk Gottes als Tempel* (SynK 1; Vienna/Berlin: Münster Lit).

Wahlen, C. (2004), *Jesus and the Impurity of the Spirits in the Synoptic Gospels* (WUNT 2/185; Tübingen: Mohr Siebeck).

Walton, J. H. (2006), *Ancient Near Eastern Thought and the Old Testament: Introducing the Conceptual World of the Hebrew Bible* (Grand Rapids: Baker Academic).

Ware, J. P. (2005), *The Mission of the Church in Paul's Letter to the Philippians in the Context of Ancient Judaism* (NovTSup 120; Leiden/Boston: Brill).

Webb, R. L. (1991), *John the Baptizer and Prophet: A Socio-Historical Study* (JSNTSup 62; Sheffield: JSOT Press).

Wedderburn, A. J. M. (2006), 'Jesus' Action in the Temple: A Key or a Puzzle?', *ZNW* 97: 1–22.

Weinfeld, M. (1985), *Justice and Righteousness in Israel and the Nations: Equality and Freedom in Ancient Israel in Light of Social Justice in Ancient Near East* (PFBR; Jerusalem: Magnes).

Wengst, K. (1987), *PAX ROMANA and the Peace of Jesus Christ* (Philadelphia: Fortress).

Wenham, D. (1995), *Paul: Follower of Jesus or Founder of Christianity?* (Grand Rapids: Eerdmans).

Wentling, J. L. (1989), 'Unraveling the Relationship between 11QT, the Eschatological Temple, and the Qumran Community', *RevQ* 14: 61–73.

Werline, R. A. (1998), *Penitential Prayer in Second Temple Judaism: The Development of a Religious Institution* (SBLEJL 13; Atlanta: Scholars Press).

Wernle, P. (1916), *Jesus* (Tübingen: J. C. B. Mohr).

Wildberger, H. (1978), *Jesaja* (BK 10.2; Neukirchen-Vluyn: Neukirchener).

Winninge, M. (1995), *Sinners and the Righteous: A Comparative Study of the Psalms of Solomon and Paul's Letters* (ConBNT 26; Stockholm: Almqvist & Wiksell International).

Winter, B. W. (1994), *Seek the Welfare of the City: Christians as Benefactors and Citizens* (FCCGRW; Grand Rapids: Eerdmans; Carlisle: Paternoster).

Winter, P. (1961), *On the Trial of Jesus* (SJ 1; Berlin: de Gruyter).

Witherington, B. (1990), *The Christology of Jesus* (Minneapolis: Fortress).

Wright, A. G. (1982), 'The Widow's Mite: Praise or Lament? – A Matter of Context', *CBQ* 4: 256–65.

Wright, N. T. (1992), *Christian Origins and the Question of God*, vol. 1: *The New Testament and the People of God* (London: SPCK; Minneapolis: Fortress).

Wright, N. T. (1996), *Christian Origins and the Question of God*, vol. 2: *Jesus and the Victory of God* (London: SPCK; Minneapolis: Fortress).

Wright, N. T. (2003), *Christian Origins and the Question of God*, vol. 3: *The Resurrection of the Son of God* (London: SPCK; Minneapolis: Fortress).

Wright, N. T. (2009), *Virtue Reborn* (London: SPCK).

Wright, R. B. (1985), 'Psalms of Solomon: A New Translation and Introduction', in J. H. Charlesworth (ed.), *The Old Testament Pseudepigrapha*, vol. 2: *Expansions of the 'Old Testament' and Legends, Wisdom and Philosophical Literature, Prayers, Psalms, and Odes, Fragments of Lost Judeo-Hellenistic Works* (ABRL; New York: Doubleday): 639–70.

Yee, G. A. (1989), *Jewish Feasts and the Gospel of John* (ZacSNT; Wilmington, Del.: Michael Glazier).

Yoder, J. H. (1994), *The Politics of Jesus: Vicit Agnus Noster* (2nd edn; Grand Rapids: Eerdmans; Carlisle: Paternoster).

Index of ancient and biblical sources

Index of modern authors

217

Index of subjects

Agis IV 140 n. 69
Alexander Jannaeus 30 n. 5, 31 n. 54
Ananus (Annas) 24 n. 28, 62, 96
Antiochus IV 8, 18 n. 2, 42, 125 n. 136
anti-semitism 2
Apollonius of Tyana 155
Archelaus 166
Aristobolus II 21, 23–4, 25, 31,
    32 n. 60

Caesar Augustus 167, 187
Caiaphas 62, 96, 101, 102
Calgacus 164
cleansing of the Temple 14, 62, 103, 105,
    106, 111, 117, 132, 142, 149, 163,
    176–7, 189; historicity of 82–3;
    intention behind 88–99, 180, 185;
    and scriptural citation 83–8
Council of Usha 12 n. 28
covenant 7, 9, 22, 34–5, 40, 53, 56,
    87, 114, 135, 164
Crassus 125 n. 36
creation *see* new creation
cynicism 124 n. 35

Decalogue 87

early Church 38, 41, 155, 160; anti-priestly
    polemic 55, 59–60, 62–3, 75–7, 92–9;
    collectivism 73–5; counter-temple
    movement 20, 45, 77–8, 109, 182–3;
    expectation of eschatological temple 6,
    9, 12, 47–79; and the historical Jesus
    1–6, 7, 20, 49, 78–9, 99, 106, 109–10,
    115, 121, 131, 132, 140, 183; prayer
    42–3, 50, 66; priestly self-identity 50–2,
    54, 61, 63, 65–70, 76–81; relationship
    to Second Temple 47–9, 51, 64, 67–8;
    understanding of tribulation 51, 52–3,
    54–7, 59, 60–1, 70, 77–8
Eli 96
Elijah 42 n. 96, 68
exile 11–12, 14, 15 n. 27, 18, 19, 23, 36,
    59, 61, 87, 98, 139, 161; *see also*
    restoration

Exodus (story of) 10, 39, 43, 53, 56, 60,
    73–4, 117, 161, 167, 176
exorcism 14, 151–2, 154–70, 171, 179;
    in antiquity 155; in the early Church
    155; historicity of Gergesene exorcism
    157–9; Jesus' aims in 146–7, 180;
    location of Gergesene exorcism 157–8,
    165, 172; significance of 'Legion'
    166–7

First Jewish War 94, 96
forgiveness 7, 41, 62, 135, 138, 140, 141,
    147, 162–3

Gentiles 11, 18–19, 22, 85, 99, 104, 109,
    111, 125, 164, 166, 168, 171–2, 173–4,
    176–8, 179
greed 22, 24–5, 27–9, 31, 35, 37, 92, 93,
    95–7, 97 n. 53, 98, 99, 126, 130, 150,
    164, 181, 182, 188

Hanina ben Dosa 155
healing 14, 151–2, 152–4, 179, 181
Herod Antipas 15, 38, 62, 173, 182
Herod the Great 95, 97–8, 103, 175
Hippos 158, 165, 166, 167
historiography 80–1, 97, 111, 155–6
Hophni and Phineas 96
Hyrcanus II 32 n. 60

idols/idolatry 51, 63 n. 72, 87, 99, 115,
    126, 130, 163, 164, 180, 182, 186–7

Jason the High Priest 8 n. 15
Jesus: anti-priestly polemic 85–8, 86
    n. 13, 92–9, 108–9, 110–13, 114–15,
    149–50, 163, 180, 185; asceticism
    127–30, 139–40, 145; and collectivism
    127–31, 133–4; counter-temple figure
    13, 15, 20, 86, 109–13, 115, 130–1,
    140, 150, 179–82; death of 4, 6, 7, 9,
    14, 15, 48–9, 52, 54, 55, 58, 61, 75, 81,
    106, 111, 128, 132, 142, 189; and the
    early Church 1–6, 7, 20, 49, 78–9, 99,
    106, 109–10, 115, 121, 131, 132, 140,

221